On the Bridges Between Heaven and Earth:
Sixty Years of Living Dangerously

By Peter William Tremayne

CONTENTS

Introduction

To keep going or to drop with a sigh
Into the soft snow of oblivion —
That is a choice. And yet what choice have I?
I must keep moving on until I die.

~ *The Climber,* Alistair Te Ariki Campbell

REMEMBERING AND WRITING the story of my life has been an illuminating experience. The obvious temptation was to play *what-if* scenarios, which I've avoided because the past can't be changed, and I've heard that the craving to do so leads to madness! Instead, I have tried to uncover the motivation behind my choices and decisions over the years. Seeking this has me convinced there have been few coincidences in the evolution from where I began to where I am now, eight decades later. Everything I've done, everyone I've known, and everywhere I've lived seem to be connected. Perhaps what I've been doing all these years has created my future. Either that or I've had friends in high places.

In this memoir, I recall 60 years of high-risk adventures, echoes from a past that are getting quieter, more distant, and sadly, often lost. One consequence has been the realization of how reckless some of those adventures were and statistically, I should already be dead. Nonetheless, I believe many of the risks I took were moderated by training, experience, preparation, no panic, and plenty of dumb luck!

In 1957, living with risk began at age 17, qualifying as

an Air Force fighter pilot in New Zealand. I was trained by WW2 flight instructors who had seen active service in the skies of Europe, North Africa, and the South Pacific, doing their best to make us like them—talented, fearless, self-confident, *immortal*, some arrogance ... and party-loving fools. My classmates and I fully embraced the *immortal* tag, believing we would never die in any airplane we were flying. Besides, at our graduation, we were blessed by New Zealand's most famous soldier, Charlie Upham, Victoria Cross and Bar, who was there to pin on our pilot brevets. How could we ever fail him or deny his courageous actions in WW2?

I've often been asked how I became a commissioned officer and military pilot at 18 without attending university or college. One of the reasons was the exceptional high school education I received in New Zealand from teachers, many of whom were WW2 veterans, though the main reason was timing. My classmates and I were born at the beginning of WW2, well ahead of the Baby Boomers who would flood the schools, the universities, and most desirable workplaces. We didn't realize at the time that the world was ours to take. That's probably why I was accepted into the Air Force pilot training program at such a young age. This fascinating relationship of success and birth years is explored in the book *Outliers* by Malcolm Gladwell.

Now in my early 80s, I often delude myself that I retain some of those attributes (perhaps just the party-loving fool?) climbing and scrambling among the peaks of the Sierra Nevada. But in case it turns out in the next few years that I'm not really *immortal*, I've decided it's prudent to prepare a requiem, which is what this memoir of living dangerously is about. I believe it's important to tell the stories of being in far-flung places, doing dangerous things with courageous people. I've been privileged on this long-life journey to be accompanied by a band of unsung heroes. You know who you are, and we all remember those who have already passed on.

My stories are about high adventure in many parts of the world: from the dazzling white glaciers and plains of Antarctica, the jungles of Southeast Asia, the fertile plains of Bengal, the high peaks of the Himalaya and Alaska, the red earth of the Australian Outback, the tropical islands of Papua New Guinea, the rugged wilderness of New Zealand's South Island, the conifer forests and volcanic peaks of America's Cascade Range, and most recently, the California mountain range known as the Sierra Nevada— where I finally came to rest.

Drawn from my aviation career of 42 years, there are stories about feats of derring-do and acts of stupidity in various airplanes—military and civilian. There are also passionate stories of alpine mountaineering, a sport I should not have been doing after age 50, but did anyway, until slowly mutating into long-distance hiking, before I fell off a high place where I shouldn't have been.

I hope you enjoy reading about these adventures as much as I did experiencing them.

Peter William Tremayne

Teasing the Tigers

D. H. Lawrence wrote that every year you pass an anniversary unaware: the anniversary of your own death. I've seen it so many times before, as adventurers circle and circle the spot marked X where they meet their own death: taunting it, teasing it, playing with the big cat. Never fool yourself thinking you can tame it.

~ *Deep Survival*, Laurence Gonzales

1957: Learning the Right Stuff

If you push the stick forward, the houses get bigger;
if you pull the stick back, they get smaller.
(Unless you keep pulling the stick back
—then they get bigger again.)

THE WONDERS OF FLYING, with hands and feet on airplane controls, soaring high above the earth, in an environment where humans were never designed to exist or have dominion over. Yet there I was, a fledgling Air Force pilot, slipping the surly bonds of earth. The year was 1957, the month January, and my training began as a pilot in the Royal New Zealand Air Force (RNZAF). If I could show that I had the Right Stuff, I expected to graduate in December that year with the rank of Pilot Officer, wearing the coveted pilot *Wings* on the left breast of my officer's uniform. Then I would be a fully qualified, instrument rated, aerobatic, close formation military pilot: a hotshot aviator with a total flight time of 200 hours, all flown in the WW2 trainer, the Harvard AT-6.

Looking back over years, I'm humbled knowing I was able to survive the training and graduate as an officer and gentleman (?) and a fully-fledged pilot. I was still very much a callow youth, but officialy had acquired the Right Stuff.

Was the training so easy that a simple country boy like me could handle it? Far from the truth. I look back on that year as the most difficult physical, academic, and mental challenge I'd ever faced before, and never since. Trying to explain what the training was like back then, I often quote a US Marine saying—*The last easy day was yesterday*—and that's the way it was for us to stay in the program. There were no easy days as flight training was alternated with ground study; half a day in the air and the other half in the classroom. Failing any of the regular airplane check-rides or written exams was not an option. Make one bad mistake in the air, then repeat it, we could be gone. As attrition began taking close comrades out, it became progressively more difficult for the survivors to *get over it* and continue to move ahead. Self-confidence, self-discipline, and determination were the tools needed to survive.

Following that year of effort to survive and succeed in the great game of military aviation, everything became relatively easy. Like my successful classmates, I'd been transformed into a highly confident individual, imbued with the knowledge that I could now achieve the impossible. We, the graduates, had every reason to feel somewhat immortal. We were the survivors of slow but steady attrition of our original group during the 11 months of training. The truth was that the weeding out had begun during the initial selection process months before we entered the training program. Many were called, few were chosen, and even fewer graduated. As you would expect, those who were selected had to be perfect physical specimens with a crooked smile, straight teeth, handsome, and charming. Just like me (?)

Some years later, as an instructor pilot within the same training program, I would convey to pilot students the reasons for success or failure from my own experience. My simple explanation was to be at least average in all three disciplines: military officer qualities, aviation academics, and flying ability. In other words, a good all-rounder. There was no advantage in being an academic genius if you couldn't fly for crap, or didn't know your left leg from the right on parade.

How good were we, the immortals who survived? It didn't take long to find out from our peers; young pilots who had preceded us by a year or two. When we showed up at our first operational conversion training units at RNZAF Base Ohakea in early 1958, we were referred to as *bog-rats*, and told not to consider ourselves real pilots

In retrospect, I was fortunate to join the RNZAF as a student pilot in the dying days of that vast knowledge learned by thousands of allied aviators during WW2. The British Commonwealth Harvard, or the USAF's Texan AT-6 quickly and expertly prepared them for combat roles in Hurricanes, Spitfires, and Mustangs, planes similar to the Harvard: all tail-draggers with large propellers producing high torque, propeller-wash and precession, particularly during takeoff. Flying the Harvard was a constant physical experience, particularly during aerobatics and high G-Force combat maneuvering. In this beast, we, the chosen ones, would become the heirs of Churchill's *The Few*, those fighter pilots who halted Hitler's invasion of England in September 1940.

In 1957, the RNZAF's Flying Training School and its big brother, the Central Flying School, embodied the very best of WW2 pilot training, using the Harvard AT-6 to teach all military flying skills, from ab-initio through to advanced. This included all-weather flying, aerobatics, air combat techniques, air gunnery, and bombing. The plane made plenty of noise, inside and out, with the cockpit cold in winter, hot in summer, and smelling of burnt gasoline and oil. Without previous flying experience, it was initially difficult to handle this comparative monster of an airplane. This was not a puddle-jumping, bug-smashing little tinker-toy Cessna trainer, as used in the civilian world, but rather a thoroughbred beast that needed a strong and steady hand.

Learning to fly the Harvard AT-6 with finesse took time and perseverance, yet it became fun to fly with experience. Possibly the steepest learning curve was instrument flight. The plane's flight instruments were WW2 vintage and the only radio navigation aid was a small AM radio capable of receiving the Morse Code signals from radio range ground-based antenna arrays. All instrument training was done from the rear seat, with its cockpit visually closed off by a canvas hood, while the instructor occupied the front seat. The most demanding maneuvers flown solely on instruments were recoveries from unusual attitudes, including spins, using limited panel, with Artificial Horizon and Directional Gyros caged.

Our *Wings* graduation of nine pilots included two for National Airways Corporation (NAC) and two for the Territorial Air Force (TAF). Three of the Regular Air Force pilots were posted to Vampire fighter jets, and two to Bristol Freighter transport airplanes. Sadly, I was one of the two pilots destined for the Bristol Freighter. My dreams as a well-trained hotshot fighter pilot had been to fly the Vampire jets, but fate and poor air-to-air gunnery results had decreed otherwise. We, the two misfits, were required to complete a conversion course on small twin-engined planes before tackling the big lumbering transport beast.

1958: Flying with Two Engines— the De Havilland Devon

THE NEXT AIRPLANE in my aviation life was the De Havilland Devon, a twin-engined trainer for pilots, navigators, and signalers in the RNZAF. The Devon was a military variant of the very popular DH-104 Dove, short-haul airliner developed in Britain in 1945. Flying the Devon was a very different experience from the Harvard; no aerobatics, no gunnery or bombing, but not a tail-dragger, either; instead, designed with a nose-wheel making for easy takeoffs and landings. This landing-gear configuration gave minimal swing during takeoffs and vastly improved directional stability during landings, particularly in cross-wind conditions. For pilot conversion to the Devon, the training program was mostly about instrument flight and radio navigation in all-weather flight conditions. Still, most notably, it was about handling in-flight engine failures at low speeds.

Two engines are better than one because the airplane can continue to stay airborne when one of those engines fail. However, there are inherent problems that must be handled by the pilot with multi-engined propeller-driven engines. To reduce asymmetric drag, a failed engine's propeller must

15

be *feathered* as soon as possible, and airspeed must be kept above a critical value to avoid losing directional control.

Back in 1958, before the evolution of flight simulators, our training program required us to deliberately fail an engine inflight by shutting off its fuel supply, then following the appropriate procedure to secure the engine and feather the propeller. Landing with one engine shut down was then expected. Like most twin-engined piston-powered airplanes, there was never excess power to operate normally at heavy airplane weights using only one engine. This limitation was the primary reason for placing at least three engines, and better four, on long-range airliners designed for operating over oceans; that is, long distances between suitable airports for emergency use. Keep that in mind when you're sitting in the back of the now-ubiquitous two-engined jet airliners of today, flying over oceans for thousands of miles. Years later, when I was piloting the four-engined Boeing 747, an instructor friend often posed the question, *Why do I fly four-engined airplanes?* And his answer would be, *Because there are no five-engined airplanes.* Having grown up flying underpowered two-engined airplanes in my youth, I still strongly agree with those sentiments.

~

The Bristol Ugly Years: *The nicer an airplane looks, the better it flies – and vice versa!*

The third airplane in my long flying career was, in my opinion, the worst of the worst. In 1958, I had the dubious pleasure of training on the Bristol Freighter at the RNZAF Base in Auckland. There was nothing glamorous about piloting the Freighter or even being a passenger in this noisy tin-can that leaked water when flying through heavy rainstorms. Alas, my future was flying the Freighter off and on until 1968, but fortunately, the majority of that flying was with 41 Squadron RNZAF, based in Singapore, a most excellent assignment. From there, we bumbled around Asia in this sad excuse for an airplane from Kathmandu to Tokyo, including airdrop operations in Malaya, Sarawak, and short-range transport support for our troops in Vietnam.

I remember the Freighter as a difficult aircraft to fly with panache: it lacked pressurization, air conditioning, weather radar, retractable landing gear, or state-of-the-art avionics. We cruised at 135 mph, always below 10,000 feet, sweating like pigs on the ground and freezing like brass monkeys at cruise altitude. I'm sure I flew through every thunderstorm that existed in South East Asia during the 1960s, and while the torrential rain spilled on my feet, oozing through the instrument panel, the passengers downstairs unfurled their umbrellas and prayed for deliverance. The truth is, I never really mastered the art of flying the Freighter to its full potential, despite 4,000 hours of trying. The tail wheel configuration and obscure aerodynamic mysteries that Bristol had built into this airplane provided a challenge that was well beyond average pilot skills like mine. For example, when rounding-out for a three-point landing in this overgrown Tiger Moth, an error of just a few inches could result in a bounce like a spring-healed rat (Qantas has them on the tail). Recovery from this rather alarming maneuver was generally a missed approach, or a teeth-shattering barely-controlled crash.

When transiting the US military bases of Vietnam, the Philippines, Okinawa, and Japan, we received comments such as: *Is that an airplane or the box it came in?* And *That's 40,000 rivets in loose formation,* or *That airplane can't really fly, it's just so ugly that the Earth repels it.* Using our best pompous British accents, we would respond with: *The Freighter might be rubbish, but at least it's British rubbish.*

In my opinion, the only good thing about operating the Bristol Freighter for the RNZAF was the job itself. Flight crews and maintenance personnel, accompanied by their families, were posted to Singapore for two-year assignments with 41 Squadron, based at RAF Changi from 1955 through to the early 1970s. I had the good fortune to be with the Squadron for two tours: 1960 to 1961 and 1965 to 1968. During those years we traveled, albeit slowly and in great discomfort, from the Maldives, Gan Atoll, Ceylon, and Nepal on our northwestern side to Japan, Korea, Hong Kong, Philippines, Vietnam, and Borneo on the northeastern side. Additionally, during my time in Singapore, we were involved in three Southeast Asian wars: two British and one American.

Operationally, we did amazing things with the Freighter, flying in and out of very short (3,000 feet) airstrips, sealed or often grass, dirt or gravel, with temperatures of 95 degrees F (or higher), and often at the maximum takeoff weight of 44,000 pounds. Miraculously, the Freighter rarely broke down, but then, except for the engines, this plane didn't have many moving parts! During the first British war—the Malayan Emergency 1948–1960— the Squadron flew airdrop missions over the jungles of the Malayan Peninsula, using RAF Kuala Lumpur as a base. During the second British war—Indonesian Confrontation 1964–1966—the Squadron flew airdrop missions over the Sarawak jungles, using RAF Kuching as the forward base.

For the American war—South Vietnam 1965–1975— our Bristol Freighter operations were from out-of-country; that is, from Singapore bases. We also used South Vietnam airfields for transit between Singapore and Hong Kong. In the early 1960s, Hong Kong passenger flights were flown northbound via RAF Labuan in North Borneo and Clark USAF Base in the northern Philippines. Southbound from

Hong Kong, we would return to Singapore with a refueling stop at Saigon. Then, from the mid 1960s, northbound from Singapore to Hong Kong was through Danang or Qui Nhon, and southbound through Saigon.

1958: Southeast Asian Days

Southeast Asia is like the Durian fruit:
prickly, strange, smelly and beautiful,
revolting, enchanting, an offence and an addiction
~ An Eye for the Dragon, Dennis Bloodworth

MY FIRST TASTE AND SMELL of Southeast Asia was landing a New Zealand Air Force (RNZAF) airplane at Kupang airport on Timor Island, Indonesia. This significant event for me at the age of 19 occurred in August of 1958, with no insight that half my working life would be spent in this exotic region of the world. Accompanied by a large crew, I had flown to Kupang from Darwin in northern Australia on a routine mission from New Zealand to Singapore. We were delivering a changeover Bristol Freighter and spare engine for 41 Squadron of the RNZAF, based at the Royal Air Force (RAF) airfield at Changi. This squadron had been assigned by the New Zealand government to assist the British Commonwealth effort in defeating the Communist insurgency in Malaya known as the Malayan Emergency, a conflict that began in 1949 and continued until 1960.

In 1949, three RNZAF Dakotas (C-47Bs) arrived at RAF Changi to serve with the Far East Air Force. The unit was named A-Flight of 41 Squadron and was the first New Zealand regular unit to serve in Southeast Asia since the ending of WW2. The Unit returned to New Zealand in 1951, eventually to be replaced at RAF Changi with a full Squadron in 1955, newly equipped with Bristol Freighters. This airplane had a maximum takeoff weight of 44,000 pounds versus the C47's 31,000 pounds, had seating for 36 troops instead of 28, but oddly, the crew configuration was designed for only one pilot, one navigator, and one radio operator, whereas the C47 required two pilots, a navigator, and radio operator. More on this enigmatic decision elsewhere.

In 1955, flight crews and maintenance personnel, accompanied by their families, were moved from New Zealand to Singapore for two-year assignments with 41 Squadron based at RAF Changi. Four Bristol Freighter aircraft were assigned to the Squadron, but subject to tail-number changeover for periodic heavy maintenance back in New Zealand. Initial crew conversion to the Freighter was accomplished at the RNZAF Base in Auckland by the Transport Support Unit (TSU), which also operated the Freighters that remained in New Zealand. TSU also had the responsibility of flying the periodic aircraft changeovers between New Zealand and Singapore, which was the reason for my first visit to Southeast Asia in August 1958. Earlier that year I'd been assigned to TSU for Freighter pilot conversion, then for local flights within New Zealand and occasionally to eastern Australia or Fiji.

There was nothing glamorous about piloting the Freighter, but it offered a unique escape to other countries from isolated New Zealand, a country surrounded by thousands of miles of ocean in every direction. In the 1950s the vast majority of world travelers from New Zealand went by sea. The country's only international airline, Tasman Empire Airways Limited (TEAL) operated limited Flying Boat services to Australia until 1954, then piston-powered Douglas DC-6s until 1961 and finally, turbo-prop Lockheed Electras until it became jet-setting time with Douglas DC-8s in 1965.

Travelers needed deep pockets to afford flying from—or to—New Zealand until the advent of the wide-bodied jets in the early 1970s. In 1958, when I flew what would ultimately become a very popular tourist route in the jet age, there was only one jet airliner in commercial operation and that was the de Havilland Comet, operating on limited routes in the world. However, big change was on the way, with the first Boeing 707s going into operation with Pan American Airlines in late 1958.

The Freighter aircraft changeover journeys were operated from 1955 through to the last years of the 1970s from Auckland to Singapore on a circuitous route that consumed 30–40 flight hours, over a period of four to five days, assuming no breakdowns en route (which were common). Then, after a few days layover at RAF Changi, the same crew would fly home to Auckland along a similar route. The number of fuel stops along the way depended on the load being carried. In August 1958, we were carrying a spare Freighter engine for the Squadron at RAF Changi, so our route was Auckland to Norfolk Island to Brisbane to Cloncurry to Darwin to Timor to Bali to Jakarta to Singapore.

In contrast, after the introduction of jet airliners, this route from Auckland to Singapore could be flown in less than ten hours! That's what millions of tourists have been doing every day since the 1970s, with no concept of what it was like to fly across the Tasman Sea, the great Australian Outback, and the countless islands of Indonesia, below 10,000 feet, penetrating unseen thunderstorms, at one quarter of their jet airliners' speed and making fuel stops every five to six hours of flight. At least the unique experience for us cost nothing, and better still, we were paid for doing it.

Though it cost us nothing, it was actually very demanding work from the early trip preparation through each day's flying to each stopover, plus dealing with refueling, flight planning, local customs, immigration authorities, and accommodation if staying overnight.

The Exotic Delights of Southeast Asia

From my first short visit to Singapore in 1958, then as a permanent resident for five years in the 1960s, another three years in the 1970s, all with the RNZAF, then ultimately as a civilian from 1979 to 1982, I learned to love everything about the environment. The sights, sounds, and smells of Asia became my real home, with a more desirable lifestyle than New Zealand, the country to which I reluctantly returned for miserable periods between assignments.

My first impression was of heat and humidity. Singapore is situated 90 miles north of the equator and has a typical tropical climate with abundant rainfall, high temperatures and high humidity year round. Many of its climate variables, such as temperature and relative humidity, do not show large month-to-month variation. 24-hour temperatures averaged 84° F, with a humidity level at 86 percent. Unlike the last four decades in Southeast Asia, air-conditioning in buildings, vehicles, and military airplanes was almost nonexistent until 1975. We and our families slept under mosquito nets, slightly cooled by ceiling fans and a daily intake of Palidrine antimalarial pills. Violent thunderstorms were a feature of mid-afternoons, bringing down deluges of water on homes and offices that lacked glass windows, only wooden shutters; the mass of water taken away by deep monsoon drains.

The next impression was the smells, good and bad. The good was the fragrance of tropical flowers such as

23

Frangipani, Hibiscus, and Bougainvillea. The bad was the stench from open drains: human excrement, rotting food, and the skin of durian fruit (in season). Often, these outdoor smells were overwhelmed by the tantalizing cooking aromas from roadside food stalls: fried garlic prawns, curry puffs, chili crab, chicken and pork satay, fried rice with prawns, and banana-leaf curried chicken, lamb, or goat.

These Chinese, Malay, and Indian dishes were washed down with ice-cold bottles of Tiger and Anchor beer, Gin and Tonic (Schweppes for its anti-malarial quinine), and Scotch Whisky to kill the stomach bugs … or so we thought. Many of us smoked high quality British cigarettes like 3-5s (Tiga-Limas in Malay speak) that came in sealed aluminum cans. Some even smoked the clove flavored Indonesian Kretek cigarettes. Another eating delight was the assortment of fresh tropical fruits: papaya with fresh squeezed lime, mangos, mangosteens, rambutans, and ultimately durian—a dubious choice that took me 15 years to try—and then became addicted!

In my earliest years in Singapore and Hong Kong, the real fun was shopping for items unattainable in New Zealand or Australia: cans of foam shaving cream, Old Spice and Mennen's after-shave lotion, razor blades that stayed sharp for two weeks instead of two days, flip-flops for the communal shower stalls, miniature transistor radios and high quality cameras from Japan—all at affordable prices for us low-paid military personnel. Most significantly, we could purchase *Playboy* magazines, an item that would be searched for, and confiscated by, the little Hitler thugs of the Australian Customs Service at Darwin during return flights to New Zealand. There was no TV in Singapore in the early 1960s, so watching movies in the downtown air-conditioned theaters, while drinking beer and smoking, was a special treat, and likewise, there were outdoor movies shown weekly at the Temple Hill Officers Mess —drinking and smoking! Local and world news came from the Singapore newspaper *The Straits Times*, and *Time and Mad* magazines from the USA. In all, it was a lifestyle far removed from dreary old New Zealand.

Did we realize how fortunate we were? Perhaps, but most of us had been volunteers in becoming Air Force aviators, and took every assignment for granted. When we joined up, we were fully cognizant that the New Zealand government had placed Army and Air Force Units in Singapore and Malaya from the early 1950s. More specifically, in my case, Bill Tremayne, my father, had been the 41 Squadron Engineering Officer in Singapore in 1955, so being there was simply unbroken family business. However, like me, some of the Squadron members who were there in 1960 were destined to return to Singapore over the next 15 years, and that was certainly fortunate for the individuals and their families. By the end of 1981, I had completed three tours in Southeast Asia with the RNZAF, and one as a civilian pilot for the Australian company, Stillwell Aviation—and loved every day of being an outlier in a foreign paradise.

1958: Australian Outback—
Drinking, Driving, and Crashing

AS A COMPANION PIECE to my drinking and flying story, I have a curious tale from the Australian Outback. In August 1958, I was flying my first international trip from New Zealand to Singapore and return in a Bristol Freighter. Onboard was a large crew of instructors, trainees, and one special passenger, Antoni (Toni) Glowacki. During WW2, Toni had been a Polish Air Force fighter pilot attached to the Royal Air Force (RAF). Flying Hurricanes during the Battle of Britain, he had shot down five German aircraft in one day. Later, he was with the RAF Polish Squadron No.303, then attached to a USAAF Squadron flying P-51 Mustangs over occupied Europe.

On the flight back from Singapore, our airplane broke down at Cloncurry for five days. On one of those days, the Senior Air Traffic Controller at Cloncurry airport took four of us for the 40-mile drive in his brand new car (a frog-green British Vauxhall) to the uranium mine at Mary Kathleen for a Happy Hour and barbecue with the many Eastern European migrants working there. Toni was in his element as he recognized many of the languages spoken. On the drive back to Cloncurry, we hit—head-on—the only vehicle coming the other way. It was 1958, so no seat belts available

26

in those days! The driver's chest and stomach managed to fold up the steering wheel, but the rest of us suffered only minor injuries. I was in the back seat with Ray Turner and Inky Collins, with Toni in the front left seat. Considering all his dangerous wartime flying Toni must have thought, *After what I've been through and survived, this is how I die, in the red dust of the Aussie Outback.*

The inebriated blokes in the Beaut-Ute (pickup truck) we had hit, kindly loaded us onto the truck bed (no sides, and cuddled up with two smelly dogs), then drove us to Cloncurry for another wild drinking party. Our badly bruised driver explained why he had hit the truck, which had been parked, facing us with headlights on, on the left-hand side of the road. That was on the correct side for us to be driving, which we were. The problem was that when our driver saw the lights, he naturally assumed the truck was parked on the right side of the road, so he jogged left of the lights only to discover we were sliding downhill in the dirt, then corrected to the right, but not far enough to clear the front grill of the truck!

Toni had many stories to tell of his wartime exploits and beyond. In England, having survived the war, he arranged to have his family smuggled out of Soviet-held Poland, then immigrated to New Zealand. Once there, he joined the New Zealand Air Force as an instructor, helping with the transition from propeller fighter planes to the new British jet fighter-bomber, the De Havilland Vampire. In 1958, he was assigned as the Operations Officer at the Whenuapai Base where I was converting to flying the Bristol Freighter. An airplane that wasn't much fun to fly, but help was at hand; being current on the Harvard AT-6, I got to fly the one assigned to the Base, a plane known as the *Station Hack.*

The Station Hack was used locally to fly simulated attack missions on New Zealand Navy ships, operating out in the Hauraki Gulf, east of Auckland. On one memorable mission, Toni was in the back seat, and after a number of dive-bombing runs, he asked to fly from the backseat and repeat the bombing runs. He was not current on the Harvard, and after handing over control, he surprised me by flying the plane erratically. He was all over the place with the flight controls until ... rolling into the dive-bombing maneuvers where his angles and controls became rock-solid. What I saw that day was a master of attack profiles, a retired fighter pilot who had been a deadly opponent of the Germans.

Unfortunately, the Whenuapai Station Hack I flew in 1958 was a replacement from the previous year. The Harvard AT-6 from early 1957 had crashed during a similar training mission for the New Zealand Army at a camp between Auckland and Hamilton. The two crew members, a pilot and navigator, on conversion to the Bristol Freighter, were both killed in the crash. Bad stuff happens when low-time pilots become too excited about thrilling their spectators.

1959: Turnbacks Can Kill You, but Girlfriends May Save You

THE VAMPIRE FB-5 CRASH LANDING involved a classmate of mine, the pilot known as Reggie. To set the stage for his dramatic accident, we need to go back to our last few months at Base Wigram in 1957. Reggie had found a most attractive girlfriend we thought looked like Kim Novak, one of Hitchcock's beautiful enigmatic actresses. Our graduated class arrived at Base Ohakea in early January 1958, where we were referred to as Bog-Rats by the *experienced* Vampire pilots. One of the senior officer's family was still living at Wigram and had commanded that a Devon flight shuttle from Ohakea to Wigram be operated every weekend. It flew south late on Friday afternoon and returned to Ohakea on Sunday afternoon. Reggie was a regular passenger because his Kim Novak still lived close to Wigram.

Early on a Friday afternoon, Reggie was just airborne off Runway 27 at Ohakea when the engine turbine failed—too low to bailout—but he quickly determined he had the airspeed and height to make a 180-degree turn back to land on Runway 09. He made the turn, only to realize the strong headwind of 25 knots had not only placed him closer to the approach end of Runway 09, but it was now a tailwind. He explained to me that he had flown over the approach end of

29

the runway with an estimated groundspeed of 200 knots. So, he made the smart decision to keep flying until the speed washed off, which took him past the airfield, over paddocks full of cattle and sheep, between a row of tall pine trees, banked to thread the needle, and finally, as stated in the accident report: *At this stage I lost control.*

When the dust settled, uninjured, he looked down beneath his feet where he could see clumps of grass mixed with many chips from the laminated wood fuselage. When the crash-crew arrived accompanied by the Base Commander, Reggie was still sitting in the cockpit. His first comment was, "Sir, I hope this doesn't interfere with my Devon flight to Wigram this afternoon?"

1959: Antarctic Dreaming

The strange case of good dreams morphing into nightmares

ONE AND A HALF YEARS into my Air Force career, I had obtained the Right Stuff, but found myself in a world of Wrong Stuff, being transferred to fly the Bristol Freighter, a plane that provided no glamour or excitement in piloting, but did offer free international travel, albeit slow and noisy, to exotic places in Asia and the South Pacific. By early 1959, I was in the running for assignment to 41 Squadron RNZAF in Singapore, having been route-checked on a flight to RAF Changi in August 1958. Then I volunteered for duty with the Antarctic Flight. Why, oh why?

I recall the primary reason was a personal dislike of flying the Freighter and its operation within New Zealand, but it was also about joining a great adventure. From what I'd read and heard about the RNZAF Antarctic operations in the Beaver and Auster airplanes, supporting Ed Hillary's race to the South Pole in 1957–58, it sounded exciting, something I wanted to be part of. From a briefing about what the training in the South Island would be like, including fun times hanging out in the Mount Cook National Park, I was hooked. I do have to own up to a third reason for volunteering (minor of course!), that involved a Christchurch girlfriend. That girl was Annette, whom I'd first met at the Wings Graduation Ball in December 1957 and kept in contact during 1958 on flying visits to Base Wigram.

Whatever the reasons for this desired posting from Base Auckland, I showed up at Wigram in early April 1959, reporting to the Antarctic flight's assigned hangar located at the southern end of the airfield. It was exciting to be there, meeting the other nine volunteers. The pilots: Les Jeffs, Bill Cranfield, Graham Derby and Pete Rule. The ground crew: Wally Tarr, Ron Fergusson, Athol Boag, Graham Hodson, and Bob Johnstone. Bill Cranfield had created a brilliant training syllabus that taught us new techniques about operating ski-planes and survival in extreme polar conditions. Bill was a natural Bush Pilot who would've been totally at home flying in the northern wastelands of Alaska and the Yukon.

The extensive specialized training included a lengthy period in the Southern Alps, learning the techniques of glacier travel and survival in extremely cold environments. By today's standards our climbing equipment was primitive: wood-shaft ice axes, ten-point iron crampons, manila ropes, no harnesses or mechanical descenders, leather boots, and inadequate clothing. To complete the preparation for Antarctic operations we began training for ski-plane takeoffs and landings on the Tasman Glacier. The flying was done in the RNZAF's Antarctic Beaver and Mount Cook Airline's ski-wheel Austers. The RNZAF Antarctic Auster remained at Wigram, although its performance was superior to the Mount Cook aircraft, but lacked the wheel-ski landing gear for use between Mount Cook airfield and the Tasman Glacier. Once in the Antarctic, this Auster would be equipped with basic skis for its landing gear.

Sadly, the training and fun was over in six months, and in the southern spring of 1959, the Beaver and Auster were shipped by the NZ Navy to McMurdo Sound with a unit complement of three pilots—Les Jeffs, Bill Cranfield, and Pete Rule, and the maintenance crew under the control of Wally Tarr. Graeme Derby and I were to remain in New Zealand. The plan for us was to return to our original units, be on standby if needed, expecting to replace Bill and one other pilot for the 1960–61 southern summer at Scott Base.

So far, so good, except I had to fly those nasty Bristol Freighters again. But I would remain on upward mobility career-wise with my Antarctic Dreams still intact. Besides, my girlfriend, Annette, had been moved to Auckland for advanced nurse training, so life was wonderful that summer of 1960. I even came to appreciate the Freighter after an international trip to Honolulu to rescue a RNZAF Hastings airplane with a destroyed engine. Steve Evison and I were the pilots, island-hopping from Whenuapai to Norfolk to Nandi to Canton to Christmas to Hickam. We laid over for a week at the Officers Club at Fort Derussy on Waikiki Beach, before returning to New Zealand on the same route. This first visit to American soil became the genesis for a long-standing desire to live in the USA.

Back in New Zealand, the news came through from Scott Base, Antarctica, that Les Jeffs and Pete Rule had crashed the Beaver near the Beardmore Glacier. They were uninjured and would not be rescued for a week, with the help of Bill Cranfield, extracting them to safety in the Antarctic Auster. Within a month I was advised to forget about RNZAF Antarctic operations, and would be posted to 41 Squadron at RAF Changi. So by mid-March 1960, I was flying the Freighter in the wonderful Southeast Asian environment: To Hong Kong (for my 21st birthday), Ceylon and Gan Atoll, Thailand, Laos, Borneo, Philippines, and Japan. Furthermore, in August 1960, Annette and I were married at RAF Changi, purchased a new car to bring back to NZ, and settled into the joys of Singapore living.

The scene was now set for something going wrong, which began with a message from RNZAF Headquarters that the Antarctic Flight was spooling up again with a replacement for the crashed Beaver, a DHC Otter, ready for the summer season 1961–62. I was required to be back at Base Wigram for training and preparation no later than April 1961. Owen Staples, the 41 Squadron Commander, an excellent boss, said he would tell HQ to leave me alone because he needed me at 41 Squadron. That's when I made the definitive decision that would destroy three years of my flying career, believing I was doing the right thing for the Air Force who had trained me to be an Antarctic Ski-Pilot. I thought that the unique training in 1959 made me someone special. What a delusion. Without fully considering the financial impact of leaving Singapore after only one year, I agreed to the request, despite Owen Staples doing his best to explain that I was making a big mistake leaving the Squadron.

Owen Staples had been right. I was a first class idiot, because one month before my scheduled return to New Zealand, the RNZAF Antarctic Flight was again cancelled and would never be reformed. Owen gave me the bad news and I implored him to have me stay on at 41 Squadron. He declined (in my opinion, rightly so), and explained that my replacement was already on his way to Singapore. That event was a lasting lesson for a naïve youth who had complete trust in the Air Force Service. Owen left me with a message to be circumspect about unquestioningly accepting assignments from HQ. Later in my career, I learned that none of these appointments were objective, so be careful what you ask for.

The disastrous outcome: we found ourselves back at Base Wigram, Christchurch. The tropical warmth and financial support for married officers in Singapore was exchanged with the start of another miserable New Zealand winter and budgetary hardship. No car, no Base Housing, no furniture, and Annette pregnant with our first son, Jeremy. I had been assigned a temporary position as the Flying Wing Adjutant, a meaningless job without further career prospects. I was permitted to fly the Harvard AT-6 up to ten hours per month, but otherwise, my Antarctic dreams became nothing but an echo of adventure.

After six months of boredom pushing paper in a dull office, I was rescued by the United States Navy (USN). They had requested a New Zealand Air Force pilot to join their Antarctic Squadron VX-6 as an observer and active ski-pilot at their Base at McMurdo Sound. I was chosen and attached to the Squadron for the southern summer of 1961–62. They checked me out on one of their DH-C Otters at Christchurch, then flew me south to the McMurdo Base on a ski-equipped C-130 Hercules to fly Otters for five months in Antarctica. The Otter felt like a large clumsy DH-C Beaver, with a propeller turning so slow I could almost count the blades! But as a single-engined workhorse, it was capable of carrying a large load.

One week after I joined the Squadron, one of their Neptune Reconnaissance planes crashed on takeoff from the Australian Antarctic base at Wilkes Station. The initial investigation blamed the bomb-bay bladder fuel tank coming loose on the rough snow surface and spraying fuel into the Jet Assisted Take Off (JATO) rocket exhausts. Some crew members were killed and others badly burned. It was a sad time for the members of VX-6, and had me pondering whether I'd made the right choice with this new assignment. It seemed like a dangerous mission to be flying with the USN in Antarctica, but the career opportunity was too good to refuse, and the increased income was a blessing for my family. During my time in Antarctica I received additional allowances for hazardous flight duty, with daily meals and lodging expenses paid by the USN.

At McMurdo, I was assigned to fly the Otter airplanes with Lieutenant Ron Bolt USN on numerous missions, initially to and from the Beardmore Glacier Air Facility, and later as far north as Lady Newnes Ice Shelf. Also, there were missions to Little America and Roosevelt Island. Our permanent home was at the McMurdo Base (known as *The City*), living in quarters with a group of US Navy pilots—all great people. However, much of my time in Antarctica was spent at remote locations, hundreds of miles from McMurdo. In the Otter, we carried full survival gear that included a three-person pyramid tent, snow shovels, gasoline stove, a large tarpaulin, and cartons of canned and boxed C-rations. We also toted individual packs of additional cold-weather clothing and personal items.

After deciding on an operating base location for five or more days, we would erect the tent, or tents—if we had passengers. Then we'd dig a deep trench in the snow and cover it with the tarpaulin, packing that down around the edges with snow blocks. With snow steps leading down at one end of the trench, snow benches cut into the side walls and a crude chimney at the other end to exhaust the stove's carbon monoxide fumes, we had a crew dining space. A short distance away we would dig a much smaller trench for use as a latrine.

Some days at the Beardmore Camp, we were entertained by the arrival of a Hercules C-130 bringing jet fuel (JP4) for US Army Iroquois helicopters and Aviation gasoline (Avgas) for the Otter. The C-130 would touch down on its skis, open the rear ramp while still moving, and roll 50 gallon fuel drums onto the snow, then close the ramp, full power on the engines, and accelerate across the snow and take off. Always an impressive display. Our Beardmore camp was situated at a beautiful location on the southern extent of the Ross Ice Shelf, 350 miles from McMurdo Base, and 30 miles from the tongue of the Beardmore Glacier, the same glacier that the British Scott Expedition had used to reach the South Pole in 1912. On one of the our many Otter missions from Beardmore, we landed close to the tongue of the Axel Heiberg Glacier, the route used by Norway's Amundsen Expedition to the South Pole in 1911. Not only did Amundsen beat Scott to the South Pole, his team survived; Scott's didn't. As a teenager I had read all the available books on the race to the South Pole, so seeing the actual locations where the dramas had played out was a gratifying experience.

During another Otter mission, Ron Bolt and I spent a week near the historic location at the Bay of Whales, where Amundsen had begun and ended his journey to the South Pole in 1911. Later, the Bay of Whales became the location for the *Little America* exploration bases originally established in 1929 by Admiral Richard Byrd of the US Navy. The last base, *Little America IV*, was established nearby in 1946. We flew over the area, but saw little sign of the base. We were using a semi-permanent camp location on the highest point of Roosevelt Island, which was not an island in the normal sense, but simply a large white bump on top of the Ross Ice Shelf. Taking off in the Otter from Roosevelt was exciting, particularly in partial whiteout conditions because it was difficult to gauge whether we were running up or down the sides of the bump. This was exacerbated by a rough snow-ice surface, and on one occasion we failed to get airborne after a teeth-shattering run that was probably uphill. The whiteouts were so bad at the camp, I recall blindly walking into four-foot high snow walls and falling into deep trenches we had made, though the visibility was perfect to see dark or colored objects: tents, the airplanes, fuel drums, and people—all floating in a void, without shadows.

Between the Otter missions, I was able to acquire some copilot seat time in the Hercules C-130 and the Sikorsky S-58 helicopter. The C-130 flights took me to South Pole Station and the New Byrd Station. The S-58 helicopter flights took me to the Dry Valleys and the historic huts on Ross Island that had been built for the 1907 and 1911 expeditions of Scott and Shackleton. Standing at the geographic South Pole was a momentous occasion, but without any doubt, I can say my visits to the Dry Valleys by helicopter were absolutely unique. These glacier-free, ice-free, and snow-free valleys are hidden amid the mountains and glaciers on the eastern side of McMurdo Sound. The valleys are deep, with near vertical walls, and with ponds of liquid-water in ambient temperatures well below freezing. Being there, it was easy to imagine I was visiting another planet.

In late February, I once again volunteered, most unwisely, to return from McMurdo Base to Christchurch on the Icebreaker USS Glacier (GB4). It was a hellish seven days at sea with malfunctioning engines and jammed roll control stabilizers. By design, Icebreakers have a rounded keel for riding up on sea-ice, and need the assistance of underwater stabilizers to reduce extreme roll motions. For much of that voyage the ship rolled up to 30 degrees left and right, requiring us to be strapped into bunks, eating only cold sandwiches, avoiding overflowing toilet sewage sloshing back and forth along the corridors. All this was just another lesson from my Antarctic dreams. Don't ever volunteer for anything in the military!

Back at the Wigram Base, and once again becoming a serving officer of the New Zealand Air Force, nothing much had changed. The same dismal office job, but at least I had accumulated enough income from the Antarctic duty to purchase a car and some furniture for an off-base rental house. This was good news for Annette, Jeremy, and new son Christopher. But for me, it was now a waiting game, hoping to get back on a career track that involved flying, which took two years. Finally, in early 1964, I was assigned a position as Qualified Flight Instructor (QFI) at Wigram's Flying Training School. I would be training ab-initio students on the Harvard AT-6 and advanced students on the twin-engined Devon. The QFI course was strenuous, but I focused on absorbing the ultimate Right Stuff after being exiled to an aviation wasteland for crimes I hadn't committed.

The instructors at the Central Flying School (CFS) were Top-Gun quality: Ted Arundel, the Unit Commander, Stewart Boys; fighter pilot, Robin Klitscher, master of aerodynamics; and my personal flight instructor, Barry Reid, who taught me the dastardly tricks of how to win the CFS Lawson Aerobatic Trophy—which I did! Something I had forgotten was the final assessment in my logbook that shows I was awarded an Above Average rating in pure flying (a first since joining the Air Force) and a Master Green Instrument Rating (also first time). It's no wonder I was subsequently considered a hotshot pilot after leaving the New Zealand Air Force, away from a few subjective detractors in that small world of aviation. In the bigger aviation world of Australia, and then the vast world of the United States, I was awarded first class status as a professional pilot by junior crew members who had flown Air Force One, SR-71 Blackbirds, B-52 Buffs, and the Nighthawk F-117.

It was a good feeling to be back in the line of normal Air Force pilot progression, and I still retained a seniority advantage, having joined at age 17, which offset the four years of being screwed around for doing what I thought was the right thing. Within one year, I was given a prize assignment—back to Singapore and 41 Squadron, still flying the Bristol Ugly, but this time in two new shooting wars, one with the Indonesians in the jungles of northern Borneo, plus the bonus of joining the Americans in fighting the dirty little Commie Rats invading South Vietnam.

Unforeseen behind those jungle ramparts of war, the RNZAF received a fleet of Lockheed Hercules C-130s that would be used for support in South Vietnam and also for a return to Antarctica. And so I found myself back on the ice in late 1968 flying C-130s from Christchurch to McMurdo on joint support missions for the US Navy and New Zealand's Scott Base. So the world turns!

1960: Vientiane, Laos—
Exclusive Memories from Southeast Asia

IN MAY, 1960, I turned 21, a momentous birthday that was spent getting inebriated in Hong Kong with my crew covering all the costs. A month later I was flying missions into Vientiane, Laos, distributing schoolbooks that were gifts from the New Zealand government to the children of Laos. My primary assignment in Vientiane was to act as our unit's Liaison Officer with an American Aid organization. My contact was Roxanne (Roxy), a beautiful young woman from California—maybe a CIA operative? Among many exciting things we did together was water-skiing on the muddy Mekong River with two MI-6 agents from the British Embassy in Laos. Fortified by bottles of excellent champagne, we skied between the carcasses of water buffalos that were floating downriver. I ended the day's activities with a bleeding rope-burned wrist and in love with Roxy after she dragged me into the shallows beneath the boathouse.

Travelling between our hotel and Roxy's apartment was a risky business at night with the sporadic sound of AK-47 gunfire from the nearby streets. Roxy explained that the two factions of The White and Red Princes' soldiers were making contact during the hours of darkness. In the restaurant below our hotel rooms a French woman waitress with bushy black armpit hair had a very erotic, pheromonal effect on this very young, simple country boy from New Zealand. Unfortunately, her boyfriend was a French paratrooper in Laos to train the White Prince's soldiers who kept a close watch on this most desirable woman. To impress her, I did learn to the use French words, "Deux Seven-Up, Une Carlsberg." We had been advised not to drink the water at the hotel and instead use Seven-Up for drinking and cleaning teeth, so I quickly determined that the price of two Seven-Ups equaled the price of one Carlsberg—for the Squadron accounting records, of course!

Six months later, I was called out for an emergency flight to Bangkok. We left RAF Base Changi, Singapore in the early hours of the morning, advised that we could expect a briefing by the British military attaché on arriving in Bangkok. Our task, given by the Attaché (an RAF Wing Commander), was to fly emergency medical supplies from Bangkok to an airfield called Udorn that was close to the Laotian border. The supplies were for the staff of the British Embassy in Vientiane. In December 1960, the information on the Udorn airfield we were given by RAF intelligence officers at Changi, then later by the British Embassy folks in Bangkok, lacked the reality of what we found.

Apart from the perfect US military-style concrete 10,000-foot runway in the middle of nowhere, nothing else was there: no buildings, no taxiways, no parking ramp, and no navigation beacons. After landing, still not sure we were at the right place, a VW Combi drove up with two Embassy personnel who collected the supplies, then left in a hurry. With the task complete, we flew back to Bangkok, spent the night, and departed for RAF Changi the next morning, only to be recalled to Bangkok after being airborne for 20 minutes. We were assigned a new task: fly back to Udorn to evacuate the families of the British Embassy staff in Vientiane and bring them to Bangkok. We did, then without receiving further assignments, left Bangkok for Singapore the same afternoon.

1960: Left to Die in the South China Sea

ONE MORNING after showing up for work at 41 Squadron's base at RAF Changi, I was taken aside by Owen Staples, the Squadron Commander, who told me to dress for flying, then climb in a Land Rover with a driver who would take me to an undisclosed location. That location turned out to be a jetty on the Johore Straits, from where I was hustled onto an RAF Rescue Launch. Still without any briefing or explanation from the crew *(sit down, hold on, and shut up)*, the Launch moved out from shore and headed east at high speed, eventually running fast below the Malayan Peninsula's southern shore, then swinging north into the South China Sea. I finally realized that I was part of a Search and Rescue training exercise as one of a three-man flight crew that had not volunteered to be the victims of a simulated ocean crash-landing. Bob Poole was a Hastings Captain with the RAF's 48 Squadron, I was with the RNZAF's 41 Squadron Freighters, and a Shackleton NCO crewman (I'll call him Bloggs) with the RAF's 205 Squadron.

The crew of the Rescue Launch didn't seem to know what the full plan was, except to drop us off somewhere in that vast sea in a rubber dinghy, and then, after the exercise was complete in the middle of the night, pick us up and take us back to Singapore. Fortunately, as the senior officer, Bob had been hastily briefed by pilots from 205 Squadron who would be flying the Shackleton maritime patrol plane that would be coming to find us … in the dark! The plan began with the three of us loaded into an inflated dinghy about two hours before dark, with the launch crew standing off some distance until a Shackleton found the dinghy by tracking in on our Portable Radio Beacon (PLB) location. Then, in the dark of night, it would fly by and drop a SAR container that would float close enough for us to retrieve. What could possibly go wrong with this half-assed scheme?

Well, as the night came down like thunder across the bay, and the first heavy rain shower filled the uncovered dinghy, we realized we had been placed in a very real survival scenario. The launch crew had left us with one small container of water, no food, no clothing apart from our tropical flight suits, no cover for the dinghy, and a PLB limited to transmitting non-directional beeps on 121.5 Mhz. We had no way of communicating with the launch crew, or them to us! And what about the sharks that inhabited those tropical waters? There was no briefing on how to handle them without shark repellent, which we doubted would work if we had it. What we desperately wished for was the Launch to come get us, but it would be many hours; they were dealing with engine problems, and like us, drifting into locations unknown.

A reminder for all you armchair reality TV survival drama watchers. In 1960 there were no communication satellites in the sky and GPS was three decades in the future. The three of us in that dinghy had no illusions about the difficulty of being found by the Launch in the dark, or perhaps in the morning, if the sharks left us alone, and our flimsy rubber boat wasn't torn apart on a rocky shoreline. Of course, there would be no video or audio operators coming to our help, because there was no TV in those days in Southeast Asia. It would have been nice to have a smarmy TV director pull alongside in his control boat and offer to 'vote us off the island'!

A few hours after dark we heard the engines of what we hoped was the Shackleton airplane flying at a low altitude above us. After a number of orbits there was a mighty splash close by, which, by meager torchlight we determined was the SAR container. At least it hadn't arrived on top of us and the dinghy, but was too far away to reach with the supplied paddles.

Before leaving the general area, we had to hope that the Shackleton crew had provided our last position to the Launch crew, because except for the sound of heavy rain on us and the sea surface, there was silence from either airplane or boat engines. Around midnight we saw distant lights on the water, which we prayed were from the Launch, so we fired off the two flares we'd been left with—and we were saved—from a survival exercise that was poorly conceived and badly run. For the three stooges assigned to the dinghy, Bob Poole wrote a scathing report outlining the near disaster that could have befallen us because of limited equipment in the dinghy, lack of communication devices, and no backup plans if the launch broke down.

1962: Flight of the Vampire Jet

THE GREATEST THRILL in my military flying career was the opportunity to fly the De Havilland Vampire, a jet-powered fighter-bomber that had been designed during WW2 and operated by the RNZAF from 1952 until 1972. In 1962 at Base Ohakea, I was checked out on two versions of the Vampire: the T-11 dual trainer and the single-seat FB-5. Both versions were more exciting and easier to fly than any of the piston-powered craft that had been my history since joining the Air Force. The Vampire was a first generation turbojet, powered by the first British jet engine, the Rolls Royce Goblin, a centrifugal compressor design. Despite its early lineage, its flight performance was breathtaking for pilots coming from piston-engined airplanes.

Fortunately, my extensive flight training in the Harvard AT-6 had involved air-to-air gunnery, dive bombing, low-level bombing, and air-to-ground rocket and gun attacks. The Harvard AT-6 had also been a platform for learning a full range of aerobatic maneuvers, close formation flying including battle formation fighter tactics. So, after the Harvard AT-6, converting to a real fighter like the Vampire was relatively straightforward. The concepts of using an agile airplane as a weapons platform were well understood; only the high speed and high altitude flight envelope of the Vampire needed to be learned. However,

47

converting from piston-engined airplanes, I needed to adapt to the slower acceleration of turbojet engine and the corresponding need to control rapid throttle movements to avoid initiating a compressor stall.

I flew seven dual instruction flights in the two-seat Vampire T-11 that included extended range navigation missions with external fuel tanks. Then another seven solo trips in the T-11, made pleasant because of the extra elbow room available in the cramped cockpit without the instructor. The T-11 was equipped with Martin-Baker ejection seats that complicated the pre-flight preparation when settling in the cockpit. These first generation ejection seats came with explosive cartridges to launch pilots skyward from the cockpit. As such, close to the ground, they required the airplane to be going faster than a minimum speed and above a minimum altitude to be used successfully. If not, the pilot would probably die connected to a partially-inflated parachute, or impact the ground still attached to the seat.

The real fun began when I was put in charge of the single seat Vampire FB.5 with its cockpit somewhat dissimilar to the T.11. There was no ejection seat, so like the Harvard AT-6, only a parachute to sit on. The instrument panel, gunsight, and control stick looked very like that of a WW2 Spitfire Fighter, so flying the FB.5 was like a Walter Mitty wet-dream from the Battle of Britain, though much faster and much higher. Having operated tail-dragging planes for so long, the incredible thing during Vampire takeoffs was the ease of staying straight on the center line because of the nose-wheel and no propeller to create a left or right swing. After leaving the ground it was not necessary to use the rudder pedals, and in normal high speed flight most maneuvering, including advanced aerobatics, could be done by use of elevator and ailerons only.

One of the glorious aspects of being an Air Force turbojet pilot in 1962 was the high altitude skies above New Zealand belonged to us—and had since 1952. The country's two airlines in those days only operated turbo-prop airplanes: Air New Zealand (ANZ) with Lockheed Electras and National Airways Corporation (NAC) with Fokker Friendships, normally flying below 25,000 feet. Our fleet of Vampires and Canberra bombers had uncontrolled freedom to operate anywhere above that height. No commercial turbojets were in competition until 1965 when ANZ acquired a small fleet of Douglas DC-8s, and in 1968 when NAC acquired a small fleet of Boeing 737s.

As an ex-pat New Zealander living in the USA the last 36 years, I must point out the irony of the current aviation scene in that country. The only turbojet-powered airplanes now flying in the skies above New Zealand are either commercial airliners or toys for rich boys—the vintage Warbird jets. The RNZAF lost its fighter, strike, and trainer turbojets to the political schemes of successive left wing Labour governments. Their Air Force is now little more than a military flying club. Cry, my beloved country.

It was another 20 years before I got to fly a turbojet powered airplane again, the twin-engined Israeli built Westwind Corporate Jet, owned by Bougainville Copper Limited (BCL). The airplane design, its navigation, and communication equipment, and particularly, its two Garrett Turbofan engines, were generations ahead of the Vampire. We operated at altitudes up to and including 42,000 feet at Mach speeds close to the Vampire's compressibility stall, and carried two crew and ten passengers in airconditioned comfort. First flying this plane in 1982 coincided with end of my 25 years of dangerous flying: 20 years in the New

Zealand Air Force, then five years delivering small airplanes from the United States to Southeast Asia, Australia, and New Zealand.

However, flying the Westwind and feeling safe in the air after those 25 years, I foolishly decided to become an alpine mountaineer in my spare time. In so doing, I exchanged one risky lifestyle for another!

1962: Scud Running for Beginners

SCUD RUNNING is loosely defined as follows: In general aviation, scud running is a practice in which pilots lower their altitude to avoid clouds or instrument meteorological conditions (IMC). The goal of scud running is to stay clear of weather to continue flying with visual, rather than instrument, references. This practice is widely accepted to be dangerous and has led to death in many cases from pilots flying into terrain or obstacles, such as masts and towers, generally referred to as CFIT (controlled flight into terrain); however, even instrument-rated pilots sometimes elect to take the risk in situations where the minimum instrument altitudes are too high for their aircraft. (FAA Information.)

In 1957, during RNZAF flight training in the Harvard AT-6, I was introduced to the mandatory flight training lesson called Bad Weather Low Flying. This was officially sanctioned scud running, designed for military pilots to remain beneath a low cloud cover, close to the ground in hilly terrain. The technique was to go as slow as possible but still maintain excellent maneuverability, which required partial extension of flaps (high lift devices) and engine power settings to provide instant climb thrust for steep banking turns, or a rapid climb if needed to avoid fast approaching (unexpected) terrain. The slower speed gave more time to recognize the end of a valley that was blocked by clouds or other hazards such as power lines and towers. This procedure also covered the possibility of reduced visibility from rain or patches of lower clouds than the main base.

During my 42 years of flying, I did my share of scud running, mainly in small, maneuverable airplanes and with the added advantage of being a qualified and experienced instrument pilot. If you can fly safely by flight instrument references only, it is an easy task to climb through a total cloud cover in the event of losing visual contact with the ground. However, there are risks to this action: Does the airplane have enough climb performance to avoid hitting high ground obscured by clouds? Are you climbing into controlled airspace and unseen air traffic? Most importantly, do you have onboard radio navigation equipment to carry out a safe letdown procedure through the clouds to a suitably equipped airfield? Unfortunately, one of the reasons you could be scud running is your airplane or your destination airfield lacked the necessary radio navigation equipment to get you safely back on the ground. Tough luck, Flyboy!

In May of 1962, my scud running days came close to a nasty end on the side of a mountain in the South Island of New Zealand. I was flying a Harvard AT-6 from Wigram Air Base near Christchurch, crossing the Southern Alps westward to the coastal town of Greymouth. Navigation in the AT-6 was limited to map reading: map to ground features if you knew where you were, or ground features to map if you did not have a clue. Radio navigation in the AT-6 was only possible in the Christchurch/Wigram area, where there was a primitive Radio Range Station and DF bearings available from the Wigram Tower. There may have been an NDB (Non-Directional Beacon) at Greymouth, but useless to me in the AT-6 (no airborne receiver), so the entire flight and arrival at Greymouth had to be in visual flight conditions.

Forty miles from Wigram, a solid cloud cover extended over the peaks of the Southern Alps with the layer topping out at 10,000 feet, but excellent visibility above the layer as far west as I could see. I made the questionable decision to continue above the clouds with navigation by dead reckoning—that's a phrase to die for—running a time hack for arrival overhead Greymouth, based on forecast winds. If Greymouth was hidden by clouds, I believed the Tasman Sea off the coast would be clear, allowing a safe descent over water and then an eastward scud run back to Greymouth.

With ten minutes to run to my ETA (estimated time of arrival) for Greymouth, I was presented with the perfect sucker-trap-for-pilots: a wide hole in the cloud cover that reached down to ground level, providing the view of a railway line running through a river valley. Consulting my paper map, I calculated I was looking at the railway that ran through the high peaks from Christchurch to Greymouth, and with little thought of the risks involved, I lowered the landing gear and flaps to begin a rapid spiral descent into the hole. I stopped the descent at 500 feet above the ground, raised the landing gear, adjusted the flap setting and determined that I was flying just below the cloud base, with the AT-6's nose pointing westward along the railway line.

One of the time-honored techniques of low-level scud running is to follow highways, rivers, and railway lines. A very real risk with following railway lines in mountainous terrain is the possibility of unexpected tunnels, and I was entirely unfamiliar with the area surrounding Greymouth, so what dangers could be waiting around the first curve I encountered? Feeling uneasy about my decision to continue this hazardous procedure, I considered the smart option of tight turning back to the hole and spiral climbing back to safety. Alas, looking back, I saw that the hole had closed, so no easy escape; I was committed to do or die along the tracks.

As I continued, I was confronted with a hard-left turn in the valley, and no idea what awaited me around that corner. The cloud base was hugging both sides of the high terrain, limiting any safe escape from the valley except to go straight ahead hoping for the best. To my delight and relief, the valley opened into flat country with the Tasman Sea in the background and the town of Greymouth under a cloud base of 1,500 feet. That was the first occasion when I believed I had friends in high places and promised myself to never do something so stupid again.

A most convincing example of why scud running can be so dangerous was the 1979 accident of Air New Zealand's Douglas DC-10, ANZ Flight 901 that crashed on the slopes of Antarctica's Mount Erebus with its summit above 13,000 feet. The flight crew decided it was safe to descend below the Minimum Safe Altitude (MSA) of 16,000 feet in poor visibility, by descending through a hole in the clouds (sounds familiar) down to an altitude of 1,500 feet above the ocean, then using as their sole navigation aid an INS (Inertial Navigation System) specifically excluded in their operations manual for the conduct of descent below safe sector or enroute altitudes.

The final act in an escalating series of crew errors was the tragic event while scud running below clouds at 260 knots (300 mph) and 1,500 feet altitude. The pilots flying that plane were like me, trained in the Harvard AT-6 with the RNZAF, so why didn't they at least slow down the DC-10 by lowering the high-lift devices, thus giving them more time to avoid the impact, following the 'Terrain-Pull Up' warning they received from the installed GPWS (Ground Proximity Warning System)? That answer lies in the Accident

Report: Their Airline Operations instructions for Antarctic lookie-loo flights included the recommendation not to extend high-lift devices in case the devices became stuck in the extended position. If so, the DC-10 would be incapable of returning to New Zealand, and the crew would have no choice but to land on the ice runway at McMurdo Sound with no cold weather clothing for the 257 persons onboard. What a shoddy, potentially dangerous operation it was!

1963: Walking with Her Majesty, Queen Elizabeth

If you can talk with crowds and keep you virtue,
Or walk with Kings – nor lose the common touch,
Yours is the Earth and everything that's in it,
And – which is more – you'll be a Man, my son.

~ *If*, a poem by Rudyard Kipling

ON MARCH 18, 1963, I had the great honor and unique privilege of escorting Queen Elizabeth the Second past the ranks of one hundred airmen of the Royal New Zealand Air Force. The occasion was Her Majesty's farewell at the conclusion of her Royal Tour of New Zealand. My part in the ceremony was as the Commander of the Royal Guard of Honour. My rank at the time was Flight Lieutenant, aged 23, and even 60 years later I don't believe that after the event, I ever lost the common touch.

I'm sure my detractors out there would say I was never the same unpretentious person again, but regardless, I was impressed that I didn't make any mistakes during the performance. There were many potential risks in what I was required to do, with all the British Commonwealth watching, and I'd be the fall guy when things went wrong. I was also the only person in the large gathering with a speaking part: calling out the commands to my Guard members, asking the Queen to accompany me, then having a nice chat with her during our walk together. I was surrounded by many others that day, any of whom could have made embarrassing mistakes, but none did. These highly skilled and disciplined individuals consisted of the one hundred airmen of the Guard, my excellent Support Officer Wally Tarr, and the brilliant musicians with the band of the RNZAF, led by Warrant Officer Simpson.

This grand performance had been planned and practiced, many times, under the guidance of my Senior Sergeant, Buck Buchanan. Buck was an extraordinary individual, having survived the battles for Crete and North Africa during WW2. He had been captured on the island of Crete, then imprisoned by the German Army in Greece, but escaped, crossing the Aegean Sea in a small boat to Turkey. From there, he was sent back to his unit in North Africa where he was awarded the Military Medal (MM) for bravery. Buck was always there to guide me with his military wisdom and help me on the parade ground in preparation for walking with the Queen. He introduced me to great military writers and was a fine companion during field and survival exercises with our aircrew students. Without his help and advice, I would not have been the officer I became in later years.

Living and working in the United States since 1985, I'm often queried by military veterans why I talk of my allegiance to Queen Elizabeth as my Commander in Chief. In response, I produce my Commissioning Parchment, which in part states: *Elizabeth the Second, by the Grace of God of the United Kingdom, New Zealand and Her Other Realms and Territories' Queen, Head of the Commonwealth, Defender of the Faith: To Our Trusty and Well-beloved* Peter William Tremayne — *Greeting:*

We, reposing especial Trust and Confidence in your Loyalty, Courage and good Conduct, do by these Presents constitute and appoint you to be an Officer in the Regular Force of the Royal New Zealand Air Force from the First day of May 1957.

From that day in 1957, aged 17, I clearly understood that my ultimate loyalty was to the Crown and Queen Elizabeth, an allegiance that could bypass all politicians, good or bad. It has been said that the real power of the Queen rests in the power she denies to others, in particular, corrupt politicians, which includes presidents and prime ministers.

For my 20 years of military service, that included operations in two wars—South Vietnam and Indonesian Confrontation in Borneo—I was awarded seven medals: four of them with Queen Elizabeth's profile on one side. The oddity about these awards was the lengthy delays in issue after my retirement. Two were available to wear during the last half of my service, but the remainder have been arriving in the US mail, sent from New Zealand over the last 40 years! I'm proud to have them in my possession, but sadly, will never wear them on my left breast on Veteran's Day parades in America. The latest generations here have no idea that New Zealand and Australia joined the USA in fighting—a just fight—against the Communist invaders from North Vietnam. Similarly, they have no knowledge of our fight to save Malaysia from President Sukarno's Indonesian military forces in the jungles of Borneo.

We were Soldiers of the Queen
Dressed in Jungle Green
Living the Dream
Flying the War Machine

As I write these memories, it is good to know that Her Majesty is still active in her nineties and making commonsense statements about the stupidity of wokeness and cancel culture. Unfortunately, her dopey grandson, Harry, has gone off the reservation after marrying an

American. I could have warned him about doing that! As for Meghan, who thought she was marrying a Prince of the Realm (good luck with that), should be happy that he was something ever better—a pilot. Anyway, looking at the photographs of me walking with Elizabeth in March 1963, I see two very young attractive people who have both since lived wonderful exciting lives. God Bless the Queen, and hope that I, too, make it into my nineties.

What a trip for a wild colonial boy from New Zealand! At that time, neither Her Majesty nor I knew that my paternal grandmother was descended from an Irish political prisoner, sent by the English in a convict ship in 1823 to the Fatal Shore (Australia) for the term of his natural life.

1964: At 25, Spin, Crash, Burn – or Not!

All the wide sky
Was there to tempt him as he steered toward heaven,
Meanwhile the heat of sun struck at his back
And where his wings were joined, sweet smelling fluid
Ran hot that once was wax.

~ *Metamorphoses*, Ovid

IN THE CLOSING DAYS OF 1964, shortly before the New Zealand Christmas vacation, I came within seconds of oblivion in an uncontrollable plane that was pointing vertically toward the ground, less than one thousand feet above impact. The plane stalled and rolled with every effort I made to ease the nose from the vertical. My vast experience as a student and instructor piloting the Harvard AT-6 Trainer had me convinced I could not recover from this maneuver before impacting the ground, probably still vertical.

What had brought me to this time and place to die?

I was flying the Number Four position within a formation of four Harvard AT-6s, practicing fighter ground attack missions within the Lake Elsmere military training area, south of Christchurch, New Zealand. We were all Qualified Flight Instructors (QFIs), employed at the RNZAF's primary pilot training school at Wigram Air Base. Our

students had been released from training for the long
Christmas summer vacation, freeing the grownups to go
have some fun in the fleet of Harvards sitting idle and fully
fueled on the ramp. All it took was throwing on a parachute,
running to our assigned plane, imitating the fighter scrambles
of The Battle of Britain. Kick the tires, light the fires, and the
first off the ground was the leader—then brief on Guard
(radio frequency, that is).

On this near fatal day, we were in the capable hands of
Trevor Bland, an experienced fighter pilot in the Number
One position as Formation Leader. The other three, including
me, were from non-fighter backgrounds. We were experienced
pilots, but mostly on large slow transport aircraft. In our
pasts, we had done fighter ground attack exercises in the
Harvard during our initial training, but for me, that was
seven years earlier.

On our way south to the aerobatic and low-level
assigned airspace over Lake Elsmere, the four of us chased
each other's tails, literally. This was air fighting action at its
most exciting game playing, where the lead plane tries to
shake the following planes by using every conceivable
maneuver—rolling, climbing, diving, turning, stalling, spinning,
or a combination of all these things, and constantly pulling
high G-forces. Great fun while it lasted, until Trevor called
us into a low-level battle formation, descending rapidly to
50 feet above the ground, leading us along the left side of a
low ridge in a simulated ground radar shadow. Trevor
advised that the attack profile on the simulated target
would be initiated with a steep pullup to 1,000 feet above
the ground, using max climb power. Then rolling into a
wing-over, perpendicular with the horizon, allowing the
nose to drop, rolling the wings back level, acquiring the
target with the gunsight, and firing the simulated guns until
pulling away from over the target. Executed correctly, the

four planes would be spaced slightly astern of the leader, each approaching the target from spread-out compass headings.

Trevor began a verbal ten second countdown to the pullup. At the five second mark, Number Three slipped back into my right-wing tip, and to avoid a collision I had no option but to rapidly reduce engine power just at the point when Trevor called 'pullup.' *Decision time for me: Either disregard the command and fly ahead level, or do the pullup, simultaneously applying full throttle power, but subconsciously knowing my plane would be close to stalling at the tip-in altitude. I chose the latter maneuver.*

And so, it was. The Harvard stalled and rolled into an inverted nose down attitude, no higher than 1,000 feet above the ground. This event was dangerous enough, until I made the stupid choice of pulling through into the vertical, instead of rolling the plane upright and accepting a slow controllable descent below the horizon. *Now I was falling to earth like Icarus, with wings no more useful than those made of feathers and wax.*

With so little time before impact, I should have panicked, but instead, called on my experience with aerobatic maneuvers, including practice spinning in the Harvard, applying that knowledge not to force an early pitch-up action that could result in a fully developed spin. The plane had to fall and accelerate, allowing the airspeed to move above the stall for the positive G-loading required to bring the nose above the horizon, at which point I would open the throttle to max power and climb away … to live another day!

With only seconds before the inevitable, a temporal illusion transpired, where time expanded long enough to ponder the effect of my death on my young wife, two young sons, and other family members joining us for Christmas within days. As I write this after 57 years, the cognitive inputs during the event are still locked in my memory. In the minutiae of that moment, I could see two fence lines, one which would likely catch the tailwheel if by some miracle I didn't hit the ground. Additionally, there was a farmer standing beside his tractor, staring up wide-eyed at my rapidly approaching plane. The crash would probably miss him, but I imagined what he would see as I hit the ground.

Obviously I survived, but the question remains: How did I pull off this survival stunt? To this day, I fail to understand how that plane, so far outside its performance envelope and so close to the ground, was capable of being coaxed back into the sky. Furthermore, how did I, an experienced hot-shot pilot, get into this death-defying act? Well, it was not entirely my fault. The pilot flying in the Number Three position initiated the near disaster by sliding back into my slot, an action easily corrected in close formation flying, except in this case when it was combined with a required full-powered climb and low level rolling maneuver.

What establishes the difference between death and survival? Is it merely good luck, risk management, professional training, task ability, experience or even divine intervention? Maybe all those things, and though I'm not a religious person, there had been moments when I felt someone out there was looking after me. At those times, the feeling had been most welcome.

I have no doubt that training and experience saved my life in the plummeting plane. At the time I had over five hundred flight hours in the Harvard AT-6, two hundred as a student and the rest as a flight instructor. During those five hundred hours, I estimate half would have been spent in aerobatic maneuvers, including recovery from numerous fully developed spins, sometimes done during instrument-only flights. This technique was part of the *Recovery from Unusual Attitudes* training that had been pounded into me by WW2 pilot instructors in 1957. In essence, the unusual attitude I'd found myself in was a normal aerobatic one, similar to completion of a stall-turn, where the last part of the maneuver is a vertical descent with power off, waiting for the speed to increase above the stall before pulling the nose up above the horizon and applying engine power.

The difference was that normal aerobatic training was done at an altitude high enough to recover above a virtual floor of 3,000 feet above the ground, and I had found myself well below that! Notwithstanding, experience made me hang in the vertical, slowly accelerating toward the ground, until the plane finally achieved a speed that allowed a pull-up before impact.

For my New Zealand aviation historians, searching for official Air Force information on this near fatal accident will provide you with nothing. Trevor was the lead pilot of this four ship battle formation, and only the two of us fully understood what happened that day. Back on the ground at Wigram, we mutually agreed to neither write about nor discuss the incident. He also helped me get my flying mojo back that day. Sadly, Trevor, a good friend and great fighter, pilot died a few years ago, keeping his word to the end.

1965: In Warzones with the Ghost Squadron

I wanted wings till I got the goddam things
Now I don't want them anymore
They taught me how to fly, then sent me off to die
Well I've had a bellyful of war!

~ *The Wild Blue Yonder,* Oscar Brand

THE RNZAF MUSEUM, located on the hallowed fields of the closed Wigram Base near Christchurch, is the repository for what the New Zealand Air Force was in its finest days, which now, hold nothing but echoes. In early 2019, I attended a 41 Squadron Reunion at the Museum. The Squadron was disbanded in Singapore in 1977, but surviving members had been gathering at appropriate aviation locations in New Zealand every two years. I was visiting New Zealand from my home in the USA specifically to be at the reunion. I had not lived or worked in New Zealand since 1979, but kept in regular communication with retired service members about the slow decimation of the country's defense forces. What I wasn't prepared for was the level of socialist corruption from successive Labor governments that had effectively neutered New Zealand's ability to defend its borders.

For example, at the RNZAF Museum in 2019 was a display board entitled *The Singapore Connection.* The second paragraph read as follows: *No. 41 Squadron RNZAF, operating Bristol Freighters was the mainstay of transport operations from 1955. Most of their work was non-military and consisted of regular embassy support flights throughout the region, logistic support, and humanitarian aid.*

This statement was total balderdash, and I suspect, deliberate, to hide the truth about the many warlike operations the Squadron had been involved in. From 1955 to 1960, it was the Malayan Emergency, the battle against Chinese Communists in the jungles of the Malayan Peninsula; from 1964 to 1966 it was the Undeclared War with Indonesia in the jungles of Sarawak; then from 1965 to 1975 it was the battle against the North Vietnamese Communist invasion of South Vietnam. The reality was that 41 Squadron had been involved in shooting-war operations for much of its time in Southeast Asia, so why was the Museum presenting revisionist history? My simple answer—tourism—New Zealand's largest income earner. And where were the majority of those tourists coming from? My best guess: Communist China, Communist Vietnam, and a smaller portion from Indonesia—people from countries that 41 Squadron had once known as enemies, with their soldiers doing their best to kill us.

Perhaps I should give the RNZAF Museum a break; after all, the Museum is not part of the Defense Department and has nothing to do with defending the country, although bizarrely, it's the home of more fighter/bomber firepower than exists in the modern emasculated RNZAF. Ominously, the Museum's apparent misinterpretation about the history of 41 Squadron illuminates an example of an Air Force unit being hidden in plain sight—a Ghost Squadron—a unit that had operated in Southeast Asia for 22 years, achieved extraordinary success for New Zealand in war and peace, but now deliberately forgotten, except by the surviving members of the Squadron, their numbers getting smaller every year.

The most scandalous example of how the New Zealand government and Defense Department treated Squadron members after years of flying into South Vietnam was the denial of the GSM 1992 (Warlike) Vietnam medal. A member from that period, Scotty Wingfield, discovered large gaps in the paper trail concerning 41 Squadron's activities between 1963 and 1975. It took Scotty ten years tracking down information about the support personnel who were onboard hundreds of Bristol Freighter flights into South Vietnam. Scotty's records had shown that the Squadron flew into South Vietnam 572 times, making 1979 landings at 21 different locations, some under fire.

The most significant lost records were Flight Authorization Books, the documents that show details and approval of each flight, including the flight crew members, maintenance support members, and the assigned mission. The Authorization Books after March 1965 were missing from Official Records, so Scotty had to cross-reference flight crew logbooks (including mine) with sworn statements, unit histories, pay and travel allowance records, personal photographs taken in Vietnam, aircraft maintenance logs, and so on. By mid-2021, Scotty's fine efforts resulted in awards of the GSM 1992 (Warlike) Vietnam Medal to 96 Squadron members (ten posthumously) most had originally been denied.

To put this rectified omission into perspective, almost 100 wartime service medals were belatedly awarded to Squadron members who had not been considered worthy, and so really never existed in this Ghost Squadron. Significantly, what Scotty discovered about lost records affects not only the South Vietnam operations, but raises serious questions about the Squadron's operations in

Sarawak from August 1965 to September 1966. If the details of the hundreds of operational missions in Sarawak were lost, then perhaps it was all forgotten and never happened in the official NZ Defense records, and therefore, no Gallantry awards were ever considered for aircrew members.

Fortunately, other Squadron aircrew (still alive) and I know what did happen, and we have our Flight Log Books to tell the story. My records from that time show that by early September 1966, I had completed a total of 162 *Operational* airdrop missions and delivered a total of 1,050,000 pounds of supplies. I can't speak for the other members involved but would guess that many of the pilots, navigators, and signalers would have all exceeded 100 operational missions. Based on my statistics, it would be reasonable to suggest that another 1000 missions were flown by other crews, dropping a total of 6,500,000 pounds. These are impressive figures when you understand the airdrops were supporting combat troops at the jungle forts, that is, on active service operations.

To my knowledge, the only award for 41 Squadron's part in Confrontation was a Mention In Dispatches (MID) for the pilot, Noel Rodger. There were no Gallantry awards, as there had been during the Squadron's participation in the Malayan Emergency in the 1950s. Although we from the British Commonwealth military joke that Americans get their medals out of cornflake boxes, I do like their objective system for determining gallantry awards. An American Distinguished Flying Cross (DFC) will be awarded to flight crew members after they have completed 100 operational missions. So, where are the DFCs for our countless operational missions over the jungles of Sarawak? Sadly, in the New Zealand Air Force of my time, you couldn't expect a commendation for a DFC if your senior officers didn't like you or if they hadn't got theirs first. For the benefit of my readers, in particular you current and past members of the New Zealand Defense Forces, I've jotted down a few memories of the Ghost Squadron's war in Sarawak. Was it really dangerous or were we just having fun in the sun?

1965–66: Indonesian Confrontation— Sarawak Theater of War

IN AUGUST 1965, I flew an RNZAF 41 Squadron Bristol Freighter from Singapore to RAF Kuching, Sarawak, to begin Air Supply operations to the jungle forts along the Kalimantan border with Indonesia. The British, Australians, New Zealanders, and Gurkhas were in a shooting war against Indonesian Regular Army units along the border, including a threat from Indonesian Air Force Fighter aircraft. The RAF's No. 20 Fighter Squadron was on hot standby, with Hunter aircraft at the end of the Kuching runway to provide air cover if our Bristol Freighter or the RAF's Argosy were attacked by Indonesian Mig-21s while we circled the forts. Many of these forts were located close to the border, and therefore, within the range of Indonesian anti-aircraft weapons.

The Squadron quickly realized a serious limitation in operating the Freighter in this hostile environment with the lack of a second pilot. Whatever the reason, from their introduction, our Bristol Freighters were configured for only one pilot. The cockpit looked like an afterthought, a cramped coffin for three crew jammed on top of the slab-sided fuselage. To access this hellhole, a vertical ladder was provided, topped with a heavy trapdoor that if accidentally unhooked would bash one's head, followed by a dead-fall back into the cargo hold. In this crawling-only cockpit was seating for three: pilot on the left, navigator on the right, and radio-operator behind the right seat.

For our Sarawak operations it was determined that during the actual air drop operations close to the border, two qualified pilots would occupy the front seats, each with a set of flight controls. Except for two Freighters that had been built with dual controls, normally used for conversion training and routine check-rides, it was necessary to jury-rig several of the single-pilot aircraft with a second set of controls in the navigator's position for aircraft that would be assigned for airdrop operations in Sarawak.

It's important that I highlight what this conflict between the Indonesians and ourselves was like: to remind those who were not there, too young to remember, or not taught the history of a conflict that became known as the *Undeclared War*. Undeclared it may have been, but it was an authentic and dangerous war for soldiers on the ground and airmen in the sky. If it had not been a serious conflict, why did we carry Sterling submachine guns, why did we require a second pilot in the cockpit during airdrop operations, and why did we need fighter aircraft cover? We attended daily intelligence briefings on the disposition of the enemy and regularly carried airdrop loads made up of Howitzer shells used by the fort gunners to fire into Indonesian territory to protect us from ground to air gunfire. Except in Nepal, very few readers will know that a young Gurkha soldier was awarded the Victoria Cross (VC) for his gallant actions in Borneo during this *Undeclared War!*

Being shot at from the Indonesian side of the Kalimantan Border was a constant threat when circling to drop at the forts, particularly those Drop-Zones (DZ)s very close to the borderline such as Pang Amo, Plaman Mapu,

Nibong, and Stass. Only a small error in circling at those
DZs over the featureless jungle was enough to be in the
range of hostile gunfire. I recall a particular airdrop at
Plaman Mapu during the first six months of our Kuching
operations. The drop load had included many shells for the
Fort's Pack Howitzer, and after a few circuits over the DZ,
their radioman requested a priority to drop all the boxed
shells before the remainder of the load. When asked the
reason, he stated that the enemy was shooting at us on every
circuit, and the fort was trying to neutralize the threat by
pounding them with Howitzer rounds. This was a learning
moment for us, that often close to the border, the British,
Aussie, and Kiwi Army guys would not tell us that we were
being fired on in case we decided to run away without
finishing the drop of food and beer!

In June of 1967, after the end of hostilities with
Indonesia, I was with a Bristol Freighter crew flying from
RAF Changi to Perth, Australia, via Bali, Port Hedland, and
Carnarvon. At Bali, we spent the night at the Hilton Hotel,
and there a young Indonesian waiter commented on our
RNZAF uniforms with the New Zealand patch on the
shoulders. He spoke good English, and after we told him
we were flying a Bristol Freighter from Singapore to
Australia, he explained his recent background as an
Indonesian Army officer serving on the Kalimantan Border
with Sarawak in 1965–66. He then surprised us by revealing
he was on the border when his unit shot down a New
Zealand Bristol Freighter. I told him the Freighter flew away
to fight another day, but he didn't believe me, even when I
explained that I'd flown that airplane back to Singapore the
night after the incident and it whistled across the South
China Sea because of the bullet holes! However, this young
Indonesian ex-soldier was correct. A 41 Squadron Freighter
did take hits from ground fire near the Indonesian border

after inadvertently straying over the invisible line in the jungle, but it made it safely back to Kuching, and I did fly it back to Singapore that night.

I recall another shooting story that ended tragically. I was having a typical tasteless British Army breakfast at RAF Kuching, trying to get my head together for Major Bloodnock's intelligence briefing at 0800 hours. Across the breakfast table from me was an RAF Flight Lieutenant, about my age, who was going on his first Sarawak mission as a Whirlwind helicopter pilot, a flight from Kuching Airfield to the jungle fort at Stass, codenamed Red 21, and he asked me whether the fort was difficult to find. So I pulled out my scruffy topographical map of the warzone, and gave him the magnetic bearing from Kuching Airfield to Stass of 256 degrees and a distance of 23 miles. I explained that in our Freighter it was a ten-minute flight from takeoff, so probably 15 minutes in his Whirlwind.

We left the Officers Mess together, in flight suits and jungle boots, stumbled to the Armory for issue of personal Stirling sub-machine guns, plus two magazines of 30x9 mm bullets, and crossed the pieced steel planking tarmac to the briefing room. We were greeted by Major Bloodnock's usual war talk: where the enemy was or wasn't; expected weather for the day to be morning clouds, poor visibility from burning hill rice cultivations, and afternoon thunderstorms. We were then given the assigned airdrop missions for 41's Bristol Freighter and 215's RAF Argosy. I parted ways with this newbie Sarawak RAF helicopter pilot, wishing him a good flight to Stass, never to see him again. That afternoon we received a report from Stass that a Whirlwind had been shot down by enemy gunfire close to the border and the pilot was last seen running through the jungle firing his machine gun at Indonesian military pursuers.

1965–1975: The Ghost Squadron— In and Out of South Vietnam

MY EXPERIENCE with 41 Squadron's many years of involvement in South Vietnam began in 1960, continuing through to the final days in Saigon in April 1975. From March to December 1960, my logbook showed eight flights in and out of South Vietnam, mostly on route from Hong Kong to Singapore, with landings for fuel at either Saigon or Tourane (later called Danang). Then, from 1965 until 1968, I operated in and out of South Vietnam with the Squadron on 40 flights; some on transit between Singapore and Hong Kong, but mostly on in-country flights between Saigon, Qui Nhon, Nha Trang, and Vung Tau. During this time the sky above South Vietnam was a dangerous place if you couldn't locate your position accurately with Tactical Air Navigation system (TACAN), or squawk a IFF-Transponder code for friendly radar to see our plane, or communicate with Americans using UHF radios. This equipment was military avionics, not available in our Bristol Freighters. The US military air traffic consisted of helicopters in large numbers, fighter-bombers, large gunships, and Forward Air Controller (FACs) planes, and artillery fire zones in locations we had no knowledge of.

74

The word *Avionics,* a linguistic blend of A*viation* *Electronics,* didn't come into common use until the late 1960s. Avionic systems included communications, navigation, and the display and management of multiple systems, all the so-called Black Boxes that are fitted into airplanes. When Bristol built the RNZAF Freighters, they knew nothing of advanced avionics, so from 1955 through to 1967, we operated around Asia making do with two fixed-card Automatic Direction Finders (ADFs), a 20-frequency VHF radio, and two archaic long-range HF sets. During those 12 years, we would arrive at US military bases in the Philippines, Okinawa, Japan, and South Vietnam like a horse and buggy showing up at a modern US Interstate truck stop needing hay for the horses and communicating with semaphore flags! The US Base Operations officers shook their heads and laughed a lot, not believing that we lacked IFF-Transponders, UHF comm radios, or TACAN radio receivers.

A reality of the South Vietnam aviation world was the presence of many older transport airplanes operated by the US military, Air America, and others. These airplanes, like the Douglas DC-3, were close cousins of the Bristol Freighter, but had been upgraded with the latest avionics, making them capable of surviving in that American warzone environment. The irony for us at 41 Squadron in our Bristol Freighters was the RNZAF had just experienced its most significant fleet upgrades since WW2 with C-130 Hercules, P-3 Orions, and UH1D Iroquois helicopters, all equipped with the latest American military avionics. So what about us at 41 Squadron, risking our necks on a regular basis over South Vietnam with avionics from the Titanic? The New Zealand government had given us only a knife to go to a gun fight, and that knife was short and rusty. They didn't seem to care what the risks were, and no medals for bravery were ever awarded. This bizarre wartime omission was pulled straight from the pages of Joseph Heller's *Catch-22*: *Since you got by without this equipment for so long, then you obviously don't need it.*

Sometime in late 1967 help was at hand, but not from New Zealand. It arrived in a most unusual way, and from a most unlikely source. A Royal Navy Scimitar fighter-bomber crashed on landing at RAF Changi; the pilot ejected before it hit the ground and survived. During the Navy's salvage operation of the wreck, our enterprising Squadron Commander, Hutch Hutchins, and ingenious maintenance team somehow *acquired* the black boxes from the wreck, stuff that we needed to survive over Vietnam. So was born the *Stretcher Case* that turned the Bristol Freighter into a modern military airplane, or a pig's ear into a silk purse. This initial avionics upgrade, not officially approved, to the Ghost Squadron's Freighters included a TACAN radio-navigation receiver, a UHF radio transceiver, and an IFF radar transponder. It's quite likely that this equipment saved the lives of crew members who could have been lost in a downed airplane over South Vietnam.

From 1968 to 1972, I continued to make flights in and out of South Vietnam, but not in the badly equipped Bristol Freighters. With other aircrew members from 41 Squadron, we had been promoted to fly the C-130 Hercules with No 40 Squadron based in Auckland, New Zealand. With this fantastically capable four-engined transport airplane, we travelled the world from the Antarctic to North America to England, but most importantly, we were regular visitors to South Vietnam. Our main mission was carrying New Zealand Army troops to and from Vietnam, which were done in two flights: Auckland to Alice Springs, overnight, then Alice Springs to Saigon or Vung Tau. The avionics fitted to the C-130 were the perfect answer for safe operations in the warzone of Vietnam. This magnificent war machine flew at twice the speed and twice the altitude of the Bristol Freighter, and was in good company with hundreds of US Airforce and US Marine C-130s, for onsite repairs if necessary.

1966: Professional Navigators
and Radio Operators

This is a comedy piece, so don't get upset, you Navs and Sigs

WHERE I CAME FROM, navigators and radio operators were crew members not trained as pilots. You may ask why we needed them, particularly since 'real' pilots were so good at everything they did? The reality was a time and motion problem. To aviate, navigate, and communicate with the available technology of that time required more hands and eyes than even hotshot pilots like me could manage.

Let me explain. In 1958 I was assigned to my first operational Air Force unit, a transport squadron equipped with Bristol Freighters. This sad excuse for an airplane looked like a mutation from a WW2 troop glider design—a glider with engines added. This horrible deformity was the quintessential British Piece of Rubbish (BPR). At the time, shortly after WW2, the British did a brisk trade in BPRs, flogging them off to their ex-colonial Air Forces in trade for butter, frozen lamb, wool, tea, gold, diamonds, and rubber.

Because the Bristol Freighter may have been planned as a glider(?), accommodation for a multi-talented crew had not been considered. As a WW2 troop glider, it would have been only designed to make one flight, towed from England to its final landing behind the beaches of Normandy, after which the pilots would run away from the wreck, a desire I often felt after a particularly bad day flying the Freighter! The pilot's job was easy to define, doing what we did in all airplanes: master of the craft, controlling this ungainly beast on the ground and in the air. Problem was, the navigation and communication equipment was so archaic, so large and badly located, that multi-talented pilots couldn't reach the apparatus without leaving their seat. And that was not practical, since the installed Auto-Pilot was another piece of WW2 junk; that is, near useless in controlling the airplane if left on its own.

So, to operate this plane effectively, it had been necessary to add two more crew members with the specific tasks of using the navigation and communication equipment, a navigator and a radio-operator, neither trained or qualified to fly the airplane, even if they'd been provided with a set of flight controls. In the last decades of the twentieth century these two job description became redundant: the navigator, following the development of Inertial Nav Systems (INS), Omega Nav Systems (ONS), and finally the Global Positioning Systems (GPS); the radio-operator, after the introduction of Single Sideband (SSB) High Frequency long-range communication equipment. Unfortunately, back in my Bristol Freighter days—1958 to 1977—these wonderful developments in avionics were not available for installation in this ancient flying machine.

For the benefit of those few retired navigators and radio operators still around, I apologize for my cynicism. I would like to think that the camaraderie we shared back in the days of yore still exist. My real problem with the Bristol Freighter was the airplane itself and the fact it was configured for only one pilot. To be entirely honest about navigators and radio operators of the past, their mastery of the arcane skills required to operate the inadequate equipment available to them was extraordinary. Often, I thought they considered a pilot's job much easier than theirs, and maybe they were right? Twenty-five years after my final flight in a Bristol Freighter, I participated in an online discussion with a few of my favorite navigators from those long ago days in Southeast Asia. We had all retired from the New Zealand Air Force during the interim years, with me living and working in the USA. The humorous email exchanges indicate that the camaraderie between pilots and navigators had not been lost.

The exchange began with an email from Terry Knight in New Zealand, with information that our old Air Force Squadron would be holding a reunion for past and present personnel. Within the details he provided was the surprising news (to me) that the current Squadron Commander was a navigator.

I wrote the following to Terry and other retired navigators: *Thanks for the information on the Squadron's milestone. A navigator in command—what's the Force coming to? I remember a time when giving a navigator command of his protractor and dividers was a dangerous thing, for fear of doing injury to himself or others in the cockpit. And what's with the spelling of navigator? According to Litton's Glossary of Terms, navigator is spelled I.N.S. (Inertial Nav System).*

Anyway, it's good to hear from you Old World navigators, particularly now that the FAA has stripped me of my wings, offering only the job of Flight Engineer on the Boeing-747. I had to turn it down; picturing myself doing walk-arounds on the Anchorage ramp in 30-degree below temperatures, getting lost in the whiteout between nose and tail, and not being missed in the cockpit until the young pilots needed fresh coffee. As an active Retired Person, I'll be down your way in January–February seeking shelter and liquid refreshment. Hope to see many of you then.

Terry responded with: *Great to hear from you after so many years and to know that you still respect navigators. It's interesting that the list of contributors to this exercise is predominantly composed of practitioners and ex-practitioners of the black art and members of the flat-earth society. We invited a few pilots to join us because they get very 'thingy' and under-confident otherwise. I'm working for the CAA down here and we can't offer you a job as Flight Engineer, but there might be one for an ex-pilot! I hope you will be either staying down here next year or coming back for the Squadron Reunion, which we are pushing to have at Labor weekend. Brian Grigg has a long list of ex-members of the Squadron that he will no doubt pass on to you, so check to see if your Alzheimer's permits you to add a few names.*

Rodney Bracefield, another navigator, also responded: *I always knew you took a long time to appreciate the value of the navigator. Good to know that you are still able to get around, and if down in Wellington, give us a call. I am currently the CAA's CNS/ATM project manager and trying to make it safer for those who fly by ensuring that when RVSM is introduced in February next year in the Pacific, the pilots stay at the correct altitude and don't wander off the assigned tracks without telling someone. I'm still explaining to pilots how to do it!*

Mick Dillon, another navigator also responded: *I gave Terry my email address last Sunday and since then my inbox has exploded! Great to hear from all of you. Like the other navigators, I was surprised to hear from Peter Tremayne, not just because I haven't heard from him in a while, but he was obviously using a computer!*

My second response to Terry : *Great to make contact with you again. I thought of you earlier this year on my last flight to Hong Kong, while stumbling around Kowloon near the long-gone Joe's Bar. Imagined you still at the bar reading the burning newspaper, flames licking up around your hands, me still holding the cigarette lighter, very shortly before we were shown off the premises. Anyway, my great days of travel are finally over and I'm doing just fine in retirement. Living the good life in the American Northwest: home of constant rain, White Supremacists, eco-terrorists, and other loonies. Is this a great country or what? Yes, I do plan on returning to New Zealand for the Squadron Reunion, but names of ex-members? I can't even remember what Alzheimer's is. 'Practitioners of the black art.' Nice line, but the only black art I remember was when the Lucas electrics failed in those heaps of British rubbish we flew before Mr. Lockheed's fine machines arrived on the scene.*

My first response to Rodney: *Good to hear from you, but I resemble that remark you made about pilots straying off course and altitude. Having said that, giving approval for RVSM operations to airlines such as Korean and Asiana is a chancy business. I know from my years of flying the North Pacific routes. Those guys are scary, even when trying to park on the ramp (Asiana B-747-400 mating with an Aeroflot AN-62 at Anchorage in 1999).*

My first response to Mick: *What can I say to an old master like you. Of course I don't do computers. Using a keyboard is still woman's work. So, I'm dictating this to my ravishing young secretary who understands these complex machines, but sometimes lets me play with her mouse. Anyway, when were you ever the user of electronic gizmos? One of my Great Flying Stories that I'd relate to my American counterparts, concerned this navigator who refused to use a chronometer for precise timing on airdrops, preferring to mutter an incantation that sounded like: "Higgledy Piggledy One ... Higgledy Piggledy Two," etc. They were always impressed, but a little confused.*

My third response to Terry: *Sorry for using this as an open forum, but it's really your fault, putting all those email addresses on your original message. I couldn't resist. I guess I've been too long in exile. Although I probably can't dredge up names of ex-members, I'll rat through my archives for photos and other mementos from those days, but I suspect I have more data on our years at 41 Squadron than at 40 Squadron. Mick Dillon will remember that I often played the role of scribe when he was composing his masterpieces in the bars of Southeast Asia. I still have the beer-stained originals of those inspired outpourings. This is also true of my years at 40 Squadron. I have yours and other's original manuscripts from Bangladesh 1972. Most of these have been transcribed into computer-speak by my lovely secretary, of course.*

1966: Drinking and Flying

Air Force Rules:
The minimum time between bottle and throttle is eight hours.

IN THE GOOD OLD DAYS before random alcohol and drug testing, drinking used to be fun, and flying with the inevitable hangover was torture—the wages of sin! This was especially true when flying ancient piston-propeller heaps-of-junk like the Bristol Freighter. Oddly enough, the one occasion that I did fly this plane shortly after a drinking session, all sounds of whirling propellers and airframe vibration were strangely muted. This experience had me thinking that we all should have flown this ghastly plane only when drunk, sweating like pigs in the tropical environment of Borneo in the non-airconditioned cockpit.

Why did my crew and I ignore the regulations by drinking and flying on a stinking hot afternoon over the jungles of Sarawak? *Upfront, let me acknowledge that it was not all my fault, nor was it a wartime, airborne scramble in our fight between the Indonesian and British Commonwealth forces.* Instead, the directive came from our imperious Squadron Commander, based back in Singapore. It was the last day of the month, and we, the Kuching Duty Operational Crew, needed to check the box for MCT (Monthly Continuation Training), because we had been too busy flying operational missions over the jungle, thereby neglecting the all-important MCT. The directive was to be actioned, despite having flown four missions that morning; we returned to the Kuching Base, had a late lunch, then retired to the Officers Mess bar for the remainder of the afternoon.

From mid-1965 to mid-1966, No. 41 Squadron of the RNZAF based at RAF Changi in Singapore, was given the wartime mission of air-supply support to British Commonwealth army forces in jungle forts along the Sarawak–Kalimantan border. The Squadron's Bristol Freighter crews were rotated on two-week assignments based at RAF Kuching in Sarawak. The daily mission routine was guided by the local weather pattern, cloudless mornings, and afternoon thunderstorms. These missions over mountainous jungle had to be flown in visual flight conditions, using the most basic navigation techniques to avoid hitting hills or the 200-foot high jungle canopy, then finding the camouflaged forts and avoiding straying over the Indonesian border, only to be shot down by enemy ground fire.

Because of the daily weather pattern, mission execution was limited to mornings only, with the occasional afternoon assignment for troop support flights to the coastal towns of Sibu, Bintulu, or Miri. As crew members, we settled into the daily routine of an early breakfast, visiting the Armory to collect our Sterling sub-machine guns, attending the daily Intel briefing, then being assigned the mornings missions: normally three, sometimes four. We would fly the missions, with short breaks on the ground while the next parachute-packs were loaded. Most days the missions were complete and debriefed with the Intel folks, all done by one o'clock. Then it was off home to the Officers Mess, returning our sub-machine guns on the way, and to the bar in sweaty flight suits to consume pints of ice-cold beer on tap, maybe with some food.

This drinking and flying day began no differently than most days on Sarawak operations, completing a tough morning over the jungle, then relaxing in the bar with two or three pints of beer. With the realization that we needed to go flying that afternoon, the option of delaying, thus giving time to sober up, was not a good choice because the daily thunderstorms would be overhead the airfield within a few hours. *Decision time. Let's go get it over with. We'll get airborne, head north to the coast, engage the auto-pilot, fly around in big circles, make no high-G maneuvers, try not to throw up, then after the required two hours we'll return for the landing—probably the most demanding task for drinking pilots.* So, that is what we did, without hitting anything, including the jungle, and I hoped no one would be any the wiser, because our circling location had been well out of sight from the airfield and Kuching town.

After the event, we discovered that our Kiwi Flying Circus near the coast had not gone unnoticed. If we had not been suffering like stunned mullets, we would have remembered that the location was used as a stealth recreation camp by the British SAS (Special Air Service), rotating in and out of the jungle forts. On occasion, we had dropped resupply containers on the beach for them, so we should have known there was every chance of being observed while wasting time and fuel circling the area. Two days later I was invited to an evening booze-up with a group of British Army and Air Force personnel at our base, including a few SAS troopers in attendance. Being the only New Zealand pilot in the gathering, I was singled out by the SAS troopers asking about a Kiwi Bristol Freighter flying haphazardly above their secret base on the northern coast. They had hoped the plane's mission was an airdrop of surprise goodies for their coming Christmas in the jungle. No such luck, lads, when I explained the embarrassing reason for the Flying Circus—a crew trying to sober up before attempting a landing back at Kuching airfield. They thought that was hilarious, and promised not to pass the story on, but those professional killers lied!

The allegedly well-trained airline pilots of today, who are nothing more than computer system operators, might be wondering why I decided to go flying immediately after drinking two to three pints of beer. First, it was wartime, so I would suggest you watch the movie *Catch-22*. War makes people crazy, and peacetime regulations and behavior are suspended, not by official decree, but by individuals who wish to simply survive ... and have fun.

Second, many of the military pilots trained during the 1950s and early 1960s had been students of WW2 flight instructors and their unique talents. During flight training, those instructors did their best to make us like them. During my time on wartime operations from RAF Base Kuching, it was a common sight to have an RAF flight crew show up at the Officers Mess for lunch and pints of beer before continuing their daily passenger flight from Singapore to Labuan in North Borneo. To my knowledge, none of us in the RNZAF participated in such a blatant breaking of rules, but for the RAF, this behavior seemed to fit their zeitgeist of the time.

When I felt backed into a corner of either refusing the directive to go flying because I had been drinking, or following the common behavior of certain RAF pilots by drinking and flying, I made the unwise decision of doing the latter. In those long-ago days, we all had been drinking and driving, many times, so the experience of going flying with nothing to run into except the jungle or ground seemed an acceptable choice. Most of us are still alive, so all's well that ends well ... I suppose.

1967: Early Warnings of a Defeat Foretold

MY FIRST WARNING: during May of 1967, I had flown from Singapore to Bangkok and then on to Chiang Mai, the beautiful Thailand city in the northwest corner of the country. A city well known for the production of Thai silk fabric and celadon pottery. We laid over in the city for two days, staying at a hotel that was being used as accommodation for American R & R military personnel. While there, we spent time exchanging Vietnam War stories with a US Airforce Colonel, a Wing Commander of F-105 Thunderchief (Thuds) fighter-bomber squadrons based in northern Thailand. Over a few drinks, the Colonel openly stated that America would not win the war in Vietnam because their bombing targets in North Vietnam were being assigned from the White House, Congress, and the Pentagon.

He gave us a very convincing example. The previous week the Wing had been given the target of a bridge over the Da River on a major route for military supplies moving south for the Ho Chi Min Trail. A flight of four Thuds were assigned to the mission, flying north at high altitude over Laos, then descending into North Vietnam through intensive anti-aircraft fire and dropping their bomb loads on the bridge, which was visually checked as destroyed. As they climbed away from the target area and turned south for home, two Thuds were hit by either gunfire or SAM missiles. One of the pilots ejected over Laos and the other limped back over the Mekong River into Thailand before ejecting. So, they'd lost two multi-million dollar airplanes, and one pilot that they assumed was either dead or captured. Were the losses worth the mission results? The Colonel said definitely not, because their best intelligence (but not from Washington) indicated that the bridge they'd destroyed was a dummy, and the actual bridge being used by trucks and tanks was one mile upriver and a foot under the muddy water.

My second warning: engraved on the Vietnam Wall in Washington, are the names of over 58,267 American soldiers who were killed in the South Vietnam war. Over 33,103 of those soldiers were only 18-years-old when they died. In October 1967, I came to know an 18-year-old American soldier whose name might be on that wall, but I've always hoped he survived the last six months of his tour. His name I've forgotten, after misplacing the notes he'd given me. Let's call him Chris after the young soldier in Oliver Stone's movie, *Platoon*.

This Chris was a Medic with the 1st Air Cavalry Division and had survived his first six months in Vietnam, despite participating in many terrifying combat missions. He was on R & R in Hong Kong for a brief period, getting around the city with two other US soldiers. I was with a 41 Squadron flight crew on an unusually long layover in Hong Kong—three days and four nights. On the first evening we headed for our favorite watering hole in Kowloon, a restaurant and pub that served genuine Lowenbrau German beer on tap. The main attraction of the pub was a piano bar with a player-singer from the Philippines who was brilliant and had the crowd singing along with the latest popular songs. My crew members—Bill Ramsey, Colin Simmons, Pete Amodeo, and I loved the place, as did the other patrons, many who were military folks like us: Chris and his American buddies, two Australian soldiers also on R & R from Vietnam, and two Royal Navy sailors from a British Minesweeper berthed in Hong Kong Harbor.

On that first night, the 11 of us had a great time, sharing a bucket-sized mug of ice-cold Lowenbrau that took two hands to hold and glug. We possibly called for refills eight times. At one point we had to make do with a glass boot, smaller than the bucket, but see-through. Pete Amodeo disgraced himself by dropping his false teeth into the boot, and the rest of us watched his teeth slowly sink into the boot, shedding food particles on the way. Pete mumbled something like, 'Sorry about that,' then reached in, retrieved his teeth, and passed the boot to me.

Since he was my crew member, I felt partly liable, so I took a drink and passed it on around the circle. Later, we staggered home to our respective hotels with the promise of meeting at the piano bar the next night, Saturday, October 14, 1967, which we did, but slowed down the heavy drinking … a little! That night I had the opportunity to talk with Chris about his Vietnam experience. He told me about his first mass helicopter attack mission into a valley controlled by the enemy. After touchdown he was out of the chopper as the last man in his squad; he was a medic, so he needed to be at the back. When the choppers and their noise lessened as they climbed away, all he heard was automatic gunfire. Trailing his squad in the high grass to a tree line, every soldier in front dived for cover in the grass, or so he thought. When the enemy gunfire was suppressed by airborne gunships, Chris stood up in the grass, but nobody else in his squad did; they'd all been hit.

On Sunday, the Royal Navy lads invited all of us to a cocktail party on the bridge of their Minesweeper anchored at the Hong Kong Island side of the harbor. The official beverage was gin and tonic, and after a few hours, still moored to the pier, the ship seemed to be wallowing in a heavy swell! It was a fun afternoon with this band of brothers. I like to think that if Chris never made it home to the United States, then in his short life he'd spent a crazy time with a bunch of Larrikins from the British Commonwealth.

On the last night we spent talking, more sober, dining well, with quiet moments and a time for thoughtful discussion. Chris explained that he came from a farming family, possibly somewhere in the Midwest. I do remember that many of the things he said were very similar to Chris's letters to his grandma in the movie *Platoon*, which I've paraphrased:

I want to do my share for my country. Live up to what Grandpa did in the First War and Dad in the Second. I know this is going to be the war of my generation. Well, here I am—anonymous all right, with guys nobody really cares about. They come from the end of the line, most of them from small towns you never heard of. Two years' high school's about it; maybe if they're lucky a job waiting for them back in a factory, but most of them got nothing. They're poor, they're the unwanted of our society, yet they're fighting for our society and our freedom and what we call America. They're the bottom of the barrel and they know it; maybe that's why they call themselves 'grunts' cause a 'grunt' can take it, can take anything. They're the backbone of this country, Grandma, the best I've ever seen, the heart and soul of America.

Before we finally parted, Chris shocked me with two revelations that have stayed with me always, indications that America would never find the resolve to win the war against North Vietnam. Chris was convinced that he wouldn't survive his last six months in Vietnam, continuing the fight in a unit that initiated deadly battles with the enemy. He wasn't scared, just accepted the fate that he was sure would happen. Of more concern to him and his fellow soldiers was the verbal abuse and contempt they were receiving from American tourists in Hong Kong. So, only two years after the war had begun, these brave young men were beginning to understand that this war they might likely die from was going to be lost on the streets of America and in the corrupt mansions of the United States government.

Dream while you may in your carefree days.
Laugh while the air is clear.
Gaze at the gulls circling overhead,
Swooping at crumbs without fear

For my boy was young once, and fished on the pier.
He laughed at the birds wheeling free.
But now he is deep in the Mekong mud.
And lonely, to gaze out to sea.
~ Anon

1967: Fastest Ride to the United States

IT WAS THE FLIGHT OF A LIFETIME, with F-104s, SR-71s, Mig-21s, Grasshoppers, and Spin-Crash-and-Burns, and a crew looking for enlightenment at every layover. In July of 1967, at 41 Squadron RAF Base Changi, a group of us were assigned a training flight from Singapore to Tokyo, with a side trip to Seoul. All of us were veterans of two Asian wars: Indonesian Confrontation in Northern Borneo, 1964–66, and the first years of the South Vietnam conflict, 1965–67. The crew was composed of two pilots, John Cotton and me; two navigators, Hugh Francis and Dave Geddes; two radio operators, Jimmy Flesher and Tom Magill, one flight engineer, Dave Rosingrave; and lastly, Pete Hughan—our money man, carrying the sack of green dollars.

Apart from the large crew complement, we were not carrying significant cargo or any passengers, therefore allowing the Bristol Freighter to depart with full fuel tanks. So, on Day One, we flew direct from Singapore to Manila in the Philippines, a flight time of eight hours. The following day was a five-hour flight to the US Airforce Base Kadena, located on the Japanese island of Okinawa. At Kadena we met two US Air Force fighter pilots who were looking for a ride to Japan. Captains Ace Rawlins and Tom Mahan had just been reassigned from their F-104 Starfighter Squadron, based at Udorn in northern Thailand, and were bound for

Luke Air Force Base in Arizona. At Luke, they would be instructing German Luftwaffe pilots on the F-104G Starfighters.

We initially met with the two American pilots at the bar of the Kadena Officers Club where they introduced us to a menu of cocktails: *Mig-21s, Spin-crash-and-Burns, and Grasshoppers.* Over these delicious but high alcohol content drinks, they told us stories of flying CAP (Combat Air Patrol) missions over Laos and North Vietnam in their F-104 Starfighters. These F-104s were fitted with air-refueling probes to provide long-linger times above the ground attack bombers they were protecting from North Vietnamese Mig-21 interceptors. They amazed us with tales of sighting the Russian operated SA-2 Surface to Air (SAM) missiles that looked like flying telegraph poles rising supersonically toward them, and then going into a steep dive to bypass the missiles in an avoidance move they called *Dead Ants.*

On Day Three of our odyssey, we were joined at our Bristol Freighter on the Kadena Ramp by the two Starfighter pilots and a US Green-Beret Officer (wounded) and his wife whom we'd agreed to carry as passengers to Tachikawa AFB near Tokyo, Japan. With all aboard and ready to start engines, Kadena Tower told us we were on a long hold for departure, so we all disembarked and stood under the wings to avoid a rain shower (no air-conditioning in the Freighter, with or without engines running). Our four passengers were considerate in not laughing at their free ride limo-plane to Tokyo. After all, they were happy to still be alive and escaping the warzone! During our wait under the wing, the Air Force Police pulled alongside in a Jeep and told us that a special airplane was about to take off, and we were to turn our backs to the runway until after its departure. Immediately after the Police Jeep left us on their way to scold others along the ramp, Ace and Tom told us to turn around and watch a unique event. We heard the noise of its engines first, then the pitch black shape at the end of the runway, followed by a rapidly approaching image out of a science fiction movie. We recognized it as a Lockheed SR-71 Blackbird, the Mach-3 plus, extreme altitude spy plane that didn't exist in those days!

What a treat and special memory, but it wasn't exactly over. Ace and Tom opined that it was probably on its way back home to Beale AFB in northern California, a flight of around three hours! We had only just got back onboard our sad excuse for an airplane, when we were advised by Kadena Tower that another delay was in place. What a surprise when we saw the Blackbird again, this time approaching to land at Kadena. We watched it touchdown and then deploy large parachutes to slow down on the runway. We guessed that the pilot had found a problem on his way to the USA, probably 1,000 miles out before turning back to Okinawa.

After all this excitement, we finally were airborne on our way to Tachikawa, a flight time of five hours. My previous visit to Japan had happened in late 1960, and I saw no change with the lack of written English on road or railway signs, and found few Japanese fluent in spoken English. This observation was not a criticism of Japanese insularity, but was a startling contrast from the Asian countries we were most familiar with: Singapore, Malaysia, Thailand, Hong Kong, and Vietnam.

After three days getting lost on the railways and roads of Tokyo, we left Tachikawa AFB for Kimpo AFB near Seoul in South Korea. On arrival at Kimpo airfield, we were met by a fellow New Zealand Air Force officer, Peter Rule, assigned to Korea for peace-keeping duties with the United Nations. For me, meeting Peter at Kimpo was a nostalgic occasion. He and I had been with the original group of five pilots and five mechanics of the RNZAF Antarctic Flight formed in 1959. Sadly, this was last time we would see each other, as Peter tragically took his own life in 1987, a victim of gay discrimination from the New Zealand government and military. I still remember Peter as an exceptional pilot, a brilliant flight and ground instructor, and a wonderful person to be around.

Leaving Korea on our way southbound to Singapore was somewhat anticlimactic after the excitement of the previous days, even with stops at Okinawa and Hong Kong, from where we flew direct to RAF Changi with a flight time of ten hours.

1968: Flying the War Machine

IF THERE WAS EVER an extreme contrast between two airplanes that had been designed basically for the same mission, it was the British Bristol Freighter and the American Lockheed C-130 Hercules. I flew both planes extensively and learned their limitations and their strengths. Simply described: the Bristol Freighter was all limitations and the C-130 Hercules all strengths.

The Lockheed C-130 Hercules is a four-engine turboprop military transport aircraft designed and built originally by Lockheed. Capable of using unprepared runways for takeoffs and landings, the C-130 was originally designed as a troop, medevac, and cargo transport aircraft. The versatile airframe has found uses in a variety of other roles, including as a gunship (AC-130), for airborne assault, search and rescue, scientific research support, weather reconnaissance, aerial refueling, maritime patrol, and aerial firefighting. It is still the main tactical airlifter for many military forces worldwide, operating in more than 65 nations.

The C-130 entered service with the US in 1956, quickly followed by Australia and many other nations. During its years of service, the Hercules family has participated in numerous military, civilian, and humanitarian aid operations. In 2007, the C-130 became the fifth aircraft to mark 50 years of continuous service with its original primary customer, which for the C-130 is the United States Air Force. The C-130 Hercules is the longest continuously produced military aircraft at over 65 years. The five C-130H airplanes that I first flew for the New Zealand Air Force in 1968 are still alive and well 53 years later, a record that speaks volumes for the airplane, the training, and the ability of the pilots and maintenance personnel.

What could this ubiquitous airplane do that made it so special? At the C-130's beginning, the US Air Force called it the *Can-Do* airplane; it could do everything demanded of a military transport, including Spec-Ops in Laos, Cambodia, South Vietnam, Central America, and Israel. As an old-hand C-130 pilot, I remember the Entebbe Raid by Israeli Commandos in July 1976 as the finest example of what could be achieved with this airplane when operated by fearless resolute professionals. Many years later, during August 2021, there was another incredible C-130 operation into Afghanistan where the US government had created a catastrophe by pulling out all combat soldiers before extracting American and other allied nations' civilians. The chaotic result was totally predictable as the Taliban rolled into Kabul and then blocked the evacuation of civilians from the airport. Near Kandahar, trapped by this US blunder was a 20-man group of British SAS special force soldiers. By secure communication links, they requested a C-130 from No. 47 Squadron RAF to pick them up at an open desert location, then fought their way out there from Kandahar in darkness. Using night-vision goggles, the C-130 pilots were able to successfully land and take off again from this extreme desert terrain, safely extracting all 20 SAS troopers.

My introduction to this mighty airplane was in a C-130

training class in mid-1968, held at the New Zealand Air Force Base near the city of Auckland. My first surprise was the availability of incredible training aids, the likes of which I had never seen in my ten years of service with our Air Force. We were presented with large movable display units showing actual cockpit panels of the airplane, that when switches were moved, internal lighting represented the flow of fuel and hydraulic fluid, of bleed-air and showed electrical connections throughout the C-130. It was a magical teaching system for those days, still years before the computer age. We were issued books called *C-130 Flight Manual* and *C-130 Quick Reference Handbook*, printed for the use of United States Air Force operators and available to us. These two books contained everything aviators needed to know, or could be accessed, to operate the airplane: Normal, Abnormal or Emergency procedures, and detailed Performance Data.

Fifty-three years after that amazing training event, today's pilots must be hooting with laughter as to why I and others in that 1968 class were so impressed with the training aids and flight manuals. Back then, the reality was that until our Air Force took delivery of the C-130 Hercules, P-3 Orions, and Iroquois helicopters in the mid-1960s, most pilot conversion training had been done flying the actual airplanes, with minimal classroom learning. The reason was a lack of study materials related to the our British airplanes still in service during the 1950s and 60s. Most of the information on how to operate planes like the DH Devon, DH Vampire, Handley Page Hastings, Bristol Freighter, and Shorts Sunderland was contained in very small books titled *Pilots Notes*. These books were little more than a pamphlet that could be placed in a lower-leg pocket of our flight suits.

Although we had the excellent ground training equipment for learning the complex systems of the C-130, we lacked a flight simulator, so all flight training still had to be done in the actual airplanes, including emergency procedures, some of which would only be simulated actions. Notwithstanding, we did require students to approach the aerodynamic stall for different configurations. These maneuvers included flaps extended, no flaps extended, and lastly, with some engine thrust that resulted in a high nose attitude—a potentially dangerous exercise that could flip and roll the airplane into a spin. Back then, there was talk of that actually happening to an Australian C-130A during a training mission. The student in the left seat lost control as the plane rolled inverted into a rapidly descending autorotation. Fortunately, the instructor in the right seat was an old hand fighter pilot, recognized the spin for what is was, and applied standard spin recovery—and it worked, but the plane was considered a wreck because of High-G stress damage to the wings.

We simulated in-flight engine failures by simply retarding throttles to the flight-idle position, with perhaps one demonstration of an actual engine shutdown and the propeller feathered. This procedure was then followed by an in-flight restart. With the airplane at training weights, it was easy to see that with one engine failed, the C-130 was still easily capable of climbing away after takeoff, possibly reaching a cruise altitude above 18,000 feet. Pilots were expected to handle the plane with two engines failed, specifically both on the same side, then making a simulated instrument approach to landing. Flight training also included a no-flaps approach and landing, a maneuver that occasionally caused a runway tail scrape because of the high nose attitude at touchdown.

One of the most demanding emergency events we trained for was dealing with rapid cabin depressurization when operating the airplane at high altitude. These events in modern airliners and military transports are rare, but are a required crew emergency procedure now practiced routinely in flight simulators. The extreme urgency of the situation requires pilots to utilize memory checklist actions to deal with the problem of sudden oxygen loss (hypoxia) to crew and passengers. This requires pilots to immediately pull on oxygen masks and turn regulators to 100 percent (pure oxygen), quickly followed by an emergency descent to an altitude where passengers can survive with or without their drop-down masks. That altitude is normally 14,000 feet (or higher if mountains are in the way!) Without a flight simulator, we would practice the emergency descent for real, but without rapidly depressurizing the airplane. In simple terms, the emergency descent is a controlled dive toward the ground using a high rate of descent, but keeping airspeed within aerodynamic limits using zero engine power, and landing gear extended for high drag.

During my four years as a line-pilot and instructor on the C-130, I experienced a number of abnormal and emergency events. Two engine shutdowns, one because of a turbine breakup and the other an engine-fire warning. Then there was an HF radio that caused significant power loss on all four engines when transmitting, because its antenna was shorting into the wing, creating spurious electrical signals to the propeller controls. This problem was not in our flight manuals!

What was the C-130 like to fly? An absolute delight, almost a sensuous experience, with the powerful hydraulic flight controls providing instant maneuverability. The thrust from the four engines with their large propellers gave immediate response in either acceleration or slowing down. It was possible to quickly and accurately shift the plane's airspeed by just a few mph by miniscule movement of the throttles. In those early days of flying this wondrous machine we observed that it seemed the throttles were directly connected to the airspeed indicator and not the engines. Clearly, this unique power and speed control provided the C-130 with outstanding approach and landing ability, particularly for short unprepared airfields, as we often found in Southeast Asia.

Occupying any of the C-130 cockpit seats was a treat, with plenty of individual space and surrounded by an ergonomic design with controls, switches, and instruments all in the perfect locations for each of the crew members: command pilot in the front left seat, copilot in the front right seat with the flight engineer between the two, sitting slightly to the rear and higher. Then there was the navigator's position to the rear of the copilot, plus one to two loadmasters normally located in the cargo hold. Many of us had transitioned from the Bristol Freighter, so not only was the C-130 cockpit luxurious, but full of toys for new boys: the latest radio navigation and communication units; weather and doppler radar; Loran-C for long-range navigation, and IFF secondary radar transponders. All those life-saving avionics that we'd lacked for years over South Vietnam in the Freighter.

Alas, my time operating the C-130 was all too short. After four years and 2,100 flight hours, I was removed from 40 Squadron to be a Base Commander. However, the memories of flying the War Machine around the world remain. Every flight was an exciting experience with the bonus feature of doing unique missions to exotic lands. Every southern Spring we would operate a series of flights between Christchurch, New Zealand and the Ice Runway at McMurdo Sound in Antarctica. For a period of time we flew charter flights for Air New Zealand from Auckland to the island of Rarotonga in the Cook Islands. Occasionally there were flights to the USA with stops at Fiji and Hawaii, and flights continued through the USA to England. Throughout the period 1968 to 1972 that I spent on the C-130, the majority of our flights were to Southeast Asia, in particular to Singapore and South Vietnam. They were good years to be a Hercules pilot with the Royal New Zealand Air Force.

1972: Joy Bangling Kiwis

I'm a joy bangling Kiwi — I've come a long way
I work very hard — I fly every day
Up to Darjeeling — And down to Jessore
I don't carry milk powder much anymore

Terry Knight, C130 Navigator and Minstrel Boy

BENGAL IS A REGION in southern Asia. West Bengal, a state of India, occupies the western part. The larger eastern section is occupied almost entirely by the country of Bangladesh. Most of the people live in rural areas. Bengal is mainly a fertile plain intersected by rivers. The climate is humid and tropical with heavy rainfall. From June to October, floods and cyclones are common. Calcutta, in West Bengal, is the chief city. Many people in Bangladesh practice Islam, and the majority in West Bengal practice Hinduism. The principal language throughout the region is Bengali. Agriculture dominates the economy. The region was first united in the 8th century AD. It was subjugated by Muslim rulers in the 1100s. Almost all of the region became a division of British India in 1699. Bengal was divided into Hindu and Muslim areas in 1947 when India and Pakistan gained independence.

Joy Bangla (meaning Victory to Bengal) was the slogan and war cry of the Mukti Bahini who fought for the independence of Bangladesh during the Bangladesh Liberation War in 1971. On March 27, Major Ziaur Rahman broadcast the announcement of the declaration of independence on behalf of Sheikh Mujibur Rahman and he finished with "Joy Bangla."

New Zealand Press Release, mid-April 1972:

In February 1972 it became New Zealand government policy to place at the disposal of the International Committee of the Red Cross (ICRC) one C-130 Hercules aircraft to fly relief missions within the Peoples Republic of Bangladesh. Two separate operations have been planned and carried out. The first operation called for two weeks activity within Bangladesh. The task comprised of the carriage of food grains from Chittagong to Ishurdi. A total of 636 tons was carried between February 26 and March 10, 1972. The second operation was mounted from New Zealand to position in Dacca on March 29. This operation is due to be completed on April 20. The task at present underway has mainly involved airlifting milk powder from Siliguri, India, to Ishurdi, Bangladesh. The milk powder is for use in the children's milk feeding programme. Since its arrival in Dacca, the single Hercules aircraft has airlifted a total of 1050 tons of relief supplies in Bangladesh. Prior to its return to New Zealand it is expected that a further 300 tons will be airlifted by the Hercules. The Hercules at present in Bangladesh is operated by a contingent of the Royal New Zealand Air Force (RNZAF). The contingent is commanded by Squadron Leader Peter Tremayne, an Air Force pilot with considerable flying experience in all parts of Asia. The RNZAF team comprises 30 personnel made up of two flight crews, aircraft maintenance and air movements members.

The real story of how this Bangladesh operation went down was much more colorful than this plain vanilla version from the *New Zealand Press*. As commanding officer for the operation, I know the story well and much of what happened is being told for the first time.

The first notable drama of the operation occurred on the positioning flight from New Zealand to Dacca, the capital of Bangladesh. Our C-130 Hercules had transited Darwin for Singapore and from there to Dacca on March 28th, 1972. One hour north of Singapore over the highlands of the Malayan Peninsula, the aircraft experienced a Rapid Depressurization event, during which the cabin pressure of 4,000 feet ascended to our cruising altitude of 24,000 feet in less than ten seconds. Within one minute of the pressure loss, the pilots did exactly what was required. We left 24,000 feet in the correct descent profile, levelling at 10,000 feet within minutes. It was a daytime visual environment, easy to see we were well clear of the jungle-covered mountains. A state of emergency was declared to Air Traffic Control with our intent to divert to the Royal Australian Air Force (RAAF) Base at Butterworth in northern Malaya.

Once safely on the ground at Butterworth, we found the Doppler antenna had broken from its mounts, the result of the high-pressure air racing out through the cavity. That explained the noise of tearing metal. Our onboard maintenance personnel, with the able assistance from the RAAF engineering staff, declared no fuselage integrity problems from the panel destruction and by the next day, had manufactured a metal panel to close the hole, pressure checked it and declared our C-130 fully serviceable, with the exception of the Doppler Navigation system, which the navigators would do without.

Now behind schedule for our expected arrival in Bangladesh, we departed for Dacca late on March 29th. Once we arrived the ICRC established the planned tasking of our C-130 would initially require the aircraft to operate from Dacca Airport to and from the city of Chittagong, airlifting a variety of foodstuffs to Dacca. While this task was underway, my main contact with the ICRC, a Swedish

Army officer, Torstein, requested I accompany him on a survey of an airfield in northern India. The airfield, situated ten miles north of the Bangladesh border was Baghdogra in an area of India known as the Siliguri Gap, squeezed between the nations of Nepal, Bhutan, and Bangladesh. Our means of transport was a Hughes-500 helicopter, operated for the ICRC by a German aviation company and flown by Werner, a competent pilot, but lousy navigator. We flew from Dacca airport to a town in northern Bangladesh called Thakurgaon, the base for a Finnish Red Cross group. We refueled the helicopter next to the Red Cross bungalow and encountered an uncontrolled mass of local humanity until lifting off and getting the heck away from there. This was the first of numerous encounters with over-curious villagers after landing on that godforsaken landscape.

Our 50-mile flight northwest to the Siliguri Gap and the Baghdogra airfield didn't take long and was easy to find, flying over the almost featureless plains toward the more obvious high country of the Himalaya. Torstein and I received a most cordial welcome from senior officers of the Indian Air Force (IAF) Base at Baghdogra, giving assurance that they would help in every way possible with our C-130 airlift operation and delighted to be of assistance to another British Commonwealth Air Force. They advised there was a massive quantity of milk powder in warehouses at Siliguri, destined for the Red Cross milk feeding program in Bangladesh. The ICRC required this relief food to be flown from Baghdogra to Ishurdi airfield in Bangladesh at a rate of four flights per day.

Our survey complete, Torstein and I climbed aboard the helicopter for the short flight back to Thakurgoan where we planned to spend the night with the Finnish Red Cross. I wasn't paying much attention to our direction of flight, now heading away from the mountains across an endless featureless landscape with the sun going down and a significant layer of haze. Werner, our pilot, suddenly got my attention when he announced we were lost, and not sure whether we were still in India or back across the Bangladesh border. (Some days later when I flew our C-130 into Baghdogra, the senior IAF Air Traffic Control officer told me that Werner had crossed the border twice and they'd considered putting up a fighter to either shoot us down or escort us back into their airfield!)

Meanwhile, back in our 'lost' helicopter, Werner said the two compasses were giving false indications and we were getting low on fuel to reach our destination. I thought this was great news; I'm possibly going to die on the plains of northern India or Bangladesh—take your pick.

I grabbed the topographical map he had on his lap, trying to make some sense of the landscape we were flying over. There were small villages scattered among continuous paddy fields with narrow dirt roads joining the various farmsteads, but nothing I could relate to the map. However, the map did show a railroad running roughly east-west and confirmed with Werner and Torstein that we'd not crossed a railroad since leaving the airfield in India. So, I suggested to Werner we take a southerly heading until crossing the railroad, then turn east and follow the rail line until close to Thakurgoan. Initially, Werner would not agree, reminding me that the compasses were kaput and not reliable. Then I pulled my Boy Scout knowledge on him, instructing him to ignore the compasses and use the position of the late afternoon sun that was going down in the west. "Turn until the sun is on our right—that's south—then keep it there until we cross a railroad." And so it happened; we came upon the railroad within five minutes, turned left, heading east, at which point Werner starting believing the compass indications were probably correct.

The next challenge was to establish our position along the railroad, so we would know when to turn off toward our intended destination, which we thought would be visible from the railroad. Werner decided to land in a small town that had a railway station and ask for directions to Thakurgoan. Bad decision: within a few minutes of settling on the ground, with rotors still turning, we had hundreds of people crowding around the aircraft, standing under the spinning blades, seemingly oblivious to the mortal danger they were in, stupidly tapping on the plexiglass canopy, touching antennas and pitot tubes, perhaps hoping to break them off. Werner attempted to converse with someone through a small opening in the canopy, but no English, German, or Swedish spoken here!

Both Torstein and I urged Werner to get us airborne as soon as possible before one or more of these village idiots was chopped by the whirling rotors. This was a very nasty accident waiting to happen, an accident that would see us stranded and possibly killed by the villagers. Many were carrying machetes and other dangerous-looking farm implements. For me, this was worse than Vietnam or Borneo, where at least we could fight back with the guns we carried. When Werner powered up the engine, these stupid people didn't move, and then, as we lifted off, I expected to hear and feel a thudding from the tail rotor, which we couldn't see from the cockpit. If in fact we did injure people, I felt no sympathy; we were free again from this scary countryside … until we ran out of fuel?

Although we'd landed by a railway station, none of us had noted the station name which was partly blanked off by the horde – and may well have been in Bengali script. My next suggestion to Werner was to hover over the next station, close enough to read the English name on the platform signboard. "But whatever you do, don't put down

109

on the ground—stay airborne until the fuel runs out!" And so, we survived, by reading the name on the next station, finding it on the map, a location close to the Finnish Red Cross bungalow at Thakurgoan, and landing there with the low fuel light flashing. After a quick refueling, Werner lifted the helicopter onto the roof of the bungalow to keep the local whack-jobs from touching it with their grubby little hands.

It was pleasant and safe to be resting at the Bungalow, protected by a walled compound from the mass of humanity outside. The Finns made us welcome with food, beer, and Scotch—and relaxing in a sauna they'd constructed in a small building in the compound. My only complaint was the presence of mosquitoes in the unscreened interior with torn and tattered bug-nets over the beds. Thankfully, like the rest of my Air Force team, I was taking daily anti-malarial medication together with powerful pills to control the dysentery we all suffered from after the first few days in Dacca. Delhi-belly, Bombay-trots, Calcutta-quickstep, and Singapore-squats were old friends of my team, most of whom had lived and worked in South East Asia for many years.

We left the Finnish bungalow the next morning, flying south with Werner to Dacca who was happy to follow the main north-south railway line into the city center. When I arrived back at our hotel, the Intercontinental, I was apprised of a nasty incident that took place around the hotel the previous day. My compatriots had a grandstand view of rioting union members breaking into the hotel to injure or possibly kill non-union hotel staff. Police arrived and then the shooting started. The rioters dispersed rapidly, leaving behind their dead and injured and hundreds of shoes scattered along the streets. The lazy little beggars are so fond of slip-on sandals! My team was looking down from the penthouse rooms that I'd organized on our arrival. On that top floor, the onlookers felt reasonably safe from intrusion into our cozy 'crew room' equipped with a well-stocked bar, comfortable lounge chairs, dart board, and a corner for our two-way radio communications with Singapore and the C-130. Conveniently, the radio team was able to easily string the antennas across the roof of the hotel. This convenience later created a near Cold War conflict when the Russians arrived in Dacca.

On April 3, we began a shuttle service between Baghdogra and Ishurdi, running four shuttles per day with the C-130, carrying 44,000 pounds of milk powder on each run. The aircrew and aircraft returned to Dacca each evening. This daily operational routine continued until April 15 when the ICRC had a special assignment for our C-130 to carry bags of corn soya milk mixture from Chittagong to Dacca from April 16 to 18. It seemed that the abundance of milk powder we'd carried from Baghdogra was not always well received because of lactose intolerance among many of the children and nursing mothers. Fortunately, the enlightened world was still far away from discovering peanut or almond allergies and the horrors of gluten; otherwise the poor little beggars of the Third World would have starved! God protect me from picky eaters.

"The Russians are Coming." On April 7, two Antonov An-22 Soviet Air Force military transport aircraft arrived at Dacca Airport from Bombay, each carrying a partly disassembled Mi-8 Soviet Air Force heavy lift helicopter. On April 9, another two An-22 aircraft arrived from Bombay, also carrying Mi-8 helicopters. There were 40 Russian personnel left behind at Dacca to assemble the four helicopters and subsequently began operations carrying relief aid (foodstuffs?) around the Bangladesh countryside.

111

These 40 Russians, who I believed to be Soviet Air Force pilots and mechanics wearing ill-fitting civilian clothes, possibly made by (quietly sniggering) Siberian Gulag prisoners, moved into our hotel. At the time of their arrival, the Inter-Continental Dacca had become our home turf where we'd set up a badminton court on the lawn, a water polo net in the hotel pool, and had total occupancy of the top floor penthouse, which gave us priority access to the roof and more importantly, where our radio antennas were strung. In early 1972, the Cold War was in full swing. More significantly, we, the Kiwis, were still fighting alongside the United States in South Vietnam, battling an enemy aided and abetted by the Soviet Union, so these intruders on our turf were proxy enemies. Did we get into mortal conflicts in Dacca? Not so; the Russians appeared so pathetic in their shitty clothing and attempts to use our badminton court or pull down our antennas on the roof, we felt sorry for them. Remember that leading up to the fall of the Berlin Wall, young Russians wanted Western fitted blue jeans and shoes that weren't made in Bulgaria. Thank you, P.J. O'Rourke. They did outnumber us in the hotel, where we dressed in our Air Force uniforms going off to fly each day, so they knew who we were and where we came from. Elevating together in the hotel lifts, we had to suffer hostile stares from these big, burly, lily-white thugs just arrived from their Siberian winter. However, they did admire our beautifully designed and built American Lockheed C-130 Hercules, far superior to any equivalent aircraft available in the USSR at that time.

I was somewhat surprised at the suppressed enmity from these Russians because my previous association with Soviet Air Force personnel had been most harmonious and pleasant. It had happened 11 years before, on Christmas Eve 1961 in Antarctica. A Soviet aircraft carrying support supplies and personnel to the Russian Base at Mirny Station had diverted to the US Navy Base at McMurdo Sound due to weather problems at Mirny. They were given a warm reception by the Navy and provided with fuel for another attempt at reaching Mirny when the weather improved. In the meantime, they joined in our celebration of Christmas with delicious meals from the Chow Hall, American beer and whisky, supplemented by excellent vodka from their aircraft. We exchanged small significant gifts and with much laughter, and a few tears, embraced each other as true Brothers in Arms.

For most of our time in Bangladesh, the weather had been conducive for safe flying over a country that had few working radio-navigation aids and airfield infrastructure for anything beyond clear day operations. One notable exception was on the late afternoon and evening of April 4 when a mass of huge thunderstorms moved up from the south of Dacca. The storm was a small, very active tropical cyclone with estimated wind speeds of 70–100 mph, golf ball-sized hailstones, continuous lightning, and heavy rain. I was flying the C-130 back from Ishurdi that afternoon and arrived at Dacca Airport minutes before the storm hit the area. Taxiing into the ramp, the immediate problem was guiding the aircraft under its own power to a suitable position for tie down.

During this maneuvering, the storm arrived overhead in full force, quickly failing all electrical power at and around the airport. Using only the illumination from periodic lightning flashes and hand signals from a ground crewman, I managed to position the C-130 nose wheel over a suitable tie-down ring. By then, the aircraft was rolling up to ten degrees each way and nose wheel periodically lifting off the ground, causing a slew to left and right—very difficult conditions for the ground crew trying to link a chain from the nose gear to the tie-down ring on the concrete ramp. Finally, the ground crew timed the movement of the aircraft until a brief pause allowed them to secure the nose wheel. However, in order to prevent the flight control surfaces from damage, the GTC (Auxiliary Power Unit) was kept running to supply hydraulic pressure, allowing the cockpit flight controls to be manually centralized for the duration of the storm.

But that wasn't the end of the night's drama. A United Nations aircraft, a four engined DC-4, parked in front of our C-130 jumped its chocks, slewed through 180 degrees and moved off down the ramp, powered by an estimated 70 mph wind. A small group of my groundcrew chased after this out-of-control beast, halted its movement, and secured it with chocks and other blocking objects. Meanwhile, the remainder of the team battled with tying down both wings of our C-130 to ramp securing points. During these actions, the ultimate test of our survival that night came with the appearance of rapidly moving spark trails across the ramp; what the hell was happening? After a brief period of confusion, we realized that an adjacent hangar upwind of our location was shedding sheets of roofing iron that were passing both aircraft at waist level … in the darkness!

Despite these extremely hazardous conditions, an ashen-faced crew methodically continued securing both aircraft, aware of the danger. Above the shrieking of the wind could be heard the ripping of roofing iron, and could be seen, silhouetted in lightning flashes, the sheets peeling back from the hangar roof. When the tasks were done, all crew took cover inside our C-130 and listened to the occasional sheet clattering against the aircraft hull until the worst of the storm passed overhead. In the aftermath, we confirmed that the only damage to our aircraft and the UN DC-4 were minor skin abrasions from the roofing iron. We had saved our C-130 from serious damage that would have finished our Relief Operation in Bangladesh. Sadly, thousands of Dacca residents were left homeless and many were killed during the storm.

Recalling this event many years later, I believe it was truly a miracle that none of us at the Dacca airfield that terrible night was killed or seriously injured. Maybe we were all sheltered by my immortality? Joking, of course, but you should know that I commended these extraordinary courageous acts by my team that night to the senior officers of the RNZAF. The commendation was totally ignored. There were no medals or letters of recognition for their fine service from the New Zealand government. This is a theme I'll return to in other sections of my Air Force history. As these often dangerous operations for the RNZAF had happened or continued, the important question became: Do you want to be a professional pilot for Queen and Country, or for money with freedom to be the real you? In the brilliant movie, *Apocalypse Now,* on his way up the river into Cambodia to assassinate Colonel Kurtz, Captain Willard (CIA) wonders, *"... why the Colonel went rogue, got off the boat, and out of the goddamn program. He could have gone for General, but he went for himself instead."*

There's a wonderful saying in US military aviation: *It's hard to soar with the eagles when you work for turkeys.* That explains much about what happened to the RNZAF during my 20-year tenure. A classic example of being big frogs in little ponds, where upward mobility was a numbers game, always controlled by an incompetent few who wouldn't retire and couldn't be fired—and would never recommend medals for junior officers, unless they'd already gotten theirs! Here's to all the unsung heroes of New Zealand's military forces, in a country that would declare itself a *Nuclear Free Zone* in 1984, in the naïve belief that national

Defense Forces would no longer be necessary.

The very best thing that happened to me and my team in Bangladesh was the opportunity to take direct action in helping a group of small children and their families at the Ishurdi airfield. As the missions into Ishurdi from Baghdogra progressed, carrying thousands of pounds of milk powder, a gathering of very young children in raggedy clothing showed up each time the C-130 landed to offload the sacks. Initially, these little kids would keep clear of the aircraft until all the sacks had been offloaded, then rush to the rear of the loading ramp, waiting on our loadmasters to sweep the dregs of powder off the cargo floor. The second day I was there, I'd noted the presence of a rather ancient looking soldier, possibly from the last days of the British Indian Army units. This man, this old soldier, in his tattered uniform, using a walking cane and moving with dignity, seemed to have control over the children, so I spoke with him about organizing the children, with their numbers increasing every day, into orderly rows along the tarmac. He indicated that wouldn't be a problem but asked how the children could collect the dregs from the cargo ramp if they remained squatting in their rows on the tarmac.

My easy answer was to have two or three sacks removed from the C-130 prior to the loading of the Red Cross trucks destined for the various villages in the area, then have the contents of these sacks distributed to the children in an orderly and fair fashion under the stern supervision of the old soldier. Unfortunately, the distribution of relief aid in the Ishurdi area was under the control of the German Red Cross Team, with their leader, Dieter, always present at the airfield during the offloading of sacks. Despite him knowing, as I did, that after the trucks left the airfield and the sacks were taken to the villages, the village headmen took control of the final distribution to his

116

villagers … for favors. I had learned from the ICRC leaders in Dacca that corruption with the relief aid, in money or food, was top to bottom in the Bangladesh government—from the prime minister all the way down to village headmen.

In Dieter's sense of his job description, no bags could be taken aside for a bunch of kids who were lucky enough to live close to the Ishurdi airfield and our arriving C-130. While I was attempting to reason with him, he made a stupid mistake, not realizing the flexible nature of Kiwis, by stating that only broken bags could be given to the children. Bingo! I briefed my loadmasters—with a wink-wink and a nod-nod—to be careful and not break too many bags! They became so careless with handling the bags (perhaps a knife was involved?) the kids and their parents had milk powder to spare. I still study the photos I took of the kids in regimental lines, squatting on that tarmac, each waiting patiently for a copious dollop of powder with the old Bengali soldier looking on and smiling, often giving us a smart military salute. It remains a moving experience, and probably the most significant act in my life.

By the end of the relief flights on April 19, we'd carried a grand total of 3,140,000 pounds of relief aid foodstuffs. We left Dacca the next day for Singapore, eventually reaching Auckland, New Zealand on April 23. In my final report to the RNZAF and New Zealand government I concluded as a tactical aircraft operation, Bangladesh Two was an absolute success. As a relief aid program, it was equally successful, bringing great credit to New Zealand and to the Royal New Zealand Air Force.

Not surprisingly, in many quarters, official and otherwise, we were treated like lepers for having had such a fun time on the government's payroll. This was probably because of a junior officer who'd been on the operation and was eagerly spreading rumors about scandalous behavior by aircrew members in Bangladesh. Was there any basis to these rumors?

The Women of Dacca

To the women in Dacca we cannot say much
They're Swedish or Finnish or Danish or Dutch
The Germans are Buxom
The Russians are Red
And the French and Italians
Eat Garlic in Bed

Terry Knight, C-130 Navigator and Minstrel Boy

Our well-stocked bar, in Dacca's grandest hotel, in the heart of the newest Islamist Republic was an apostasy to the people we'd come to save, but was a huge draw to the visiting European members of the ICRC, Red Cross units, and other benefactors from Western countries. We were happy to entertain the men and absolutely delighted to entertain the women—who to us wild colonial boys from New Zealand, were an exotic collection of real winners. And we made the most of their unexpected presence in this Islamic backwater.

My favorite was Jolene, a sweet girl from Wales. During our time together I never fully understood what her function was in Dacca. She may have been with the British Red Cross Team, but more likely with the British Legation that had been established from the British High Commission in India. She had talked of living and working in Delhi before coming to Dacca. Ten years later, in 1982, Peter Weir's movie, *The Year of Living Dangerously* came out in theaters. I couldn't help but romanticize that the story, set in Sukarno's Indonesia, was like the accidental relationship of Jo and me. Ever since those dangerous, but exciting days, I've speculated that we were both in the intelligence game. She from British MI6, and me, who'd been directed to gather military intelligence from Bangladesh for the New Zealand government. Whatever our secret functions were, being with Jo in exciting times was a breathtaking experience and the first scintilla of an epiphany that was to change the future direction of my life.

Our beginning came during a trip to the fabled town of Darjeeling, set high in the Indian Himalaya, north of the Siliguri Gap. It was thanks to my recent contacts within the Indian Air Force at Baghdogra who'd suggested giving my team members a break from the heat, humidity, squalor, and infections of Dacca by sending them up into the mountains to Darjeeling. And so it happened: team members, some accompanied by the exotic women from Dacca, were invited to ride our C-130 to Baghdogra, then take a bus or the famous Toy Train up to Darjeeling. Jolene and I were lucky to be offered a ride in a Land Rover from Baghdogra to Darjeeling with the New Zealand Red Cross team, Bob McKerrow and partner. We spent two days in the town, situated in a conifer forest at an elevation of 7,000 feet, very beautiful and unbelievably pleasant with its cool temperatures and low humidity. The peak of Kangchenjunga, the third highest point in the world, was visible 50 miles to the north of Darjeeling. How could I not be seduced by this karmic intersection of long suppressed aspirations. A future not controlled by military bureaucracy, living among mountains, becoming a permanent expatriate New Zealander, and accompanied on the journey by an enchanting adventurous partner.

So went the dreams of a simple country boy from New Zealand who'd made the big time, but naively ensnared himself in traps of long-term Air Force service from age 17, early marriage at age 21, and two children by age 23. Would I find it acceptable to leave all that behind? To walk away from the Air Force would be an easy decision. The system had its pound of flesh from me, paying peanuts for doing dangerous jobs: Antarctica, Borneo, Vietnam, Bangladesh, and all the hazardous stuff in between. Don't misunderstand; often it was fun and adventure, but why not take my skills to a higher bidder? As it transpired, I'd given up on the Air Force, but it hadn't given up on me. As to my family, I could not—and would not—forsake them until my two sons had finished high school.

In the meantime, I put my bright exciting future on hold. It would become the story of a life delayed—without the far mountain peaks, without flying the world for profit, and without a partner like Jolene. She was an inspiration, with her unequivocal love, her Simon and Garfunkel music, and the surprise gentle touch of her hand when we first met. Five years would pass before leaving the Air Force; two more years to find an international flying job; another four years to be back in the Himalaya mountains; then finally in 1985 to achieve the dream ... an expatriate in a country full of mountains and flying the big jets for a world class airline.

1974: The Hantus of Pulau Rawa

PULAU RAWA (RAWA ISLAND) is a small island ten miles east of the town of Mersing, situated on the southeastern coast of the Malayan Peninsula. Despite its small size, half a mile long by a quarter mile wide, it's western shore contains a beautiful beach and a shallow water coral reef.

The Johor Royal family owned Rawa Island, where a modest resort was built in 1971 by Tunku Mohammed Archibald, one of the sons of the then Sultan of Johor. The Tunku was married to an Australian woman and their three children were the product of that marriage. The woman once told me that the island was very active with bad spirits, including a poltergeist that inhabited their hut, or in the tree that hung over the hut at the southern end of the resort. Household items, such as clocks and dishes were regularly thrown around the interior. Her stories about Malay animistic Hantus (spirits or ghosts) were very convincing.

I recall a scary incident that occurred on our second visit to Rawa in 1974. The weather wasn't great. There were rough seas between Mersing and the island with occasional thunderstorms, limiting the frequency of travel between the island and the mainland and making it difficult to escape from the craziness happening at the resort. Two young Malay boys had gone gila (crazy), apparently possessed by

121

the spirits of two old fisherman who had drowned off the island many years before. One of them had stolen a piece of red cloth that was still desired by the other and the young Malays were acting out this drama. Tunku Archibald's eldest son, aged about 18 and on a break from his oil rig job, attempted to keep them subdued by wrapping yellow cloth bands (with words or symbols) around their heads and using a particular piece of wood to exorcise the spirits.

My family and I arrived on the island shortly before this drama was in full swing. We still remember the ignorant American tourists watching the proceedings as if it was put on for their enjoyment. Annette and I tried to play down what was happening so not to scare our young sons, Jeremy and Christopher. We were told that the possessed lads wished to *machete* every person on the island, so we were very concerned on the last night before help arrived from the mainland. After a sleepless night of waiting for the inventible and armed only with a big stick in the bedroom, a boat arrived in the morning with the local Mersing Imam (Islamic teacher, cleric, and prayer leader at the Mosque) on board. He had come to exorcise the animistic demons that possessed these Malay lads, but that end of the drama was played out in Mersing. For us, the boat's arrival and subsequent departure with the crazy boys onboard was a great relief. We breathed a little easier after the boat had gone, and slept soundly the following night.

A sad footnote for Pulau Rawa: The eldest son died, possibly by suicide, shortly after the incident, perhaps on his oil rig or elsewhere, but I don't remember. A few years later, in 1979, I was told that Tunku Archibald had died of a gunshot wound a year after his son had died. Bad karma and bad Hantus?

1975: The Jungle Running Club for Idiots

AS A COMPANION PIECE to the Rawa Island incident, my knowledge about the Hantus of Malaysia was expanded during a six-week stay in the capital city of Kuala Lumpur (KL). At the time, based in Singapore with the New Zealand Air Force, I was given the temporary assignment as the military attaché in the New Zealand High Commission (Embassy) for Malaysia. My wife, Annette, and I moved into the attaché's residence in KL, a multi-level bungalow with air-conditioning in every room. We had servants, cooks, and a limo driver to get me to and from the High Commission, or both of us to cocktail parties. A very pleasant change from our non-airconditioned military bungalow in Singapore.

As part of the diplomatic corps for New Zealand, it was expected that I would play golf, placing me in locations where I could mingle with the military attachés from the other embassies in Kuala Lumpur. I was probably a disappointment after explaining that when I was too old to climb mountains, I might consider the silly game of golf. Instead, I became a regular at a club playing tennis and squash, but most notably, was introduced to running in the jungle with the Hash House Harriers (the HHH) late afternoons every Monday. In the decades since 1975, the HHH craze has spread across the world, with many stories told about this athletic aberration. Back then, when I began running with the founding fathers of the HHH in the jungles and rubber tree plantations surrounding KL, the organization was described as either *a running club with a drinking problem,* or more cynically as *a drinking club with a running problem.*

Whatever the description, I loved the fine madness of chasing a paper trail cross country through the jungle—avoiding poisonous snakes, huge spiders in their webs, and wading through swamps inhabited with all kind of nasty critters like leeches. Then at the end of the run, with darkness falling, being chewed on by mosquitos, sweating profusely and quaffing ice-cold cans of Anchor beer, anticipating the flavors of satay and prawns at a roadside makanan stall. For me, this craziness was the beginning of a renewed physical fitness, first achieved in the jungles of Malaya, running and drinking with fellow idiots.

After our wonderful sojourn in Kuala Lumpur, Annette and I returned to our military home in Singapore, where I was invited to run with the HHH group in Johor Bahru across the Straits of Johor in southern Malaya. Morrie Robinson, a neighbor and fellow New Zealand Air Force officer, introduced me to the Johor Bahru Hash that ran in a wilder jungle environment than around KL. Morrie also had me eating the Durian fruit, which became an addiction, but you had to be quick to beat the elephants, orangutans, and other monkeys to the feast.

The majority of the Johor Hash runners were locals—Malays, Chinese, and Indians, with far fewer Europeans than in KL. Which brings me back to the subject of Hantus. It was not unusual with Hash running to still be stumbling around in the jungle after dark, and the Malays, and a few Chinese (and me!) could get spooked by being lost in there until we found our way out, often with the help of a villager on his motor scooter. They would talk of the Hantus, for example: *the Pontianak, a female ghost who will stop a man on a jungle path and asks the man to follow her. The offer is not usually refused, but when she turns to go the man sees she has an enormous hole in her back. Then she melts away. At night before heavy storms, she can be heard weeping in the banana groves.* Paul Theroux 1977, his novel, *The Consuls File*.

In late 1975, Annette and I returned to Wellington in New Zealand, and while there, I became one of the three founding members of the Wellington HHH, a Hash group that has been highly successful thanks to Peter Adamson and others from that time. Amazingly, after retiring from the Air Force in early 1977, I was fated to return to Singapore in 1979, and among other things, rejoin the HHH group in Johor Bahru, seeing the same faces and great friends. So, I was back home with the Hantus from my formative years in Southeast Asia. Was I a believer? Well, I still don't laugh in front of butterflies and a number of other bad-luck behaviors that the Malays of the jungle taught me to avoid.

1975: The Last Days in Vietnam – 41 Squadron Was There

MY LAST FORAY into the war zone of South Vietnam was as a safety pilot on 41 Squadron's Bristol Freighters in April 1975. This assignment took place during the final days of the South Vietnamese people's freedom from Communist domination and the fall of Saigon. As a participant and New Zealand witness to the terrible tragedy that would befall the people of South Vietnam, this final 41 Squadron mission was the most dangerous days for any New Zealand Air Force Unit since WW2. After the earlier betrayals of 41 Squadron it was no surprise to me that the New Zealand government and Defense leaders would continue to ignore the fortitude and courage of the Squadron personnel involved in Saigon during those last days. The Detachment Commander, Squadron Leader Bob Davidson ran this final and hazardous Vietnam mission superbly, and deserved a commendation for his service. *Sorry about that, Bob; you and your team should not have volunteered to be part of New Zealand's Dad's Army.*

Remembering the best and most dangerous moments during those last days in Vietnam, my best was discreet planning to relieve the South Vietnam Air Force of at least one of their Hercules C-130s before the fleet was captured by the North Vietnamese Invaders. I had made overtures to

126

the US Lockheed Rep to determine the fuel loads, security measures, and door locks, if any. My derring-do plan was to get the plane started in the quiet hours of the night (no such thing with low-level tracer crossing the airfield!) and leap into the sky, then head south to our base in Singapore. One of the 41 Squadron pilots, Denis Monti, and I were experienced C-130H pilots, but had no idea how to start a C-130A model. We would need to read the flight manual— probably in the dark? Unfortunately, (or fortunately?) we never executed this exciting air-pirating act, but someone else did in a most dramatic way.

Ten years later, in 1985, I was flying Boeing 727s for Orion Air, based in North Carolina, and crewed with First Officer Kim Pham. Kim had been a serving C-130 pilot with the South Vietnam Air Force when he hijacked a C-130A from Saigon, flew it to a small Delta airstrip, picked up his family and village friends, and flew to Singapore. He told me he had a total passenger count of around 300, with 30 in the cockpit. They're small people, but thinking about that boggles the mind!

My worst experience was flying to Vung Tau from Saigon, an airfield we all knew well from Freighter and C-130 flights during the actual Vietnam war. Until this flight, most of our refugee supply missions had been to An Toi Island; the Vung Tau mission was considered a little dodgy from the outset, lacking good intel on its status. On April 8, acting as the backup pilot (no seat or controls!) I flew to Vung Tau with pilot Don Carter and crew on what became the most frightening of those final trips. After we landed at Vung Tau, without Tower control, nobody was seen on the ground. Then, after shutting the engines down, we heard continuous automatic gunfire surrounding us! That got our attention, so with great haste we climbed back aboard, started the engines, and took off still carrying the cargo.

127

During that takeoff, with constant gunfire coming from our left side, I'm not ashamed to admit that I crouched down on the step behind Don Carter, expecting the left window to shatter with incoming rounds, and planned how to reach the control wheel if Don was hit, then to firewall the throttles and get help from the navigator and/or signaler to remove Don from the pilot seat.

The initial camp for the 41 Detachment was adjacent to the Tan Son Nhut Control Tower, a location I was not totally comfortable with, because I had seen the mortar damage to the Tower on February 18, 1968 during the TET Offensive. We had the camp there to stay clear of active ramp traffic, and with access to water and toilets. One morning at first light, I came close to shooting one of our signalers with my personal FN 9mm handgun. The stretcher I was sleeping on was in a section of our kitchen tent, and I been woken by someone moving stealthily near the end of the bed. With my gun under my pillow, I pulled it out, chambered a round, and pointed it between my feet at the intruder, who shouted, "It's only me, don't shoot, I'm brewing an early morning coffee." If I had fired the gun, while still supine, there's every chance it would have taken off a foot, or at least a few toes!

A major advantage of our camp position was the view we had of the dramas constantly unfolding on and over the airfield. One of those moments was the arrival of a US Airforce C-5 Galaxy. I took a photo of the Galaxy preparing for takeoff after it was loaded with Vietnamese orphans and their nurses. One hour later it returned after the loss of rudder and elevator flight controls. The rear cargo door had blown off at around 30,000 feet, disabling the rear flight controls. The crew were able to return the crippled plane to within a few miles of the runway at Saigon, but then lost pitch control and skidded along the paddy fields on fire.

Standing by the Control Tower on the ramp, we were witnesses to this terrible tragedy as the helicopters flew in the dead and dying.

During the 1990s, I often flew with a retired C-5 Galaxy pilot, who had known that Saigon crew. He explained how they'd managed to control the airplane by differential power, and probably would have reached the runway if they'd not lowered the landing gear at the last moment, an action that messed with the damped pitch oscillation they'd achieved during the long careful descent.

Another memorable event, that didn't last long, was the unexpected appearance of two F-5 fighter-bombers passing overhead the airport. We could still see them over the city center, where they suddenly tipped in on dive-bombing maneuvers; then we saw smoke and debris from the hits. The story that followed was that two F-5s planes of the South Vietnamese Air Force had come from the Bien Hoa Air Base, dropped their bombs on the Presidential Palace, but missed the target, then fled west into Thailand.

The most disturbing happenings for the Squadron's activities leading up to the last days in Saigon was the rapid encroachment of the North Vietnam Army (NVA) into areas and towns that were thought to be controlled by South Vietnam forces. We were still being tasked to fly refugee food supplies to An Toi Island, using a route pattern that avoided known NVA positions, but the intelligence information coming from the US Embassy was too late and useless. I presumed the Americans didn't want the South Vietnam military forces to realize further US military hardware was not coming! We need to remember those treacherous actions in April 1975 by the Democrat Party held US Congress, and the dramatic moment when their Senator Jacob Javits told President Ford, *I will give you large sums for evacuation, but not one nickel for military aid.* We had already been fooled into flying to Vung Tau, so following that scare, Bob Davidson made arrangements with Air America to obtain their latest intel on the security status of each airfield we'd been tasked for—and disregard information from the US Embassy.

One of those airfields was Phan Thiet, a town on the coast east of Saigon. It all seemed okay until Air America advised that one of their aircraft had taken 20mm anti-aircraft fire while approaching to land that morning. So that was the end of Phan Thiet flights. On the subject of anti-aircraft threats, the NVA and Viet Cong had possession of shoulder mounted surface-to-air Strela SA-7 missile launchers, and we were advised they would use them to bring down airplanes close to airfields, including Saigon. On flights from Saigon to the island of An Thoi, a Flight Following service, originally established by US Forces, with the callsign *Paddy Control,* had been useful in keeping our Freighters and the Australian C-130s clear of artillery and ground attack fire zones. The problem was that as it got closer to the last days, an Aussie crew with more precise navigation equipment than our Freighters realized that *Paddy Control* was giving them directions into hostile territory, possibly where they could be brought down by a Strela missile. It became obvious that *Paddy* had been taken over by the NVA.

On April 13, 1975, I left Saigon for Singapore on a 41 Squadron Bristol Freighter operated by Roger Holdaway and crew. Bob Davidson and the remainder of the Detachment left South Vietnam for the last time on April 21, 1975, returning to the Squadron's base in Singapore.

1977: Welcome to Commercial Aviation, Flyboy

No matter what else happens, fly the airplane.
Forget all that stuff about thrust and drag, lift and gravity;
a plane flies because of money.
Capital Air Services and the Cessna 402 Airplane

RECENTLY RETIRED from the Air Force at age 37, I was adrift without a rudder, but confident that I could make the big time in commercial aviation in whatever role and wherever. It began with flying small twin-engined Cessna 402 planes on passenger flights into basic airstrips situated along the margins of South Island's mountainous terrain. The combination of New Zealand's extreme weather, mountainous country, and poorly-equipped older planes often created hazardous flying moments. I found this surprising, having just left the inherently high-risk world of Air Force aviation. As a former military pilot, I thought I knew everything about flying, but began learning lessons far beyond the military rules and regulations of my professional training and skills. My commuter airline required pilots to fly single-pilot all-weather flights with a specific pilot's license approval known as *Single Pilot IFR*. In addition to the flying, pilots were required to drive a fuel tanker, refuel the plane, write tickets, and load the passenger luggage. For these multiple tasks, we were paid a paltry sum.

131

To illustrate some of the wild events at Capital Air, here are a few extracts from a journal I kept during those extraordinary days:

May 19, 1977: Flying yesterday from Nelson to Westport to Greymouth, with a sunny weather day that turned into the depths of Hell. Airframe and propeller icing, turbulence, rain and a 60-knot headwind. The weather on landing at Westport was marginal, and at Greymouth worse. Flew low level at 500 feet along the coast to land at last light, in heavy rain and high winds, at Greymouth. Pleased to be on the ground, thinking why I had left the comfort and security of the Air Force desk job for this? I must be mad, because I had already lived like this in my early aviation career. I just didn't know when to quit flying. Fellow pilot Don tells of experiencing severe turbulence over the Marlborough Sounds on his flight from Wellington to Nelson. Up and down 2,000 feet!

June 13, 1977: Heavy frost on the airplane overnight at Christchurch. No de-icing available and scratch windscreen with brush, trying to clear off the ice crystals. Arrive overhead Greymouth when still dark to land on the runway without lighting. On touchdown, my peripheral vision senses something moving beside the plane, and realize it's a black horse keeping pace with me. Fortunately it stays to one side, far enough to clear the wing-tip and whirling propeller blades of the left engine. Someone waiting for passengers calls the local police, who arrive for the big roundup, then a control van shows up to clear the runway and grass verges of horses.

Arrived at Palmerston North late due to ATC clearance problem. Hassle with James Aviation about refueling. I lose my cool and taxi back to the Terminal, fast, then run off the side of the taxiway, becoming stuck in the muddy grass. It takes five hefty guys from Field Air to lift under wing, putting the plane's wheels back on the hard surface. I should never have got up this morning!

June 29, 1977: A red letter day. Made a late run Nelson –

Wellington – Nelson, arriving at Nelson to be told by local manager Bill that the bubble had finally burst: the end of the road for Capital Air Services, my job, and all the others in the Company. Required to make one last flight sequence from Nelson to Blenheim to Wellington and back to Nelson, arriving after dark but still making a high speed low pass with a 60-degree banked break over the Nelson airfield - fighter pilot habits are hard to lose! After landing, given a letter of termination of employment with one month's notice. Typically, for shoe-string airline operators, this first civilian flying job didn't last long. I was back on the street within four months after bankruptcy and a hostile takeover of the airline. There was no redundancy or vacation pay. I had just been introduced to the uncertain world of commercial aviation at a time when civilian pilots were flooding the market worldwide.

June 30, 1977: There are ten pilots at Capital Air, half of them with flying experience in Papua New Guinea, and as expected, can be a wild bunch at times. So, on the day after being fired, we decide to celebrate instead of shedding tears. It was now drinking and getting drunk time. Freddie and I start early at the Rutherford Pub, listening to his story from the previous day. He'd been apprehended by the police and tried to escape custody by leaping from the police car. But too drunk to succeed, then handcuffed, and freed after sobering up. Later we join the others at the Trailways restaurant for an afternoon and evening of drinking and some eating. Someone tries to set the restaurant on fire, so we're all asked to leave the premises!

I learn from my Nelson girlfriend, who also worked for Capital Air, that she was distraught when called into the manager's office the previous night, thinking that I may have crashed, but when told that the Company has been closed down, says, "Thank God that's all!"

July 4, 1977: The reality of losing my job is rapidly sinking in, but some good news is a job offer as aircraft sales rep for James Aviation based in Hamilton. I've been living in a caravan at a public campground near Tahuna beach, and now thinking of the impact of departure from Nelson and what it has all meant. I'll be running the sandy beach for the last time and find that sad. I'll miss being at the campground and its glorious location. I've been happier here during the past months than for many years. The everyday business of living was simplified to the essential basics – no hassles, no interference – just life. However, I'm not really bothered by moving on. It's been a pleasant uncluttered interlude, and I feel very fit and mentally relaxed. I'm prepared for the hardship of the battles ahead.

The Risks of Flying with Only One Engine.

At my second civilian job, as a sales rep for James Aviation in Hamilton, New Zealand, I found myself flying a variety of single-engined Beechcraft airplanes. Two of them were the smaller four-seat versions—the Beech Sierra with retractable landing gear, and the Beech Sundowner with fixed landing gear. Both were equipped with basic flight instruments, but neither were approved for operating under Instrument Flight Rules (IFR); therefore not at night, nor in clouds. Essentially, they could only be flown during daytime and in good weather under Visual Flight Rules (VFR).

How safe, and what levels of risk are there when flying single-engined airplanes? The foremost risk is inflight engine failure, caused by mechanical breakages, fuel starvation, oil leakage, icing, or perhaps bird strikes. Once that engine fails and can't be restarted, the airplane becomes a glider that demands an urgent landing, preferably on a long flat surface that is visible. If a pilot has been trained to practice forced landings without power, and it's daytime, in clear weather, flying over grassy fields, highways, or parking lots with few vehicles, then the risk factor is reduced. If an inflight engine failure occurs at night, in clouds, or over mountainous terrain, then chances of survival are remote—unless the occupants are wearing parachutes ... and use them.

Top-of-the-line in the single-engine fleet at James Aviation was a Beechcraft Bonanza A-36. This superb six-seat plane had the lineage of an airborne limo, a delight to fly and fully equipped to operate IFR. So, as a Single Pilot IFR qualified pilot I was soon chauffeuring management and customers around New Zealand in bad weather conditions, and often at night, without any real concern of the risks involved. Now, as a self-confessed professional pilot looking back to that time, I ponder why I was so cavalier to take those risks. Maybe I needed the job and loved the smell of real leather seats? Whatever, one justifiable reason was my background of flying single-engined military trainers and fighters like the Harvard AT-6 and D.H. Vampire. I had flown those planes often at night, and in clouds, strapped into parachutes, knowing that if the engine failed I had the option of bailing out—or ejecting (Vampire T-11 only).

I realize my justification for operating the Bonanza at night and in clouds doesn't make sense, because there were no parachutes for pilot or passengers, so the risk was extreme in the event of engine failure. This was particularly true for New Zealand, a country covered in high mountains and deep valleys, where gliding down at night or through clouds, expecting to arrive at a suitable place to crash-land had a probable survival chance of 0-5 percent ... if that!

I imagine many of you hotshot aviators out there are reading this, rolling your eyes, and thinking what an idiot this guy was. Well, it gets worse, much worse. My Flight Log Book for the two years at James Aviation shows Beechcraft Bonanza total flights of 35 night hours and total in-cloud time of 50 hours. Now, for the best part: 15 night hours and 25 in-cloud hours were accumulated on one mission—two-thirds of the way around the world from Gander, Newfoundland to Hamilton, New Zealand … solo! The total flight time was 100 hours, with so many opportunities for the engine to fail, and it did once—fuel starvation over the Atlantic!

In those far-off years from 1977 to 1979, the most secure place for pilots was on the big jets with international airlines, but getting hired by them was a crap-shoot even for someone like me with extensive flight experience and the appropriate pilot licenses. The government-owned airline, Air New Zealand, would have been a sinecure, but the Company didn't want me, thanks to some bad blood between me and other retired Air Force pilots flying for the airline. As the years progressed, moving farther away from the small aviation world of New Zealand, I realized how fortunate to have been rejected by its national airline. With perseverance, hard work, ingenuity, and some danger, I became a highly successful pilot in Australia's bigger aviation world, and ultimately, in the USA.

In the meantime, this bright future in commercial aviation was nothing but an unattainable dream, so to help make it happen, I began pursuing the hazardous business of small airplane delivery flights from the USA. This critical risk-taking began with flying a single-engined Beechcraft Bonanza two-thirds of the world from North America eastbound to New Zealand. It had been a reckless decision: a 20-day odyssey filled with danger, but an undertaking that secured me a position with one of the largest general aviation companies in Australia. This company hired me as a delivery pilot of twin-engined turboprop airplanes from the USA to Australia and Southeast Asia.

Obviously, two engines are safer than one over oceans, especially when planes are fitted with long-range navigation equipment, as these were. However, the level of risk on these flights was still high because of overweight flights when carrying additional fuel to span the Pacific's remote islands. A typical departure from San Francisco with enough fuel to reach Honolulu required an overweight takeoff in a Sweringen Metro airliner, which would result in a splash-down on the sea after an engine failure during the first five hours of flight. That's a long time to rely on good luck, isn't it? I had become addicted to risk, but each flight was an adventure, and the challenge of planning, executing, and completing each journey was most rewarding. Not in monetary gain (the company paid me a modest salary), but as a one-person pilot, navigator, and radio operator circling the world many times, I became a significant aviator, a pilot who had reached out and touched the void many times—and survived.

After four years of risking my neck on these delivery flights, safe harbor arrived with the offer to work for a Papua New Guinea mining company, Bougainville Copper Limited (BCL). Based in Townsville, Australia, I was hired as one of five pilots operating the company jet on scheduled passenger flights across the Coral Sea between Townsville, Brisbane, and Bougainville Island. The jet, an Israeli built Westwind high-performance twin-engine Turbofan, was the best airplane I had flown since the four-engined War Machine, the C-130 Hercules.

1978: Around the World on One Engine

The only time you have too much fuel is when you're on fire.

LEAVING GANDER for the short flight to St. Johns was to establish the performance of the heavily loaded Beechcraft Bonanza at cruise altitude, cruise speed, and fuel consumption on a short flight, and most importantly, while over land. Apart from studying and recording the cruise parameters, flying low over the mostly barren tundra landscape of Newfoundland was a fascinating experience. On arrival at Torbay Airport, I was impressed with its location and the city of St. Johns sitting five hundred feet above the ocean on a peninsula, close to Cape Spear, the easternmost point of North America; a sensible place to launch across the Atlantic Ocean to Europe.

My findings from this first flight indicated that the Bonanza was performing as expected with the extra weight of fuel. However, I needed to uplift another 60 gallons for the flight to the Azores, so I knew the cruise speed would be lower than what I'd experienced on the trip from Gander. Landing at St. Johns, I was treated well by airport staff and at the Airport Inn close by, a stopover location I would remember and use for the next four years.

Staying at the inn overnight, I made the acquaintance of a group of US Air Force Reserve pilots from the First

Provisional Airlift STOL Squadron based out of Westover AFB. They had a flight of military transport aircraft to take across the Atlantic, and planned to leave the following morning for Lajes AFB in the Azores. They were surprised and suitably impressed with my intention to fly a single-engine airplane, not only to the Azores but for another 14,000 miles to New Zealand. At this start point of my epic journey, I needed that boost to my ego from these military aviators because I was having grave doubts about the sheer lunacy of my mission.

The next morning at the Flight Planning Office, they presented me with a bountiful boxed lunch with a note on top—"For the Bonanza Bonzer, compliments of the 1st PAS"—signed by their senior officer, William N. Jackson, Smyrna, GA 30080. If any of you guys are still out there, I've never forgotten your kind support. Forty-three years later, I still retain the signed lid off that lunchbox!

With the maximum quantity of fuel (159 gallons) onboard, it was finally time to test whether the Bonanza and I could cross the Atlantic Ocean, both a mechanical and mental challenge. After takeoff and turning to the departure heading it was apparent that the climb to my planned cruising altitude of 8,000 feet was going to take time, but not unexpected at the heavy weight with full fuel. I was able to confirm the outbound track using the radial from the St. Johns Visual Omni Range (VOR) out to 100 miles DME (Distance Measuring Equipment). This gave me some idea of the wind effect along and across the track, but this would be the last useful information for the next 700 miles. During the early part of the climb, I'd switched the engine fuel supply from the main tanks (used for takeoff) to the other three tanks—the auxiliary tank behind my seat, and the tip tanks—to ensure all provided a positive feed to the engine, then began using the tip tanks as the main supply.

The standard fuel usage technique for ferry flying, particularly over extended time over water, was to burn all fuel from any auxiliary tanks in the early stages of the flight, leaving the fuel in the main wing tanks for last. Once in level flight at 8,000 feet, I discovered the IAS (indicated airspeed) for the best cruise power was ten knots slower than planned. I knew it would increase with fuel burn-off, but for re-planning purposes I adjusted the total flight time from 8.5 to 9.5 hours to reach Santa Maria, and advised Gander Oceanic Control accordingly. By this time, I had good contact using the long-range HF transceivers. Both installed units worked fine, but the one with the trailing antenna had the best reception.

To remain on the Great Circle track that I'd plotted, it was necessary to keep changing the magnetic compass heading to maintain the changing True track. The total shift was 15 degrees to the right over the 1,000 miles between St. Johns and Flores. During planning I'd also taken into account the wide magnetic variation in the northern Atlantic. For example, in 1981, the Magnetic Variation at St. John's was 26 degrees West, and at Santa Maria it was 15 degrees West. What I couldn't correct for was any changes in the forecast winds from those I'd used in flight planning. Where I actually was over this big ocean was now a guessing game until I had a lock-on to the Flores Non Directional Beacon (NDB), which I could track to, but not know the distance to the beacon. With the auto-pilot engaged, navigation pointing in the right direction, and fuel transfer underway, I was finally able to relax two hours after takeoff … *until the engine stopped!!*

The sound of silence was deafening. I couldn't believe it. I must have been dreaming, but I wasn't sleeping, so how could I be dreaming?

But that was the problem. I'd dropped off to sleep while flying this single-engine Bonanza across the endless Atlantic Ocean. *Single-engine.* That was a reality to grab onto, and a reason to wake up fast. It had become so quiet because there was only one engine and it had stopped working. It was all downhill from that point, quickly, down—down to a sunlit sea and not far to go. On the sea's surface, were huge swells, white caps, strong wind lanes, and it would only be minutes before splashdown.

It flashed through my mind that if I failed to survive the impact on that wild-looking sea, I'd be in good company with the ghosts of the RMS Titanic located somewhere close by, 12,000 feet below the waves. Amazing how years of training in aircraft emergencies can come back to save the day. So many times I'd practiced the 'forced landing without power' procedure in the single-engined Harvard AT-6, and there it was, immediately available:

Close the throttle, convert excess speed to height, trim for 90 knots, look for a suitable landing area, plan a tentative approach, and check engine controls: fuel selector to main tanks, mixture control to full rich, propeller control to maximum rpm.

All done, now to see what happens when I open the throttle … slowly!

Happily, the engine sputtered back to life, its life, and more importantly, mine! My best guess was fuel starvation because the last thing I remembered before it got quiet was cross-feeding from the tip tanks. I'd been cruising at an altitude of 8,000 feet when the engine stopped, and had recovered at an altitude of 5,000 feet above the ocean; then setting the engine to full climb power, dragging the overweight Bonanza back to 8,000 feet. With that underway, I had re-engaged the autopilot, checked the direction of flight, and re-established some semblance of navigation along my original track. Once back in stabilized level flight,

I very carefully switched the fuel selector from the main tanks to the auxiliary cabin tank, since it had become apparent that the tip tanks were empty. Then it was time to unwind from the fear and near panic of the incident. Falling asleep at the wheel was unacceptable and definitely not professional behavior for this stranger over a strange ocean!

With adrenaline dissipating, I began to contemplate the perilous situation I had placed myself in, fully cognizant of the dangerous implications of flying single-engine airplanes across two thousand miles of ocean. It had scared the living shite out of me, giving rise to the thought of turning the aircraft around and heading the 250 miles back to Newfoundland, the closest landfall. But I knew I wouldn't make that choice, and the decision to continue became a life-changing moment, not exactly an epiphany, but rather a slow march to the gallows with the fervent hope that I would be spared at the last moment.

What was I doing out there?

My reasons for being there were complex, but mainly crucial for a future *laugh out loud* in commercial aviation. Therefore, I decided to fly another 15,000 miles to reach New Zealand: over oceans, deserts, mountain ranges, and hostile territory with only one engine keeping me airborne. To continue on my epic journey, I had to ignore the single-engine reality with a confidence that it would not be a factor in my future survival. After all, the engine failure had been my error and not a mechanical problem, so if I kept my act together, the aircraft would keep me alive ... or perhaps not?

And so it went on, hour after hour droning across the endless ocean, maintaining good radio contact with Gander, and then Santa Maria Oceanic Control. I'd expected to have reception from the Flores radio beacon after six hours from St. Johns, but that didn't happen for seven hours, with a bearing showing me some distance south of track, and probably behind schedule. Sure enough, after flying a curve of pursuit to the beacon, I arrived overhead Flores one and a half hours behind my flight planned timing, and estimated the total flight time from St. Johns to Santa Maria to be ten hours. It was dark, but accurate navigation was finally possible; flying between radio beacons on fixed tracks from the islands of Flores to Horta to Santa Maria, where the landing conditions were reported as rain showers and strong wind from the south. Not a problem after ten hours of being nowhere. I made the approach using the Instrument Landing System (ILS) for the southern runway, touched down, taxied to the terminal, and shutdown feeling a great sense of relief. I had successfully completed the longest overwater sector of my journey to New Zealand.

Early the following morning, I was on my way for an nine-hour flight to Valencia in Spain. This involved a five-hour overwater transit to reach Lisbon, Portugal. Usefully, there were VOR radio beacons at Santa Maria and Lisbon that gave me tracking and groundspeed information for departure and arrival, but still left a gap of 550 miles with no navigation information. Flying over the Lisbon beacon, I was delighted to acknowledge I had successfully crossed the Atlantic Ocean. My thoughts were that nothing from here onwards to New Zealand could be as dangerous or as complicated as what I'd just achieved. How wrong I was.

Beyond Lisbon, navigation was simply following the established airways from one radio beacon to the next, crossing the Portuguese border into the high country of central Spain, passing within a few miles of Madrid, then a turn southeast to Valencia on the Mediterranean coast. Flying this sector turned out to be anticlimactic after the long haul from St. Johns the previous day, until I landed at Valencia, where I was greeted by a squad of bureaucratic

Customs and Immigration Officials (probably Guardia Civil) telling me that I would be required to spend one month in Spanish custody until I was granted a visitor's visa. Although there were shouting and verbal threats in Spanish, which I didn't understand, after some haggling and a few dollars changing hands, they let me go free to spend the night in a hotel. I believed the problem was my New Zealand citizenship, which apparently required an entry visa, conflated with piloting a US registered aircraft inbound from Portuguese territory (the Azores). I departed Valencia early the following morning, and I never went back!

My next destination was Athens in Greece, and the flight-planned route took me across Majorca, Sardinia, Sorrento, the toe of Italy's boot, and finally over the Ionian Sea to Athens. The way was along established airways between a series of VOR radio beacons. It all seemed very easy and straightforward, including flying in the clouds for three of the eight hours total flight time. What I hadn't planned for, and should have, was operating this all-weather equipped Bonanza through clouds in icing conditions, because, like most small general aviation aircraft, it lacked anti-icing systems for the wing leading edges and propeller blades. Fortunately, the rate of ice accrual was insignificant on the wing leading edges, but the propeller's efficiency was definitely affected, resulting in reduced airspeed, then a forced descent to a lower altitude where I could maintain a safe cruise speed.

However, the lower height created a dangerous situation for me, and perhaps other air traffic. I'd dropped below the Minimum Enroute Altitude (MEA), passing in and out of clouds with glimpses of peaks below, most likely seeing the high terrain of Corsica. In restrained panic, I called Air Traffic Control advising them of my new altitude and requesting radar vectors to the south of the high Corsican terrain, which they provided. Shortly after, I broke clear of the clouds and without further icing, was able to climb back to my original altitude, probably 9,000 feet. The remainder of the flight to Athens was uneventful and pleasantly picturesque, seeing the Mediterranean's northern shore and numerous islands from this relatively low altitude.

I found Athens to be an excellent stopover, both from the friendliness of the people and adequate support from the airport authorities. I decided to take a day off there, providing time for oil and filter changes on the Bonanza, and for me to catch up with some laundry and purchase some creature comforts to see me through the expected difficulties of the Middle East and India. I treated Athens as the last outpost of western civilization before reaching the distant inviting shores of Malaysia and Singapore.

My foolhardy journey in a single-engine plane, two-thirds of the way around the world, was filled with potentially hazardous events, mostly beyond my control because the very nature of the task created a high level of risk. Yet some of the worst moments were the result of my own stupidity, and 43 years later, I'm still ashamed of those unprofessional actions. I guess it goes without saying that the first mistake I made was accepting the job. The next was falling asleep while cross-feeding fuel that resulted in engine-failure at a low altitude over the Atlantic Ocean. Then, at the hotel in Athens, the scene was set for another self-made risky event the following day flying from Athens to Luxor in Egypt.

The problem began when I walked into the hotel bar-restaurant, a small cozy nook in the basement. The oil change and refueling of my Bonanza were complete, and I had the airborne food supplies for the next few days, to be finalized in the morning with bottled water and soft drinks from the airport terminal. So now it was time to relax, imbibing richly deserved alcoholic refreshment, something I had not done since Toronto, Canada. Having just sat down at the bar, a US Navy P3 Orion crew showed up, and any plans I had of going to bed sober were shattered. They were a good bunch of lads with whom I relived my days serving with the US Navy in Antarctica, and then we mutually refought the war in Vietnam. After spending the first 20 years of my working life in military service, times like that were magical moments, especially with US forces.

My last morning in Athens was not a happy one. I had awakened late with a hangover, with no time for breakfast, and hurried through the airport terminal, with time only for submitting a flight plan, paying the landing fees, but failing to pick up extra liquids. I did not think that as a problem because the flight time to Luxor was less than seven hours, and knew I had a few cans of soda already in the Bonanza. I was airborne a little behind my planned schedule, but it was a cool morning, so was able to climb to my expected altitude of 9,000 feet, taking up a radio beacon route southeast over the Mediterranean Sea. This established airway would take me across the southern Greek Islands, including Crete to cross the coast of North Africa at Marsa Matruh, then over the endless sands of Egypt to the city of Luxor on the Nile River. By the time I was overhead the eastern end of Crete, I had consumed whatever remaining liquids I had onboard, a thirst driven by my hangover.

Sometime later, I was wondering why I couldn't maintain airspeed without descending from my original cruise altitude, a descent that continued as I closed with the coast of North Africa. The problem was the rapidly rising air temperature, which in turn had reduced engine performance. Once over the desert, the temperature stabilized, and the Bonanza was able to maintain an altitude of 4,000 feet. Fortunately, that altitude was above the Minimum Safe Altitude (MSA) for the area, not that it mattered in the crystal clear daytime weather, but it was another performance lesson to retain in planning the remainder of my flights over the Sandbox countries. With the airplane problem temporarily solved, I took in the view below.

There was nothing but endless sand, and many miles to go before reaching Luxor without liquids to quench a terrible thirst. This was when I contemplated the most bizarre epiphany, that if the engine did stop over the desert, I would definitely survive a forced landing, only to die of thirst! Up until this point, most of the risk from engine failure had been ditching on endless oceans, where I'd considered the chance of surviving the impact no better than 50 percent. It had not occurred to me that over flat sandy terrain on a sunny day, that survival could be marginal. If I'd been carrying a few gallons of water in the cabin, the prospect would have been quite different—sitting on the sand under the shade of a wing, nibbling food, sipping water, and waiting for rescue after putting out a Mayday call on the HF radio. Looking back, I could have improved my possible survival chances by turning left to intercept the Nile River between Cairo and Luxor. There would have been no shortage of water over there.

I did make it to Luxor, where my first request after landing was for canned sodas, which were provided at a hefty price! Luxor had always been a tourist attraction because the city was located at the site of the Valley of the Kings, including Tutankhamen's Tomb. I experienced considerable delays on arrival in Luxor, dealing with Customs and Immigration officials, so eventually I had to grease a few palms to obtain fuel, accommodation, meals, and an outward clearance from Egypt.

My next destination was Dubai, located in the United Arab Emirates in the Persian Gulf. The route from Luxor took me across the Red Sea, Saudi Arabia, and Bahrain. Nothing to see except sand for nine flight hours, but I was able to maintain a higher cruise altitude than the previous day because of lower temperatures. On arrival at Dubai, I was pleasantly surprised to be greeted by friendly faces, old comrades from the RNZAF and Air New Zealand working with a ground handling company called AeroGulf Services. As a result, official formalities were minimal, and anything I needed from this stopover was done with efficiency. What a difference from Luxor, and from what I could expect transiting India via Bombay and Madras.

I had no illusions about the difficulties of the next two days, which involved the transit of India in reaching Malaysia and Singapore. My first landing in India was at Bombay International Airport, where my purpose was only to uplift fuel, and then continue on to the eastern coastal city of Madras. My scheduled one-hour stop turned into three, dealing with petty officials, tropical heat, ancient refueling machinery, and fuel with water contamination. I was eventually airborne again close to dusk and completed a night flight to Madras, threading my way through thunderstorms and landing four hours later.

My decision to fly over an extensive section of India in the dark was a mistake but forced on me by the long delay at Bombay, and a desperate desire to get away from the stench of hovels and trash surrounding that airport. Without weather radar I was at the mercy of the numerous thunderstorms with a high level of risk, being brought down by severe turbulence, lightning strike, or engine failure because of dirty fuel. This was another self-inflicted act of stupidity, but the Hindu gods had been on my side, touching down safely at Madras in rain showers and gusty winds.

The total flight distance from Madras to Kuala Lumpur was 1,500 miles, with an overwater section of 1,100 miles before crossing Banda Aceh on the island of Sumatra. By this stage of my epic journey I felt quite relaxed, even about the possibility of engine failure over the Bay of Bengal. It was a daylight crossing over warm tropical water, with a calm surface, and plenty of high altitude jet traffic that could respond to emergency radio calls. *But don't think about sharks!* There was also an en route alternate airfield at Car Nicobar, an island 800 miles from Madras, and a place I knew well from the 1960s. The flight took just over nine hours, landing at Subang, Kuala Lumpur's international airport, shortly before dark. Filling in time during this somewhat laid-back flight, I reflected on my hassles at Bombay and Madras, with the thought that if I ever did this regularly, I would need a checklist of methods to beat their system.

Landing at Subang International Airport near Kuala Lumpur was delightfully nostalgic. I'd lived and worked there in 1975 as the New Zealand military attaché, and routinely jogged through the surrounding rubber plantations with the Hash House Harriers. The first thing I did was treat myself to sumptuous comfort in the downtown Hilton Hotel, ordering and scoffing a banquet of tasty local food, washed down with pints of Tiger Beer. What a contrast to the crap-hole places I'd been over the last week, and still be alive to enjoy all that after taking so many risks.

It was a blissful moment on my journey, but one that was upset the next day by another self-inflicted idiot decision. The night before at Subang Airport, I'd been advised by the refueling crew that there was no aviation gasoline (Avgas) at Subang, the fuel that the Bonanza used. The only option they suggested was to fly the ten miles from Subang to the older Kuala Lumpur airport where Avgas was available. Because my next sector to Singapore was only a short distance down the Malayan Peninsula, I figured I could make it with the remaining fuel in the tanks— perhaps enough for two hours flying? So the next morning, arriving at Subang Airport, I discarded the suggestion of further fuel uplift and filed a flight plan direct to Seletar airport on Singapore Island.

Once airborne and heading south, the aircraft with its low fuel weight climbed smartly to cruise altitude into an almost cloudless sky. It was pleasant and quietly exciting to be on a route I remembered so well, a route I'd flown at least 50 times in Bristol Freighters during the 1960s. Looking down on the green landscape that was so familiar and passing over the city of Malacca, with an airport I knew well, a location that I had considered for a fuel uplift, just to be safe?

I guess I was suffering from get-there-itis, urged to reach my old Singapore stamping ground, even if it meant engine failure before I arrived there! South of Malacca, with another 100 miles to reach Seletar airport, I began closely watching the fuel gauges of the tanks with remaining fuel, and the low readings were a frightening reality. What to do … keep going as planned and hope for the best? As the gauges continued their drop to the empty mark, I couldn't believe I'd been so negligent, placing myself in this position to run out of fuel. There was no excuse for failing to obtain a refuel in Kuala Lumpur, or at the last opportunity, at Malacca.

As divine justice for my stupidly I deserved to run out of fuel before reaching Seletar but was saved by the smell of an oily rag that kept the engine running until I landed.

When the refueling was completed at Seletar I accurately calculated that the fuel remaining in the tanks was 5.5 US gallons, which translated into 25 minutes of flight time. This omission and near accident of mine is being told for the first time. I was so ashamed of my *Flying for Dummies* performance that I had never before related that event in my 42 years of professional aviation.

Eventually, on October 17, 16 days after leaving St. Johns in eastern Canada, I departed Singapore on a 7.5 hour flight to the island of Bali, a place I'd first visited in 1958 when the airport was still called Tuban, near the town of Denpasar. Back then, Bali and its beaches were so beautiful, so pristine, with the people and environment exotic to the eye. There were no tourists, and I could never imagine the island littered with moronic drunken Australians, who had forsaken the beaches of Bondi and the Gold Coast for a bit of action in Southeast Asia. Sadly, that change did come, and 40 years later, there was nothing else there but Aussie Bogans in Paradise.

For reasons I can't recall, after a quick and efficient refuel at Bali, I decided to continue through the night for another 7.5 hours to Darwin in Australia's Northern Territory, landing there at midnight. It was evident that the lengthy rest period in Singapore had refreshed my flying mojo and my self-confidence that nothing could touch me now. This would explain why I'd happily flown a long night sector along the chain of the Sunda Islands and across the Timor Sea to Darwin. Once there, back on home turf, I was off the ground at daybreak, heading southeast across the desert to the town of Longreach in western Queensland. That took another eight hours of flying over the waterless landscape that makes up the Australian Outback,

Then another quick refuel at Longreach, and back in the air for a short night flight to Brisbane on the Queensland coast. After spending the night resting in Brisbane, I set off for the final sector of this hazardous journey, all over water, crossing the Tasman Sea to Auckland, New Zealand. Thanks to favorable winds, I covered the 1250 miles in 7.5 hours, an average groundspeed of 167 knots. I'd planned the route to take me overhead Lord Howe Island, and its radio beacon at the 400-mile point from Brisbane, so unlike my Atlantic Ocean crossing, provided excellent track and distance navigation. Arriving at Auckland Airport was a typical homecoming, landing in high winds and heavy rain, after flying 15,000 miles with mostly clear skies all the way.

My odyssey from Gander in Canada to Auckland had required 100 flight hours (85 day, 15 night, and 26 in clouds) over a total of 18 days, with 11 of those days devoted to flying. The final three days from Singapore to Auckland had taken a total of 33 flight hours, an average of 10.1 hours per day to cover almost 5,000 miles. Not too bad for a small single-engine piston airplane, flown by a questionable pilot.

Flight of the Bonanza Self-Debrief:

• Don't ever again fly a single-engine airplane from North America over the Atlantic or Pacific Oceans, particularly without a long-range navigation system.

• Always carry gallons of drinking water when flying over oceans and deserts.

• Develop techniques to deal with the Kafkaesque bureaucracy of India and the Sandbox countries.

• Carry lawyers, guns, and money to assist escape from hellhole prisons, personal security, bribes, and for personal fun!

• Don't fly without drinking, or should it be: Don't drink without flying? Whatever works!

In the small community of pilots hired to ferry small aircraft from North America across the Oceans, there was a story, a rumor, or perhaps an urban myth, that ferried aircraft hull insurance was underwritten by Lloyd's of London. And the most significant factor in determining the premium cost was who the ferry pilot would be, so Lloyd's had a list of pilots who had been successfully crossing the Oceans, and the more trips a pilot made (without falling in the water), the lower the premium. If the story was true, then I had just bought myself a future as an aircraft delivery boy … and that actually happened in mid-1979.

1979: Stillwell's Delivery Boy

I ENJOYED WRITING this section because the act of remembering this most exciting period in my life was full of nostalgia for what we did, what we achieved and all the things we saw circling the world many times in small airplanes.

In the North American summer of 1979 I found myself in San Antonio, Texas, on an individual assignment from Stillwell Aviation, who had hired me out of New Zealand one week before. My first mission was to be checked out on the Swearingen Merlin 4 aircraft at the Flight Safety training facility based near San Antonio airport. On the completion of that training, my next task was to supervise and assist the Royal Thai Air Force (RTAF) pilots during their training on the same model at Flight Safety. Stillwell's, the Australian distributor for Swearingen Aviation Corporation, had sold three Merlins to the RTAF, due for delivery to Thailand during the next few months. Two of those flight deliveries from San Antonio to Bangkok would be my task before settling into a new home and office in downtown Singapore. That was definitely something to look forward to—away from the miserable weather of New Zealand and back into the tropical delights of Southeast Asia.

This job in Singapore was also an excellent opportunity

to escape the small aviation world of New Zealand, where, except for its Air Force that I'd left in 1977, the only professional flying job in the country was with Air New Zealand. At the time, there was no place for me at that airline despite possessing the right flight experience and qualifications. "So sorry, Peter, the airline is not hiring pilots right now or into the foreseeable future." I'd always known that Air New Zealand was a retirement home for ex-Air Force pilots—a cushy number if they hired you to fly their DC-10s on international routes. To be honest, Air New Zealand had never been my first choice as an airline, apart from providing a convenient move from one small town to another in little New Zealand.

Probably sounds like sour grapes because I wasn't hired by the airline, but I'd known that being there would be just an extension of the Air Force: *same big frogs in a little pond*. My real concern was being forced to fly in junior positions, with ex-Air Force pilots I disliked or remembered for their limited flying ability, and that had me doubting whether it was the right place for me. Two years later, any reservations I had about Air New Zealand's credibility as a first-class airline were confirmed with the entirely avoidable crash of their DC-10, Flight 901, that flew into the high ground of Mount Erebus in Antarctica on November 28, 1979, killing all 257 persons onboard.

My arrival in San Antonio coincided with the USA's Independent Day celebrations for 1979. It was mid-summer, and outdoor festivities for the occasion were everywhere in the city. At the airport, I was met by Ron Zelinski from Swearingen's Aviation Sales Department, then dropped at the La Quinta hotel and told to rest for the next 24 hours, something I really needed after a series of flights from Sydney. I believe I slept for a solid 15 hours before seeking food and drink at Denny's restaurant adjacent to the hotel.

This accommodation and dining location, close to San Antonio Airport, became my home for the next six weeks.

As expected, Ron collected me from the hotel one day after arrival and drove to the nearby headquarters of Swearingen Aviation Corporation (SWACO), in a building that also housed the Flight Safety Training Center. Ron introduced me to the CEO of the corporation, and the department heads of Sales, Finance, Training, Aircraft Assembly, and Flight Testing. As the newest representative from Stillwell Aviation, I was warmly greeted by everyone in the building. They were thankful to hear that I'd been assigned by David, my immediate boss in Australia, to look after the visiting Thai Air Force officers and pilots during their training and delivery preparations in San Antonio.

For the next 20 days, I was with the Flight Safety training instructors, initially with a week devoted to classroom lectures about the surprisingly complex systems of the Merlin aircraft. Surprising, because this small twin-engine corporate-commuter plane was equipped with systems very similar to the four-engine Lockheed C-130 Hercules that I'd last flown in the Air Force. The satisfaction and excitement of returning to the world of advanced aviation from which I'd been torn in 1972 was exquisite. After leaving the C-130, I could still make the moves but had lost the soul of flying, and now in the heartland of Texas, it was all coming back.

With classroom studies completed, it was time for the fine art of simulation. After 26 years of professional flying, this was my first experience in a full-motion flight simulator, this one designed for Merlins and Metros. Many pilots don't enjoy simulator rides and don't do well when forced to handle multiple emergencies, the primary function of the training. It has been said that a good simulator check ride is like successful surgery on a corpse!

Perhaps because of the ten exercises I did learning to operate the Merlin and Metro, and enjoying every minute of the experience, I became a longtime fan of simulators. A decade after this introduction to simulation, I was FAA approved as captain of a Boeing 747 without ever flying the actual aircraft. That happened on a revenue flight from Kentucky to California, a trip that was an amazing and memorable experience.

The Merlin 4s ordered by the Royal Thai Air Force were equipped for the photo reconnaissance role that included both conventional cameras and infrared sensors. In addition to standard commercial avionics, the planes were fitted with military specialized communication radios and navigation equipment, including a Long Range Omega system. As a Vietnam veteran pilot of the Lockheed C-130 Hercules, I felt very much at home in these three airplanes, one of the reasons Stillwell's had hired me. Besides, I had the recent track record of delivering a single-engine Bonanza from North America to New Zealand on an eastbound course across the Atlantic and beyond. I had recommended that Stillwell's use the same route for the Merlin 4s, in particular transatlantic: from St. Johns in Newfoundland to Santa Maria in the Azores Islands, to Portugal or Spain. The most extended overwater sector would be from St. Johns to Santa Maria, a distance of 1385 miles, a range that could be done safely without supplementary fuel tanks for either the Merlin or Metroliner.

By the end of July 1979, I'd been signed off as a Merlin/Metro pilot by the instructors at Flight Safety, in time to meet and greet the first two Thai Air Force pilots. I got them checked into the La Quinta Hotel and provided transportation between the hotel and Flight Safety for their training in the classroom and flight simulator. The first

RTAF Merlin 4 off the production line had been test flown, but for the next three weeks was being fitted with a large-format camera and infrared sensors below the floor and other specialized military equipment. I received a detailed briefing from the Norden System's techs on their Omega Navigation Unit that was being installed, a system we would be using for long range navigation during the flight from San Antonio to Bangkok. I was reminded that Norden had developed the famous bombsight for WW2 allied bombers.

During this hiatus between completion of training and the tentative departure date of late August, I was mostly occupied with looking after a senior Thai officer, Group Captain Cherd, or Colonel Cherd as the Americans addressed him. The Colonel was the RTAF's head of its Photographic Wing in Bangkok and responsible for the final camera and infrared installation in the three Merlin aircraft. He was ten years my senior, but because of my extensive Southeast Asian military background, we became fast friends. He appreciated my knowledge and Air Force participation in Malaysia, South Vietnam, and Laos and, of course, Thailand. The spinoffs working with the Colonel were many. He introduced me to Texas Barbecue diners, some north of the city in hill country covered in mesquite trees and shrubs, the wood used for smoking the meats. He'd discovered on an earlier visit to Texas that the meat was so tender it could be easily swallowed with little chewing, a limitation with his dental implants.

The Colonel was also indirectly responsible for me meeting my future American wife. The SWACO folks involved with the camera installation advised the Colonel that if he wished to run some airborne tests with the camera, he'd need to obtain rolls of large format photo film. They pointed us to a professional photographic store in downtown San Antonio, so off we went on a hot and humid summer day in my rental car to make the purchase. The young woman who served us was casually dressed in what looked like a character from the Monty Python *I'm a Lumberjack* skit.

Despite the southern Texas heat, she was wearing a red and black plaid flannel shirt and heavy blue jeans, probably because it was air-conditioned chilly in the shop to keep their film stock from degrading. She introduced herself as Marilyn, was curious about my accent, Colonel Cherd's ethnicity, and our need for large format photo film. Cherd gave the details of the airborne vertical mounted camera and a brief explanation of its military application in Thailand. The film was not in stock but would be ordered and sent to the appropriate office at SWACO. I gave Marilyn our contact information at the hotel, believing that our business was complete.

A few days later, I was with the finance officer of Stillwell Aviation visiting from Melbourne who requested a tour of downtown San Antonio. This included the Alamo, the 18th-century Spanish mission preserved as a museum, and a stroll along the River Walk, the landmark pedestrian promenade lined with cafes and shops. Back at the hotel during dinner with the Colonel, he told me that the young woman from the photographic store had stopped by the hotel, discussed the photo film delivery to SWACO, and asked after me. I thought it odd that the bundled up, shapeless lumberjack woman could be interested in my whereabouts.

The next morning at breakfast in Denny's, I was left in no doubt when a most attractive young woman in shorts and tank top came in through the door, walked over to my table, sat down, and asked for coffee. I can say that the rest was history, but the path to married bliss is never smooth.

Back in the misery of a New Zealand winter I'd left behind my first wife waiting on a divorce settlement. All so bloody sad, but in America, I was finding a new life and possibly a new wife.

Marilyn had been born in the Territory of Alaska before Alaskan statehood in 1959. She came from a family of Bush pilots based in the wilderness town of Talkeetna, one hundred miles north of Anchorage, under the shadow of the massive peak of Denali. Given this knowledge, I then understood why she had been dressed as a lumberjack in the steamy heat of southern Texas.

At the time of my first visit to San Antonio, I met with folks from the Pentagon or State Department for briefings on some of the aerial snoop equipment being fitted to the Thai Air Force Merlin aircraft. I doubt they had reservations about my security clearances. They would have done their homework on my 20-year New Zealand military history as a senior officer, including time as the military attaché in Malaysia. The same applied to clearances from the Royal Thai Air Force. They knew where I'd come from and trusted me with their sensitive information.

Soon it was time to go to work with Neil Morris, aka Neddie, the senior pilot at Stillwell's for Swearingen Merlin and Metro aircraft, and the two Thai pilots, airborne on the first segment of the delivery flight to Bangkok. Our planned route had been finalized in Melbourne by Neddie and Barbara Pearson, our gal to go to for landing permissions, diplomatic clearances, and fuel uplift. Our first stopover was at Indianapolis Airport, four hours northeast of San Antonio. This short flight was the opportunity for all crew members to familiarize themselves with the cockpit layout, in particular, checking out the communication and navigation radios. The following day we first flew to Bangor Airport in Maine for immigration and customs clearances, including export of the aircraft from the USA. Then it was across the border into Canadian airspace on a four-hour flight to St. Johns, Newfoundland. And there, in less than a year, I was back on familiar turf.

We spent a quiet night at the Airport Inn, but awoke to a raucous morning with two drunken women stumbling and shouting through the corridors, offering all of us a good time for a special price! I must say it was most disconcerting, especially for the Thai pilots, but we couldn't afford the delay, and the women were neither young nor beautiful. Maybe the night before, if we'd been really drunk, they may have looked more desirable. But in the cold light of morning and 1,500 miles to go before our next stop, it was a time to cut and run!

Having escaped the rapacious clutches of the women of St. Johns, we quickly flight-planned for Santa Maria in the Azores, kicked the tires, lit the fires, and fled over the Atlantic Ocean. The bad memories of my desperate journey on the same route the year before were quickly dispelled in this powerful twin-turboprop plane. We were flying at almost twice the speed and cruising at twice the altitude, but the very best thing was using the Omega Long Range Navigation system, continuously showing us where we were across the endless seascape. It was my first experience using Omega and I thought it was magical. Neddie was more dismissive of the Norden Omega performance because of his extensive use of a competitive unit made by Global Navigation, the GNS-500A, which had the capability of receiving both the eight Omega stations and also the nine US Navy VLF communication stations. After completing these RTAF Merlin deliveries, I would be introduced to the GNS-500A unit that was the primary Long Range Navigation system in use by Stillwell Aviation.

This first journey to Santa Maria in a Merlin 4 took just

over six hours, whereas my second delivery was an hour less because of strong westerly winds. Handling at the airport was done by SATA Airways, the refueling by Shell, and accommodation at the Airport Hotel. All these procedures were done efficiently and smoothly compared with my confusing experiences in the Bonanza the year before. This was the difference between handling at all airports being requested by Barbara Pearson back in Australia versus showing up at airports without prior notice or approval. With these en route changes in place, and operating a twin-engine pressurized aircraft equipped with a long-range navigation system, this type of ferry flying looked good to me.

This new job was infinitely safer than what I'd experienced and ultimately survived in the Bonanza, but there still remained high levels of risk in operation because of using takeoff weights well above the approved FAA limits. Ferry operations of USA registered airplanes were granted exclusion clauses by the FAA to operate above standard takeoff weights and could be as high as a 30 percent increase. The purpose was to allow full fuel loads in the integral and supplemental tanks, sufficient for extended flight over water, such as the Atlantic and Pacific Oceans. Using these high weights meant that with an engine failure on takeoff, the result would be a controlled crash, and an engine failure at cruise altitude during the first few hours would probably mean ditching in the sea—unless there was a built-in system for dumping fuel.

Neddie's schedule had us flying from Santa Maria to Barcelona, Spain, taking six hours, which for me was a pleasant surprise after Valencia, where I'd been mistreated by the airport officials. The only drama I recall in Barcelona was the crazy-ass taxi drivers in their constant battle to outperform all other vehicles on the city roads. Very scary after the risky business of ferry flying! The next relatively short flight was to Athens for good Greek food and drink, a pleasant overnight, and to be well handled by Athens Aviation Services. Then it was off to Bahrain with a fuel stop at Cairo, a mistake because of Egyptian bureaucracy at the airport, followed by a scary takeoff in the midday heat. The heavily loaded Merlin 4 staggered into the air after using most of a 10,000-foot runway, narrowly missing sand dunes after liftoff. I struck Cairo off my future stopover airports, believing that Luxor was a better option.

The stop at Bahrain was acceptable but not as friendly as Dubai, where my New Zealand friends could provide excellent handling services. So Bahrain was another stopover removed from my future list. From Bahrain, we flew to Karachi in Pakistan for a fuel stop and then continued to Calcutta in the dark of night. Neddie and I were puzzled by the Thai pilots reluctance to fly at night, an action that seemed to spook the heck out of them. Something to do with sky monsters in the darkness?

We ignored their concerns because they would have been trained as day/night, all-weather Air Force pilots. So through that long scary night filled with lightning flashes and avoiding the thunderstorms using our Weather Radar, we arrived at the hellhole that was Calcutta Airport in those long-ago days. The image of masses of homeless people sleeping and defecating in the terminal and along the city streets is a scene that 40 years later has been replicated in San Francisco, Los Angeles, and Seattle. So much for progress in the West!

The final sector from Calcutta to Bangkok was a short easy four hours. Like the Thai pilots, I knew I was coming home, and the reception by senior officers of the Royal Thai Air Force was impressive and festive. Wreaths of sweet-smelling tropical flowers were hung around our necks, glasses of Mekong whiskey thrust into our hands, and a Buddhist monk blessed the airplane and the pilots. It slowly dawned on me that I was really home, back in Southeast Asia, after a short absence of only four years, thanks to Stillwell Aviation.

My favorite Thai Colonel from San Antonio, Cherd, was there to meet me and to see his unique airplane in Bangkok, still in one piece without scratches or other damage. Also, there to meet us was Colin Bushe-Jones, known as CBJ to the Thais. He was a retired Australian Navy Fleet Air Arm aircraft mechanic and would be responsible for maintenance support to the RTAF for their three Merlin aircraft. I was interested in meeting CBJ because back in San Antonio, the RTAF pilots told me he often asked them, "How are you going to die?" A question they found bizarre and rude, and obviously never knew how to answer. The problem was solved on this first meeting with CBJ. He spoke with a heavy Australian twang, so what he had been asking these Thai pilots was an everyday greeting in Aussie Land: "How are you going today?"

Neddie and I spent two fun days in Bangkok visiting nightclubs, meeting and dining with CBJ, his charming wife, and Stillwell's Thai Representative, Rachada, with his beautiful wife. Then it was time for the two of us to go home—Neddie to Melbourne and me to my yet unseen residence in Singapore. Arriving at the International Paya Lebar Airport, then the ride in a taxi to the city center and my high-rise apartment block of Peace Mansion was full of nostalgia. I remembered so much about Singapore that I first visited in 1958, and from 1960 had resided there for six of my formative aviation years.

In his book *The Enigma of Arrival*, V.S Naipaul poses the question of the strangeness arriving at a place you may have been before, but it seems like you are seeing it for the first time. During the six years that I had previously lived in Singapore, my accommodation had been on British Military Bases, and the city was just a place to visit. For shopping, for entertainment at movie theatres or clubs, or for dining out. This time, I was taking up residence in the heart of the city, in a luxury apartment on the 15th floor of a tall building at the southern end of Orchard Road. It may have been strange, but being there in that new environment was an exciting prospect and one that would continue into the foreseeable future.

Stillwell Aviation had two apartments in Peace Mansion, one for my use, and the other for Tony, the general manager for the company's Southeast Asian division. My apartment was spacious with a large living room, two bedrooms and an office. There was central air conditioning for every room and a large balcony that looked out over the southern shores of Singapore Island. Tony had purchased a small car for my exclusive use and provided basic furnishings for the office and bedrooms. The rent and utilities for the apartment were to be met by the Company. In all, this new life in Singapore looked like being very comfortable and definitely affordable. The only problem was the Company's requirement for me to be absent for long periods, either back in San Antonio or on delivery flights from Texas to Asia and Australia.

I had little more than three weeks to enjoy my new home before flying out with Pan Am on their long-range Boeing 747 to San Francisco via Hong Kong. Then across to San Antonio and the La Quinta hotel for another extended rest period, and to catch up with Marilyn again. This task for Stillwell's was to ferry the third and last Merlin 4 to Bangkok with another two Thai Air Force pilots who had just completed the training with Flight Safety. The second

Merlin 4 had already been flown to Bangkok by another Stillwell pilot, John Flynn, based out of Melbourne. The route plan I built for this delivery was much the same as the previous one with Neddie, but I happily changed the stops at Cairo and Bahrain for Luxor and Dubai.

After an acceptance flight around the San Antonio local area, we left for Indianapolis and Bangor in the last few days of September 1979. At the hotel restaurant in Bangor, I noticed the Thai pilots shaking an unusual looking condiment from a glass container onto their food. The appearance was of shiny black particles, that if they'd been red would have been chili flakes. Captain Ronnachai, a pilot I came to admire as our journey continued, patiently explained that the chips were crushed beetles. When offered, I said thanks, but no thanks.

Our flight to St. John's the next morning was uneventful, with all radio/navigation equipment essential for the Atlantic crossing checked out as fully operational. The night and morning at the St. John's Airport Hotel were peaceful, without crazy Viking women marauding through the hallways. As it happened, we were back in the Airport Hotel for the next four nights, thanks to a broken airplane. There was a problem with the landing gear after takeoff on this particular Merlin; the wheels would not fully retract, a situation that was an obvious no-go for crossing the Atlantic, or anywhere. Fortunately, before returning to St. John's, the landing gear fully extended into a locked position, and after burning off extra fuel weight, we landed safely.

Innotech Aviation was our handling agent at St. John's, providing refueling and essential maintenance, but for this mechanical problem with the Merlin, they had no immediate solutions. I spoke at length on the phone with the Swearingen's support team back in San Antonio, explaining the problem we had experienced with the landing gear. Their suggestion to Innotech was to pull the aircraft into a hangar and use jacks to lift the plane clear of the ground; then using an external hydraulic pressure source, try raising the landing gear. The good news was that the gear correctly retracted into the wheel wells. But the bad news was this test had not simulated an airborne – airflow environment, so I was not convinced the problem was solved. A quick test flight over the airfield proved that my guess was correct; the landing gear refused to fully retract.

For some reason, the San Antonio team couldn't provide any further suggestions on how to troubleshoot the issue and in the meantime, we were running behind schedule. I had had plenty of time to study the training manuals we were carrying on board, reading sections on the safety features built into the landing gear retraction system. One of those devices was a micro switch on the main landing gear that prevented inadvertent retraction when the weight of the aircraft was on the ground. After takeoff, the switch opened, allowing the wheels to retract, so I figured that either the switch was faulty, or some other force was at work? On the third morning, frustrated with no further input from Swearingen or Innotech, I stood outside the hangar looking directly up the rear end of the Merlin and observed a subtle tilt to the right. On closer inspection, it was evident that the right wheel strut had less extension than the left.

There's a saying that 'you live and learn,' but in my long flying career, survival became 'you learn and live.' After wasting three days looking for answers from Swearingen and Innotech, I knew I had solved the problem with landing gear retraction. I advised the Innotech mechanics to check the hydraulic/hydrogen pressure in both main wheel struts, and if necessary, bring the pressure up to usual specification. The pressure in the left strut was normal, but the right strut was well below normal. With the pressures of both struts brought to normal, I took the Merlin on another short test flight confident that the wheels would retract correctly … and they did! My best Holmes deduction had been the low pressure in the right strut allowed the 'do not retract' micro switch to be activated by airstream on the right wheels as they approached the horizontal, just before entering the wheel-well. In all Swearingen airplanes, the main wheels retracted in a forward motion.

Before we left St. Johns for Santa Maria, there was one last question to answer: Why did the right wheel strut leak pressure after leaving San Antonio and would it continue? My simple plan was to have the strut pressure checked at every stop before departure. It felt good to be on our way after the four-day delay, and thanks to strong westerly winds over the Atlantic, we reached Santa Maria in five hours, and the next day to Barcelona in the same flight time. The Omega long-range navigation equipment worked splendidly, providing an accuracy that I found impressive, so different from my previous 20 years of overwater flying with professional navigators. It was a sad reality for their profession that they were no longer necessary. Inertial Navigation Systems (INS) had replaced them on the wide-body airliners: the Boeing 747, Douglas DC-10, and Lockheed L-1011. In the smaller corporate jets and turboprops like the Merlin, the easy to use and low-cost Omega/VLF receivers met the challenge of long overwater navigation. Ultimately, 20 years later, GPS would become the navigation for dummies!

Getting to Barcelona earlier than scheduled, I decided to continue to Athens after a quick refuel, flying through that night to catch up on one of our lost days. At Athens, we took a rest day, with the opportunity to have local mechanics check the status of the wheel struts and deal with several minor radio issues. In the meantime, I was able to enjoy delicious Greek food washed down with Retsina wine. For some reason, the two Thai pilots didn't share my enthusiasm for the local delicacies. They informed me that Bangkok and Thai food beckoned, with only a few days to go. "Please, Colonel Peter, get us home as soon as possible."

The following day we left Athens for Dubai, with a refueling stop at Luxor on the Nile. I had hoped to spend as little time as possible on the ground at Luxor, but got into a pissing contest with a debonair Egyptian Air Traffic Controller, western educated, probably in England. He was a pleasant fellow, but a shyster, demanding that the landing fees would be 500 US dollars. I explained that I'd passed through the airport one year before in the small Bonanza aircraft and only been charged 25 US dollars. I pointed to the Merlin sitting on the ramp and its registration number, which was from Thailand, a Third World country like Egypt, and that the Merlin was no more than twice the weight of a Bonanza. He made the point that I was not a Thai, so I explained that although I was a New Zealander, I'd married a Thai, and she was a very demanding woman; *Wink, wink, nod, nod, you know what I mean?*

The result was an offer with a new price of 50 US dollars for the landing fees. This simple exercise in dealing with the thieving bureaucratic rascals of the Middle East, Pakistan, and India was the beginning of my little list of ways to beat these scallywags at their own game.

I came to understand that the significant problems faced on these delivery flights around the world were on the ground, in particular across the wastelands between Greece and Southeast Asia. The only reason to land at these undesirable locations was for refueling; otherwise, we lacked the desires of moronic Western tourists for taking holidays in hell. If only the planes we flew had extended range, we would happily overfly every country that lacked western civilization. An exception, even in those days, was Dubai in the United Arab Emirates, a desert oasis of airport efficiency, luxury hotels, clean streets, and low-key bureaucracy. Better still, our chosen handling agent, AeroGulf Services, was operated by a team of ex-New Zealand Air Force pilots. Arriving from the corruption of Egypt for a most pleasant layover at Dubai became something to look forward to on these trips, resting up for the skirmishes through India.

As on the previous journey with Neddie, on the flight eastward from Dubai, we made a fuel stop at Karachi, followed by another night flight across India to Calcutta, a night operation these two Thai pilots didn't seem to mind. The stopover in Calcutta did not go well, thanks to a significant disagreement I had with an immigration officer. Before we could leave the airport, he demanded the Thai pilots relinquish their passports. I strongly disagreed, but the officer wouldn't budge, so we spent a most unpleasant night at the airport, sleeping with the homeless defecating locals. At first light, we carefully threaded our way through a minefield of human excrement, lodged a flight plan (in the right order this time), and launched into the polluted skies over Bengal. We then turned east, instructing the Omega System to get us out of India and take us to Thailand. I took one rest day in Bangkok, said farewell to the two Thai pilots, then arranged a commercial flight to Singapore and my home at Peace Mansion.

1979: Exploring the Northern Pacific

Having Fun Doing Dangerous Things

THREE WEEKS AFTER RETURNING to my home in Singapore, after delivery to Bangkok of the last Thai Air Force Merlin 4, I was on my way back to San Antonio, flying from Singapore with Pan Am. This time, I joined Stillwell pilot, John Flynn, in delivering a Swearingen Metro across the northern Pacific to Singapore. Then, from Singapore, my task was to operate sales demonstration flights in the Philippines, Malaysia, and Indonesia. This Metro was ultimately destined for an Australian-based commuter airline, so my final mission would be to deliver it from Singapore to Melbourne Australia.

The Metro was identical to the Merlin 4 in its size, weight, engines, systems, and performance, except for the cabin, which was equipped to carry 20 passengers on airline commuter operations. John Flynn explained how Stillwell's had traditionally been delivering many Metros to Australia, all done westbound over the Pacific: from San Francisco to Hawaii, to Samoa, and then Australia. All these segments involved long overwater flights that required a 50 percent increase in fuel capacity. To make this possible, the Metros had been fitted with five auxiliary fuel tanks attached to the passenger cabin floor, providing a maximum endurance of

171

12 hours, enough time to cover the distance from San Francisco to Honolulu. In San Antonio, my introduction to the Metro we were taking to Singapore was to learn the complexity of the auxiliary fuel tanks installation and inflight operation. Another new feature to study was the temporary installation of the Global Navigation GNS-500A VLF/Omega system, with its control unit placed on the cockpit floor between the two pilot seats.

With the Metro, John and I left San Antonio for San Francisco in the last week of November 1979. It was beginning to get cold in Texas and even colder in central California, which was a plus for operating an aircraft that was well above standard operating weight. We covered the two thousand, two hundred miles to Honolulu in ten hours, with highly accurate navigation from the GNS 500A. It consistently provided actual wind vectors, our groundspeed and the time remaining to reach Honolulu. I believe our takeoff weight at San Francisco was 30 percent higher than the standard limit, which was noticeable by a slow climb to cruising altitude, reduced cruise speed and increased hourly fuel burn. The technique in handling the transfer of fuel from the auxiliary tanks was to use all that fuel before switching to the integral wing tanks, which had only been used for takeoff and initial climb.

Although impressed with the efficacy using this method of ferry operation, I was well aware that in the event of an engine failure during the first three to four hours, we would inevitably end up in the sea, unable to maintain height with only one engine. Otherwise, I was so happy to be back in a region of the world I knew well, with stopovers at locations where only English was spoken, the seafood delectable, and Mai Tais were mixed and poured.

I had first flown an airplane into Honolulu in 1960. That journey from New Zealand had taken four days in that piece of British junk, the two-engine taildragger known as a Bristol Freighter. The first stop after leaving Auckland was Fiji, then Canton Island, then Christmas Island, and finally Honolulu. At the tender age of 20, the sights and sounds of tropical America were a delight. We spent most of our five-day layover on the beach at Waikiki, with US military accommodation at Fort Derussy. We had access to the Officers Club and military commissary at Derussy and Hickam Air Force Bases. At the clubs, I was introduced to grilled one-pound New York cut steaks, washed down with Mai Tais and other American cocktails.

Over the 20 years returning to Honolulu on periodic occasions, nothing much had changed except for an increasing flow of tourists flooding the city streets, beaches, hotels, and restaurants like a plague of locusts. John and I stayed at the Airport Holiday Inn to avoid the crowds and high costs of Waikiki. On this occasion, for my eating pleasure, I was introduced to small slices of raw tuna fish, sashimi, dipped in soy sauce and wasabi mustard. My guess was that the prevalence of Japanese tourists in Hawaii accounted for this new cuisine. It was tasty but needed to be washed down with beer, not cocktails. After two nights of fun, we left Honolulu for Majuro Atoll in the Marshall Islands. The distance was slightly shorter than the previous segment, taking us nine hours over an isolated region of the northern Pacific, except for Johnston Atoll, which we crossed for a navigation fix. There was a radio beacon and a runway on the Atoll, but prohibited for landing unless for an emergency. In the early 1960s, Johnston was the center for Operation Fishbowl and Starfish Prime that involved nuclear device detonations in space. Supposedly, residual radioactive contamination still haunted the place.

Being at Majuro was a special occasion for me, having arrived in Micronesia for the first time. It was a part of the vast Pacific Ocean that I knew only from reading about the battles of WW2 and America's nuclear testing sites at Bikini, Eniwetok, and Kwajalein, atolls that we would fly close to on our route to Guam the following day. At the small hotel at Majuro, seafood was again on the menu, either sashimi or grilled yellowfin tuna. Our flight to Guam the next day was quickly done in seven hours, followed the next day with a demonstration flight for the local commuter airline to the island of Saipan and return.

Back in Guam, on the evening of November 28, 1979, I saw on the local TV station the stunning news that an Air New Zealand DC-10 had crashed in Antarctica. My immediate response was to phone my parents in New Zealand, concerned that my father may have ignored my warning one month previously, about these poorly planned Antarctic flights. Many desperate hours passed before the call went through from the somewhat primitive system in Guam. What a great relief when Dad answered, only for him to provide a horror story of the crash as early reports arrived in New Zealand from the US Naval Support Force at McMurdo Sound. The foreboding and prescience that I'd experienced from a Singapore meeting with Airline friends had saved the lives of my parents, but sadly not the 20 crew and 237 passengers that were on this doomed flight.

In the 42 years since the crash, I've often pondered whether I could have influenced the fatal outcome of these poorly planned and executed charter flights. In reality, if ANZ management wouldn't listen to their own pilots, some of whom had excellent Antarctic flight credentials, they'd never listen to a misfit like me. So, if anyone's wondering why I've only now surfaced to make informed judgments on the fate of TE 901, it's because I'm writing a memoir about my 42 years as a professional aviator. Part of that story is about my foresight, based on an extensive Antarctic history, to warn my parents not to go on any of the ANZ charter flights. But who was I to know so much of Antarctic flight operations? Read my next chapter—*1979: Death on The Ice.*

~

Another drama at Guam was discovering that our new airplane was peeling paint off sections on the wings and nosecone, a warranty problem for Swearingen. John discussed the issue with Stillwell management in Australia, and the upshot was, "Fly it back to San Antonio for Swearingen to do a full repaint." I was somewhat stunned by this decision, with the personal opinion that a few dabs of paint would hold us over until finishing the demonstrations in Asia, and a full repaint at Swearengin's cost could be done in Australia. The value in time and money to fly almost eight thousand miles back to Texas, and then start all over again flying back to Guam, and onward to Singapore was crazy. But I wasn't paying the bills, or making the decisions, so I went reluctantly with the flow. I had been looking forward to being home in Singapore for Christmas, and that now looked doubtful.

On November 30, we left Guam for Majuro, refueled there, and continued through the night to Honolulu. And so it went, day and night until reaching San Antonio on December 3. Once there, John Flynn told me he was going home to Australia for Christmas, climbed on a big jet plane, departed, leaving me in limbo as to what was expected of me. Fortunately, my newfound Alaskan friend, Marilyn, helped me fill in the next ten days waiting for the repaint to be completed. My simple instruction from Stillwell's in Australia was to stay in place until the repaint was complete, then begin the delivery on the same schedule as before. I asked who the replacement pilot for John Flynn would be, and when would he or she arrive. The answer was, "Don't be silly; it's the long Christmas holidays in Aussie, so find someone locally."

The Metro was still in US registration, so I figured (without checking) that the FAA probably wouldn't care whether I had a backup pilot or not on this delivery flight. After all, the previous year, I had flown solo in the US registered Beechcraft Bonanza from Canada to New Zealand … the long way! Admittedly, on this operation, it would be useful to have a spare pilot (or just a warm body) to sit in the right seat while I took a pee in the cabin, or made adjustments to the five auxiliary fuel tanks. As it happened, one of the warm bodies was my new girlfriend, Marilyn, who flew with me from San Antonio to San Francisco. My brief flying lesson was: if the autopilot clicks off, put your hands gently on the control wheel, keep the blue sky above, and don't touch any other levers, switches, or buttons. And don't panic if red lights start flashing with aural warnings of impending disaster—just ignore!

By mid-December, winter had arrived in North America, bringing strong westerly winds across the Pacific Ocean between central California and Hawaii. From what I recall, I could accept a maximum average of 12 knots headwind component to make it to Honolulu from San Francisco without falling to the sea—fuel tanks dry! Each morning for three days from my room at the Airport Hilton, I would contact the Oceanic Forecast Service for a read on the expected wind component at 15,000 feet for the route to Honolulu. On each of those days, the wind speed was above what I could accept for the crossing. During this same waiting period, I was able to find more than just a warm body to join me as a safety pilot. Mike Hance was a flight attendant based in Honolulu with United Airlines. He was also an Instrument Rated Commercial Pilot, often employed as a ferry pilot of small airplanes across the Pacific.

Five days before Christmas, Mike and I checked the headwind component as a go for that morning, and off we went to Honolulu, only to return to San Francisco four hours later. A combination of higher winds than expected and extreme airframe icing slowed our progress so much our GNS 500 navigation system provided the bad news that we would run out of fuel three hundred miles before reaching Honolulu. Even that information was optimistic because at our turning back position, the plane was so loaded with ice, we had descended from 15,000 to 11,000 feet cruising altitude.

Three days before Christmas, we tried again, this time successfully, with a total flight time of 11 hours because of headwinds. On this attempt, there was a lack of mid-level clouds, so no airframe icing. During the last two hours of our flight, I had begun planning survival options of landing either at Hilo or Maui, as our remaining fuel endurance counted down toward the absolute limit of 12 hours. The distance to Hilo was 60 miles shorter than continuing to Honolulu, and Maui was another choice once we passed Hilo. However, neither option was required because the headwinds finally dropped off as we descended toward Honolulu.

It was great to be flying with a pilot who lived in downtown Honolulu. Mike invited me stay with him at his apartment for the two nights we had scheduled before continuing our journey. He introduced me to his group of exotic Hawaiian friends. Some were from United Airlines and others from a local flying club, who invited us to a Christmas Eve party near the airport on the night before our planned departure for Majuro. Since nothing had gone as planned with this Metro delivery, I was not surprised when I was approached by the local FAA Office asking if I could change my next destination to Wake Island before proceeding to Guam. The reason: to uplift an injured US government worker on the island and take him to Guam. I made some quick calculations on the distance to Wake, which was similar to the San Francisco to Honolulu segment, but without the headwind problem. I responded with a yes, and asked about clearances and fuel availability at this US military airfield. The answer was no problem, no worries, everything would be cleared for our arrival and departure, and there would be fuel at no charge. Merry Christmas. God speed and be safe out there!

Since there was some urgency to this Casevac mission, I decided to leave Honolulu on Christmas Eve, after making a quick appearance at the Flying Club party, cautiously supping eggnog that was supposedly alcohol-free, but doubtful. We departed Honolulu airport shortly before midnight, crossed the International Date Line two hours later, putting us into the day after Christmas. No Christmas Day, so no Christmas for 1979. Nevertheless, Mike had not forgotten the moment, bringing forth small gifts from his luggage to the cockpit under a nightscape of brilliant stars. We turned down the cockpit lighting to better look upon what I'll always remember as the most magical Christmas night I've ever known. Mike and I were probably the only people within a thousand miles, and perhaps forever blessed by this unique experience.

Not long after daybreak at Wake Island, we tracked into the radio beacon on this remote coral atoll in the middle of the North Pacific. Approaching the airport terminal, we could see an ambulance and a small group waiting on our arrival. Mike and I had been airborne for nine hours and been awake for much longer, but it was apparent these folks on Wake expected us to be underway to Guam without delay. The plane was quickly refueled, boxed lunches and soft drinks provided, and our patient on a stretcher tied down on the cabin floor between fuel tanks. One other passenger, acting as a medical assistant, added to our cabin complement. In less than an hour, we were airborne again, turning southwest toward Guam 1,500 miles away. We landed at Agana airport on Guam Island after a short flight of only six hours.

We were back to where John Flynn and I had left off many weeks before. The small airline on Guam requested another demonstration flight from Agana to the islands of Rota and Saipan. On the way back to Agana, I took the opportunity for a low pass over Tinian Island to observe the massive runways used by the *Enola Gay* and other B-29 bombers for the raids on the Japan homeland in 1945. Then it was time to continue the original journey toward Singapore, with a stopover at Manila in the Philippines. Finally, we arrived at Seletar Airport in Singapore on December 28, one month later than expected. Mike Hance stayed at my apartment for a few days before flying home to Honolulu on a business class ticket provided by Stillwell Aviation. I was sorry to see him go because our air adventure had been an exciting ten days from San Francisco.

With the Metro now in Singapore, Stillwell's local aircraft engineer, Colin Bewley, with the help of Singapore General Aviation, our handling company at Seletar, removed the five auxiliary fuel tanks and associated piping from the cabin. I had determined that the planned demonstration flights around SE Asia, including the final run to Melbourne, Australia, could be done with just the integral fuel tanks. After the tanks were removed, I carried out a local test flight, then spent a week at the apartment, planning for the extensive demonstration schedule that began on January 9 in the Philippines. I had no backup pilot for any of this flying, which was not a problem. Instead, I was accompanied by Colin Bewley, a more useful person than a spare pilot to take on this trip, because he could fix things that broke!

Using Manila as a base, Colin and I did demonstration flights to Baguio, Fernando Air Base, Legaspi, and Virac. During the 1960s, I did have experience flying in and out of the Philippines during my New Zealand Air Force days but enjoyed visiting these new locations. After Manila, we flew south to Kota Kinabalu, which I'd known as Jesselton, in northern Borneo. I was now very much on home turf, having spent many years flying to Jesselton, Labuan Island, and Kuching, from Singapore. We made a short stop at Kuching on the way home to Singapore, where we were granted a day off before heading south to Jakarta, Indonesia. Once there, we used it as a base for three days, doing demonstration flights at Bandung, Jogjakarta, and Bali. With those tasks complete, it was finally time to take this well-traveled Metro to where it ultimately belonged— in Australia. But the fun and excitement of this two-month odyssey were still not over, until an inflight engine shutdown, halfway between Bali and Darwin. There had been a momentary indication of a turbine over-temperature, and in case it continued, I did a precautionary shutdown. We flew on to Darwin, lower and slower, but with the knowledge that the engine could be started again in the unlikely event of the other engine failing.

After threading our way through numerous thunderstorms, we reached Darwin, still operating on one engine, landed safely, and were met by the airport crash crew with nothing for them to do! Colin and a local maintenance crew did a check on the offending engine, found no internal damage, did a few ground engine runs, and declared the Metro fully serviceable. The next morning we were airborne early for a flight to Alice Springs, a quick refuel, and then the very last segment of this fantastic journey to Melbourne.

My first three delivery flights, with their associated dramas, set the stage for the next two years I was with Stillwell's. Nothing was easy, and every trip was a challenge, in part because I was accepting these airplanes straight off the assembly line. There was never time for extensive shakedown flights, resulting in minor to significant equipment failures en route from San Antonio to Thailand and Australia.

1979: Death on The Ice

Trespassers over the Last Place on Earth
Altitude is life insurance. No one has ever collided with the sky.
~ Chronicle of a Disaster Foretold

THANKS TO A FORTUITOUS MEETING in early October 1979 at my Singapore apartment, I was able to save the lives of my parents by advising them not to make reservations on any of the Air New Zealand (ANZ) charter flights to Antarctica planned for the southern summer of that year.

The chance meeting was with longtime friends from New Zealand Air Force days who had joined ANZ in the mid-1970s and were now flying DC-10 airliners on the Pacific routes. I'd been absent from the New Zealand aviation scene for a few years but had heard the rumors of the Antarctic charters for 'tourists in street clothes,' and couldn't believe the New Zealand Civil Aviation Department (CAD) would continue approving these potentially dangerous flights. My visitors told me otherwise: the airline had advertised four Antarctic charters during November 1979.

My visitors were like me, coming from similar backgrounds in the RNZAF. We'd trained on Harvard's in Christchurch in the mid to late 1950s. Then moved on to fly

Bristol Freighters in Auckland and Singapore with No. 41 Squadron, then the C-130 Hercules with No. 40 Squadron in Auckland. Every springtime at 40 Squadron, we took part in Operation Ice Cube, which involved multiple flights between Christchurch and McMurdo Sound, landing on the ice runway at Williams Field. When my friends raised the subject of the next scheduled ANZ Antarctic flights, I assumed that they, and other RNZAF Ice Cube veterans then flying for ANZ, would be involved in planning these flights. Sadly that was not the case. From what I recall, they said that none of the experienced RNZAF Antarctic pilots were volunteering for the trips and had not been approached for their input by ANZ flight operations staff.

Whatever the case, hypothetically placing myself in their shoes, I imagined ANZ ignoring even my experienced input, particularly if I recommended that they scrap the whole idea unless they corrected some serious omissions. For starters, I was astounded that ANZ had no intention of placing extreme cold weather survival clothing and equipment on board for passengers and crew. Were they planning to request experienced Ice Cube C-130 pilots from the RNZAF to fly in the DC-10 cockpits (or vice versa), who could make valuable suggestions on the approach and descent to McMurdo Sound? Had they planned to install a temporary TACAN radio-nav receiver in their DC-10s that would enhance their low-level navigation in the McMurdo area? I believe the answer was no to all. I could only assume that ANZ flight crews didn't need any help from either the New Zealand or United States military aviators.

Maybe they were too arrogant for that, or more likely, ANZ management realized that briefing passengers about cold-weather clothing and survival equipment (tents, gas-stoves, ropes, ice axes, etc.) onboard would expose the company's unspoken concerns that these Antarctic flights were potentially hazardous. The result would be a race to get off the airplane before departure, and a subsequent loss of interest by future passengers. In my opinion, it was a public relations decision not to have the equipment onboard. Nor was it in the company's best interest to have their crews checked out on RNZAF Ice Cube flights because of a real possibility that these ANZ pilots would return from these exploratory flights demanding many necessary fixes to reduce the level of risk. In the idiom of the home computer world two decades later, a handbook produced by ANZ for the charter crews would have been called *Antarctic Flying for Dummies.*

When the ANZ visitors left my Singapore apartment, I wasted no time in phoning my parents in New Zealand. From a recent letter I'd received, my dad had expressed a plan for him and Mom to take the last November charter flight by ANZ to see a small piece of the Antarctic continent. Dad was a retired Air Force officer, so when I explained my reservations about how ill-advised these flights were, he took my concern seriously. A few days later I had to leave Singapore on a flight to San Antonio in the USA, hoping that Dad would bow out of his Antarctic dreams.

~

My association with Antarctic aviation operations began in 1959 as a member of the RNZAF Antarctic Flight, training for six months in Christchurch and on the glaciers of Mount Cook National Park. I was one of five pilots selected for a unique and high-risk mission on 'The Ice.' Our mentors were experienced Antarctic fliers like Bill Cranfield and alpine mountaineers like Harry Ayres, both of whom had been with Sir Ed Hillary's Antarctic expedition in 1957–1958. We spent months studying how to live, fly, and survive in the extreme environment of Antarctica. I was 19-years-old at the time, a qualified Air Force pilot, and budding alpine mountaineer, thanks to Harry Ayres expert instruction on the Tasman Glacier. We were taught astro-navigation, advanced Morse code, the use of ropes, ice axes, crampons, cross-country skiing, advanced first aid, the dangers of Polar white-outs, frostbite, and carbon-monoxide poisoning from cooking in tents, snow-trenches, snow-caves, or igloos.

Later, in 1961, I was attached to the United States Navy Squadron VX6 to fly their DHC Otter airplanes in Antarctica. Based at McMurdo Sound for five months during the southern summer of 1961–1962, I flew extensively along the coast of the Ross Sea, around the rim of the Ross Ice Shelf from Cape Hallett south to the Beardmore Glacier and to Roosevelt Island. I visited the South Pole and Byrd Stations in VX6 ski-equipped C-130s, flew the entire coastline of Ross Island in VX6 helicopters, and alpine climbed from McMurdo Base up to the southern ridge of Mount Erebus. During those early adventures on and around the Ross Ice Shelf in Antarctica, I experienced many white-out events—on the ground and in the air.

From 1968 to 1972, I flew RNZAF C-130s with No 40 Squadron based at Whenuapai, near Auckland. During my four years with the Squadron, I'd operated the four-engined C-130 around the world, including operational troop lifts from Auckland to Saigon in South Vietnam and many other missions in Asia. Each October, I would command Operation Ice Cube flights to and from McMurdo Sound in Antarctica. Based on the safety protocols of the US Navy Squadron VX6, who had refined them for more than a decade, we at 40 Squadron adopted similar operational techniques for our flights from Christchurch to the Williams ice runway at McMurdo. Unlike the future trips by ANZ in their DC-10s, operating our C-130s we utilized a Point of No Return (PNR) about two-thirds along the route from

Christchurch to Williams Field. Once south of that point, we were committed to continuing regardless of how bad the weather would become by our expected arrival time at McMurdo Sound, because we did not have enough fuel to get back to New Zealand—even Invercargill or Dunedin.

The harsh reality of a weather-obscured runway at Williams, either by ice-fog or more likely, blowing snow (50 knots of wind lifting snow to a height of 50 feet), meant a wheels-up landing under radar direction onto the Ross Ice Shelf. If this event was necessary, we planned to stay airborne until the fuel remaining gave us approximately 30 minutes of flight, sufficient time to conduct a power-on forced landing. If it was our lucky day, during the fuel burn down to 30 minutes, a clear weather window might open over the Williams runway.

When past our PNR, crew and passengers would don extreme cold weather clothing, including placing a 'go-bag' close at hand. This bag would contain additional clothing and other survival items that would be available in the event of an aircraft emergency situation (smoke, fire, multiple engine failures) that resulted in a forced landing on sea-ice, ice-floes, or the northern ice shelves (Tucker Inlet, Lady Newnes, or Terra Nova Bay). The worst-case scenario was the plane burning, then personnel could quickly exit with their go-bags and shovels (for digging trenches and igloo construction). Even dressed in extremely cold weather clothing, without shelter from the wind, death is close at hand on The Ice.

Assuming no in-flight emergencies and suitable weather for our arrival at Williams Field, we followed the laid down approach procedure for US military airplanes. During my time at 40 Squadron our C-130s were not equipped with Inertial Navigation Systems (INS), but we did have a far superior long-range navigation system ... a crew member known as a Professional Navigator. These 'Navs' as we called them, had a seat in the cockpit (where they could see forward) and used a combination of Doppler Radar, Sextant, paper maps, plotting charts, and access to TACAN receivers, ADF/NDB receivers, weather/ground mapping Radar and Secondary Radar Transponder (IFF). The Nav would direct us south from over Cape Adair to intercept the 165° E meridian of longitude, continuing True South inbound until receiving the established approach TACAN radial, descending from cruise altitude, setting the altimeters to the advised QNH (sea level pressure) at Flight Level 180, then continuing the descent to not below 16,000 feet.

If I recall correctly, the approach procedure allowed a further descent after crossing 40 miles DME on the inbound radial from the TACAN. Although this approach procedure kept us well clear of Mount Erebus, even in excellent VMC (Visual Met Conditions), I can't recall ever reverting to a visual descent and breaking the published approach pattern. The primary reason was helping the McMurdo US Navy air controllers fit in their own traffic coming from the south and their slow-moving helicopters from all directions. Another reason was we had no spectators on board requesting close fly-bys of Erebus and Ross Island! In those years, all personnel on the ground or in the air near McMurdo were professionals and committed explorers. It was no place for Adventure Tourism, and in my opinion, it should have remained that way.

In my professional opinion, what followed next was a disaster looking for a place to happen. The flight crew decided it was safe to descend below the Minimum Safe Altitude (MSA) of 16,000 feet in poor visibility, unsure of their actual position, using as their sole navigation aid a system (AINS) *specifically excluded in their Operations Manual for the conduct of descent below safe sector or enroute altitudes.*

Ron Chippendale's Aircraft Accident Report No. 79-139 as Chief Inspector of Air Accidents for the Ministry of Transport, New Zealand, released on June 12, 1980 contains the most logical reasons for the crash of ANZ Flight 901. I believed the findings of that report, and still do in this year of 2021, 42 years after the accident. The final act in a an escalating series of crew errors was the tragic CFIT (Controlled Flight Into Terrain) event while scud-running below clouds at 300 mph and 1,500 feet. It's still hard to believe that the crew could be so reckless.

My opinion on the Royal Commission's erroneous waypoint theory: Since the AINS was excluded explicitly for use as the sole method of navigation below the MSA of 16,000 feet, all waypoints entered in the system were irrelevant and should have been ignored. However, if any of the crew had been plotting on a paper chart, the readily available latitude-longitude position reading from the AINS, they would have seen that Ross Island was coming up fast, and straight ahead.

Having recently reread the tedious nonsense sections in the report of the Royal Commission compiled by a bunch of ambulance chasing lawyers, what I see is the deliberate obfuscation of factual information provided in Chippendale's report. After the accident I absconded from the small aviation world of New Zealand, realizing that any desire I'd had to be hired as a pilot with ANZ was gone. But I've wondered all these years, what was the purpose of creating a false narrative about the reason for the crash? I can understand the pilot's union, NZALPA, trying to protect their turf and the families of the Flight Deck Crew, but that surely didn't justify a Royal Commission Inquiry.

So what was it for? Perhaps to ensure that ANZ

continued to be seen as a safe airline, and not put on the 'Don't Fly With' list with Garuda, Korean Air, and other Third World ragtag operators. Or maybe it had something to do with compensation payments when the litigation lawyers showed up from the USA, Europe and Japan. My best guess has been that it was an attempt to hide the ultimate responsibility of the Prime Minister, Minister of Transport, the Civil Aviation Division, and Air New Zealand's management, and in my humble opinion, these four entities had blood on their hands. If this simple country boy from Papatoetoe had the professional knowledge to warn his parents about flying over Antarctica with ANZ one month before the worst air accident in New Zealand's history, then what were these entities thinking when they approved the flights?

While the victims' families still search for the truth behind this totally avoidable tragedy, forty years later it seems that the New Zealand government still has limited control and oversite of adventure tourist activities. On December 9, 2019, a group of tourists were taken into the crater of an active volcano on White Island, with the only available escape option by boat. What could possibly go wrong with this potentially dangerous activity? Just like the Antarctic flights by ANZ in 1979, the White Island operation lacked common sense risk assessment. How could the tour operators justify landing 47 lookie-loo tourists onto a volcanic island that had a history of periodic eruptions? When it did erupt, 22 of the tourists died and 25 were badly injured. How's that for an exciting adventure in New Zealand?

1957: Flight student night training with the Harvard AT-6 RNZAF Base Wigram, Christchurch, New Zealand.

1957: RNZAF Harvard AT-6 in a four-ship formation over Birdlings Flat Air Weapons Military Operations Area, south of Christchurch, New Zealand.

December 18, 1957: age 18, my Wings Graduation Day at RNZAF Wigram, Christchurch, New Zealand, standing proudly by a metal friend, a Harvard AT-6.

1958: An RNZAF Bristol Freighter on a five-day journey between New Zealand and Singapore, being refueled at Cloncurry, Queensland, Australia.

191

1961: A US Navy DHC Otter from VX6 with wheels/skis flying in a formation of two Otters between McMurdo Sound and the Beardmore Glacier, Antarctica.

1962: A US Navy S.58 helicopter from VX6 in one of the dry valleys west of McMurdo Sound, Antarctica.

1962: A US Navy C-130 Hercules with wheels/skis from VX6 at the South Pole Stations, Antarctica. The engines kept running at the 10,000-foot elevation of the Station.

1962: Me at the South Pole Station, Antarctica, as a member of the US Navy Squadron VX6.

1962: A De Havilland Vampire FB5 single seat fighter/bomber of the RNZAF, the jet I flew from Base Ohakea in New Zealand. (*RNZAF Official*)

March 18, 1963:
Her Majesty, Queen Elizabeth II, escorted by me as Guard Commander at the Christchurch Airport, New Zealand. (*RNZAF Official*)

1965: At war with Indonesia, airdropping supplies to our jungle-based soldiers in Sarawak, Borneo. The RAF 20 Squadron Hawker Hunter fighters were for our defense against Indonesian Mig 21s.

1965: 41 Squadron Bristol Freighter airdrop operations over the jungles of Sarawak, Borneo. (*RNZAF Official*)

1968: Flying one of the five RNZAF C-130H Hercules. This photo was taken over Auckland City, New Zealand. (*RNZAF Official*)

April 1975: The last days in Saigon. The RNZAF 41 Squadron was there, and so was I as a backup pilot for the Bristol Freighters. From left: John Richards, John Hansen, Roger Holdaway, me, Tony Gainsford. (*Bob Davidson Collection*)

1978: The actual Beechcraft Bonanza V35 I flew from Newfoundland to New Zealand, a solo flight of 15,000 miles over 20 days and 100 flight hours.

1980–1981: A promotional photo of a Swearingen Merlin 3B, the high-performance corporate turboprop airplanes that I flew around the world for Stillwell Aviation. (*Swaco Aviation*)

1979: The very busy cockpit layout of a Swearingen Merlin 4, similar to the two airplanes I flew from San Antonio, Texas to Bangkok, Thailand. (*Swaco Aviation*)

August 1979: Arrival at the Royal Thai Air Force (RTAF) Base at Bangkok with the first of three Swearingen Merlin 4 airplanes. A warm welcome from their base commander with flowers and Mekong whisky. (*RTAF Official*)

January 1979: At Baguio Airport, Philippines, for the demonstration of a Swearingen Metro 2, with Stillwell's Philippine agents and my airplane engineer, Colin Bewley.

November 1983: From our camp at Bengas Tal on the Annapurna Circuit. The peak in the background is Annapurna 4, with an elevation of 24,700 feet.

1984: Flying the IAI Westwind corporate jet for Bougainville Cooper. Bruce Walker and me at Townsville Airport prior a routine flight to Kieta Airport on Bougainville Island.

1984: On the approach to the 5,400-foot runway at Kieta Airport, Bougainville, in the Westwind jet. There were crocodiles in the swamps at both ends off the runway. (*Shaun Davis*)

Spring 1987: Mount Hood, 11,200 feet, in northern Oregon near the city of Portland. This photo is from my first summit climb.

September 1990: A UPS B-727 night flight from San Diego to Dallas Fort Worth with Christine McKinley and Joe Moon. (*Joe Moon*)

October 1987: My first command of a Boeing 727, during an Emery Worldwide flight from Dayton, Ohio to Scranton, Pennsylvania. This was a brief stopover at Scranton.

June 1989, age 50: Surviving Denali at High Camp on the West Buttress climbing route. At 17,200 feet with temperatures down to minus 40F, trapped there with weather for seven days.

June 1989: Me ascending the last section from the 14,300-foot Ice Bowl camp to the Headwall Notch at 16,000 feet on the Denali West Buttress route.

March 1992: Me standing near the 21,500-foot summit of Mera Peak, Nepal, at age 52. Mount Everest is directly behind me.

May 10, 1999: Beginning my last flight from Anchorage, Alaska to Louisville, Kentucky in a UPS Boeing 747. I would turn 60 (too old to fly the big jets!) in six days. (*Mary Jude Hayes*)

May 10, 1998: Relaxing, but not sleeping, in the cockpit of a Boeing 747-200 somewhere over the Northern Pacific Ocean.

2003–2008: An evening view from The House at the End of the World, looking out over Frenchman Bay, near Albany in Southwest Australia. We were happy residents there.

2017, age 77: The hut that saved my life in the forever rain while hiking the Saint James Walkway, New Zealand.

1980: Airplane Delivery Professional

Now he had a straight run of well-paid, exciting work to get his teeth into – a hard job, maybe, but not more than he could manage. He would increase his reputation if he pulled this off successfully.

~ *An Old Captivity*, Nevil Shute

Flight of the Three Bees

DURING THE TWO YEARS 1980–1981, still employed by Stillwell Aviation, based in Singapore, I had the opportunity to deliver two Swearingen Merlin 3B aircraft from San Antonio to Australia. Very unlike the Merlin 4s that I'd flown to Thailand, the Merlin 3B was a shorter, higher performance version, with more powerful engines driving four-bladed propellers. It was said it possessed a better-power-to-weight ratio than a P–51D Mustang. Compared with the Metro and Merlin 4, it could fly higher, cruise faster, and go considerably farther, using only its integral fuel tanks. It was designed for the high-end corporate airplane market, could be flown legally with a single pilot, and was definitely in a performance class of its own.

The cockpit and its controls were identical to a Metro or Merlin 4, which made the transition to this different model very easy. In late January, John Flynn had given me

206

a brief check ride in one of the two Merlin 3Bs that were then operating in Australia. We flew from Melbourne to Sydney and return, a total time of two and a half hours. I remember it as an exciting introductory flight in this high-performance turboprop airplane. My first 3B delivery was scheduled for departure from San Antonio in April, an airplane that was destined for use by an Australian corporation. It had been fitted with all the bells and whistles as a luxury, six-passenger company plane, and radio navigation equipment that would allow extended overwater flights in the Pacific region. My delivery plan was to again use the Atlantic Ocean route that I was familiar with, but would overfly airports that were no longer required because of the long-range capability.

I traveled from Singapore to San Antonio during the last week of April, and flew one local flight in our Merlin 3B with Jim Humphries, one of SWACO's test pilots. Being back in San Antonio wasn't the fun it used to be when my new best friend, Marilyn, was living there. Two months before, she had moved to Singapore as my partner, and my priority now was to get this plane flying on the long way back home to Peace Mansions. Not really convinced about the charted performance figures for the 3B, by the end of the first trip segment direct from San Antonio to Bangor in Maine, I became a believer. We had covered the 1,800 miles in less than seven hours at a cruising altitude of 27,000 feet. In reality, I was operating as a single pilot but had a warm body forced on me by Stillwell's back in Melbourne. James was a commuter airline pilot who had just completed the Flight Safety simulator training for the Metro, and Stillwell's had cut a deal with James's airline for him to accompany me to Australia. Unfortunately, he wasn't a happy camper, continually complaining about his assignment and an urgent need to get home to Brisbane.

If James had known what would befall us on the first half of our journey to Australia, he would have bailed out on me in Bangor. On the morning of the second day, we discovered an engine oil leak that had to be repaired. SWACO in San Antonio advised me to make the relatively short flight to Islip Airport on Long Island, New York, where Airesearch Aviation, a maintenance company for Garrett engines, would repair the problem. They did, but because we'd arrived on a Friday, nothing could be done until Monday! Donny, the Service Manager at Airesearch, was most helpful. He provided us with a courtesy car for the weekend and accommodation at the Old Mill Inn, and even offered to arrange attractive ladies from Manhattan for our amusement. Despite turning down this kind offer, we still had a good time driving around the western end of Long Island, including a drive-by of the Amityville Horror house. We wined and dined at a couple of excellent Italian restaurants and did some jogging to work off the calories. Come Monday, it was back to work, with a short local test flight, followed by a four-hour flight north to St. Johns, Newfoundland.

While at Islip, I had scribbled out a tentative flight plan for a route from there, over Nantucket Island, then direct to Santa Maria in the Azores, but luckily opted for an Atlantic crossing from St. Johns, from where we could fly direct to Lisbon. The luck was in discovering another problem while inbound to St. Johns, thanks to being in the habit of checking the long-range HF radio with Gander Oceanic Control. This vital communication radio for crossing the Atlantic was found to be inoperative, so another day delayed at St. Johns while Sealand Helicopter Avionics workshop fixed the problem—a broken antenna!

The next flight segment remains in my memory as the ultimate in my extensive aviation career. I'd studied the

Merlin 3B performance charts in some detail, and concluded that I could safely fly the plane from St. Johns to Lisbon, Portugal, without a fuel stop in the Azores. I was confident that the flight plan would work, operating over two thousand miles and still retaining approximately two hours of fuel on touchdown at Lisbon. Somewhere, over the vast expanse of the Atlantic, I began thinking that it all seemed too easy. Cruising at 27,000 feet, with a groundspeed of over 300 mph, the installed Collins LRN-70 VLF/Omega Navigation System showed precisely where we were, and confirmed an estimated total flight time of seven hours. Besides, we were in constant radio contact with the Oceanic Control Centers at Gander, Santa Maria, and Shanwick.

I needed to keep pinching myself, making sure I wasn't dreaming this unbelievable career experience: a single-pilot operation from one side of the Atlantic to the other, in a warm pressurized cabin with luxury sniffing leather seating, and the latest state-of-the-art radio and navigation equipment working its magic so well. All that, without the need for those pesky co-pilots, navigators, and radio operators. Not that I'm demeaning their function in the Air Force transport airplanes I flew for 20 years. Sadly for their trade, the introduction of this latest radio and navigation gear, long-range overwater flights could be handled safely by one pilot alone. I must say that the experience was exhilarating.

We passed overhead the Lisbon radio beacon with an error of two miles showing on the VLF/Omega system. Not too shabby for a two thousand mile flight without ground navigation beacons. We landed at Lisbon Airport after a total flight time of seven hours, with two and a half hours of fuel remaining. This was my first time using Lisbon as a stopover, and it was not a disappointment. The Lisbon Airport Authority provided transport to and from the terminal, arranged customs and immigration clearances, and actioned payment of landing and parking fees. They made it all so effortless and at a ridiculously low cost. My decision for future flights eastbound across the Atlantic would be Lisbon, and definitely not somewhere in Spain. The Portuguese airport officials, taxi drivers, and hotel staff were a delight to deal with. Lovely people.

I'd determined that our next destination would be Iraklion Airport on the Greek Island of Crete, and not Athens. This decision dated back two years to a discussion at an Athens hotel about using Crete as a possible stopover. The suggestion had come from a US Navy P3 Orion pilot who'd landed at the joint Greek military / civilian airport at Iraklion on the northern coast of the island. He'd opined that it would be a better alternative than the large Athens Airport; far less busy, and smaller aircraft like mine could be parked close to the terminal. Besides, it would be easy for aircraft handling, and a friendly layover event, being treated as someone special by middle-aged Cretans who would remember the New Zealand soldiers who fought the German paratrooper invaders on the island in 1941.

The flight from Lisbon was going smoothly until a few amber warning lights illuminated on the front control panel, with hydraulic fluid observed streaming back from the leading edge of the right-wing. The two warning lights represented the left and right hydraulic pressure pumps. Within 30 seconds, the hydraulic pressure gauge needle dropped to zero. It was an easy decision to discontinue flight toward Crete, and instead make a diversion to Athens, no more than one hour flying from our present position. Besides, there were additional advantages to landing at Athens. Without hydraulics, we would be unable to deploy the high-lift flaps for lower landing speeds, and the wheel brakes would be inoperative, so the long runways at Athens were essential. The other consideration was the availability of known airplane maintenance if I got it on the ground in one piece! There was also the unknown as to whether the landing gear, without hydraulics, would extend manually.

As we approached the airport, I declared an emergency and proceeded to move the landing gear manual release lever to the 'free-fall' position, which happily allowed the three struts to drop into the extended and locked position. I then switched off the nose wheel steering and anti-skid systems, increased the approach speed to compensate for the 'no-flaps' condition, and executed a fast but safe landing on the longest runway at Athens Airport. So finished just another day at the office for ferry pilots.

Once comfortably installed at my favorite hotel on the beach, I phoned SWACO in San Antonio, and a call to Barbara in Melbourne for her to relay our delay to our next stopover airports. An initial inspection of our once again broken airplane by mechanics of Athens Aviation Services determined that a hydraulic pressure line near the right-hand engine had fractured. The folks in San Antonio arranged for their Europe based Tech Rep, Dick Miller, living in Cologne, Germany, to come to my assistance in Athens. Dick arrived with a few spare parts for the repair, including new hydraulic pumps. One pump had seized after the loss of fluid, and its replacement was an easy fix, but not so the fractured line, which took two days for Dick to repair because of difficult access. The total delay at Athens was three days before we were airborne again, this time direct to Dubai.

As on previous round-the-world ferry flights, I found Dubai to be an excellent stopover, thanks to the help of AeroGulf Services, well managed by George Sobiecki, an RNZAF student pilot of mine from back in 1964 Christchurch.

On past trips through Dubai, I had dreaded the next few days, required to land for fuel at Karachi, Bombay, Calcutta, or Madras, but this time with the 3B's extended range, only one stop at Madras would be necessary for a return to western civilization in Singapore. Still, with all the aircraft mechanical problems experienced with this 3B since leaving San Antonio, the possibility of another event, this time stuck on the ground in India, was a chilling thought.

Luckily, there were no more dramas to Singapore, where my questionable 'co-pilot' decided to jump ship, buy a ticket on a big jet plane, and fly home to Brisbane. What a relief; no more whining to listen to, and a nice bonus having an uncomplicated fuel stop at Madras. After years of frustrating stops in India, I'd finally broken the code on how to deal with their airport officials. An old friend in the airplane delivery business working for De Havilland Canada in Toronto had provided me with a checklist to be used before landing at Indian airports, and most importantly, before leaving. Following this checklist at Madras was a winner for me, but it noticeably upset some of the officials because I had all the answers to their deliberate pedantic questions.

Arriving back in Singapore was a happy occasion for me; I was back home and in the company of Marilyn, my partner. I contacted Stillwell's in Melbourne requesting a replacement safety pilot be sent to Singapore to fly the final two sectors from Singapore to Darwin, and Darwin to Melbourne. *Sorry, not available, find someone local.* On many occasions working for Stillwell's, I had enjoyed the freedom they gave me in problem-solving and making independent decisions regardless of where I was in the world. Fortunately, they also continued to provide the necessary financial support with business-class air travel, credit cards, and bundles of green dollars.

Finding a local pilot I could trust was easy. An RNZAF helicopter squadron was still on the island, based at the Singapore Air Force Tengah Airfield. I knew the commanding officer of the unit, a compatriot from my RNZAF days in New Zealand. I called him up and explained what I needed: one of his well-trained pilots for a fun flight in a high-performance luxury airplane from Singapore to Melbourne, all costs met including a business class ticket back to Singapore. There were probably plenty of volunteers, but the lucky winner, Ian McClelland, was an excellent young pilot to have on the last stages of this journey. Also, Marilyn joined us for her first visit to Australia. So off we went—three happy people—in our own private airplane for a seven-hour flight to Darwin in northwest Australia.

Landing at Darwin, Ian and I were presented with a surprising coincidence. Parked on the ramp was a C-130 Hercules from No. 40 Squadron RNZAF, the last unit I'd flown with in 1972. Also, no coincidence that we ended up staying in the same Darwin hotel as the Hercules crew, getting together with them in the most likely place ... the hotel bar. What a wonderful gathering. Ian and I knew most of the crew, and Marilyn was well-received as my lovely young American partner. Although not shared with others, I made an error that night in the bar, a small mistake that bothered me for some years. A young enlisted man I spoke with was so pleased to meet me again after being his base commander in New Zealand in 1973. He was complimentary with his observation that I had been an excellent boss, and what a privilege it had been to serve on the Base during my tenure. Perhaps because I was in a braggadocio mood about my newfound status in aviation, accompanied by an attractive young woman, flying the world in a luxury private airplane, I told him my truth about the time as his base commander. "For me, it was a shit time in a shit city

(Wellington), doing a boring, tedious administrative job, and I hated every day I was forced to be there. All I wanted was to be back in a flying job."

It was a shameful response to the young man's complimentary remarks, but sadly, I had exposed my hidden feelings, despite knowing I had done the job well, and been ultimately rewarded with a prime assignment back in Singapore, ironically, to another ground appointment. He was visibly upset at my response, so much so, that I'm surprised he didn't hit me. He walked away, never to speak to me again. This unfortunate episode marked the conclusion of the gathering with old friends and resulted in an early night before our final flight segment the next day.

The outstanding range and speed capability of the Merlin 3B allowed for a direct flight from Darwin to Melbourne, a distance of 2,000 miles, which we covered in six hours. The total flight time from San Antonio to Melbourne had been 57 hours over an aggregate length of 18,000 miles. The staff at Stillwell's Australian headquarters were pleased to belatedly receive this airplane, and finally able to transfer it to the eager new owners. The three of us were wined and dined by various staff members, including Barbara Pearson, the delivery pilot's go-to-gal, and Neil (Neddie) Morris. Our mercenary Kiwi Air Force pilot, Ian McClelland, enjoyed these moments in Melbourne, a place he'd not visited before. The company provided him with an air ticket, and some cash, to return to his squadron in Singapore.

This was Marilyn's first visit to Australia, a tour which we extended to New Zealand for a week before Marilyn flew home to Singapore on Qantas Airlines, and I returned to San Antonio on Pan Am for another delivery. This time it was a Metro 2, for which I'd convinced Stillwell's not to install auxiliary fuel tanks (necessary for the Pacific crossing) because I planned to use the Atlantic route, eastbound to Australia. The airplane was destined for Solomon Airways, based at Honiara, the capital of the Solomon Islands. On this journey, I was lucky to have a fully qualified co-pilot join me. He was Bruce Kirkwood, the chief pilot of Solomon Airways, taking delivery of the airline's first 19-seat turboprop commuter aircraft.

The trip went without a hitch, taking only ten days from San Antonio to Melbourne with the opportunity of finally spending a delightful night in Iraklion, Crete. Because of the reduced range capability compared with the Merlin-3B, it was necessary to make additional fuel stops at Santa Maria, Luxor, Bombay, Surabaya, and Alice Springs. After the hand-off to Stillwell's in Melbourne, I left Bruce with his new plane and took a commercial flight back to Singapore and my favorite partner. What followed was a hiatus from delivery flying for three months, traveling on commercial flights to Taiwan in the north, and Indonesia in the south, on sales missions with Tony, Stillwell's general manager in Southeast Asia. It's worth mentioning that our reason for visiting Taiwan had something to do with Air Asia, the giant aircraft maintenance company for the CIA 'secret' airlines and air forces, such as Air America, that operated in Vietnam, Laos, and Cambodia in the 1960s and 1970s.

By early October of 1980, it was time for me to return to San Antonio for the delivery flight of another Merlin-3B, this one belonging to the Royal Thai Army in Thailand. A few of their pilots had already completed the Flight Safety training but had no interest in being involved with the delivery flight. Colin, our maintenance man in Bangkok, was in San Antonio to finalize the acceptance of the plane from SWACO, and then accompany me, together with his wife, Judy, on the 12-day flight to Bangkok. When I learned of this arrangement, I phoned Marilyn in Singapore to suggest that she join us on this once-in-a-lifetime trip halfway around the world, in our private corporate airplane. She happily agreed, flew to the US, had time to visit her mother at Fort Wayne, Indiana, and then joined us in San Antonio.

Knowing so well the eastbound route across the Atlantic and beyond, I decided to make a few adventurous changes after reaching Newfoundland. Instead of a stop in Lisbon, I knew it was my time to fly direct from St. Johns to Ireland, a distance of 2,000 miles to Shannon Airport. Aided by strong westerly winds, we made the crossing in less than six hours, only to find that the Irish fuel-truck drivers were on strike. *So sorry, lads and lassies, but no fuel for you in Shannon.* It was suggested we fly to Belfast the following morning, but after checking the remaining fuel in the tanks, I said we'd go to Cardiff in Wales, a one-hour flight from Shannon. That evening we decided to do the tourist thing by visiting Bunratty Castle for an Irish banquet, being entertained by classical Irish dancers and singers.

I had never visited Ireland but often listened to put-down jokes about how stupid the Irish could be—usually told by Englishmen. Incredibly, this night we experienced a real-life demonstration of gross stupidity by the driver of our tour bus. Perhaps he'd drunk too much Guinness, because when we boarded the bus in the hotel parking lot, it took at least 30 minutes for him to find an exit. It seemed that every direction he chose ended in a blind alley, or 'no exit' sign. Finally, once on the open roads, which were narrow two-lane highways, the headlights began to blink on and off—mainly off. He explained it was just a minor electrical fault, but not to worry, he'd leave the internal cabin lights on so that oncoming traffic would see the bus along this otherwise pitch-black narrow road. The problem was, with the interior lights on, none of us, including the driver, could see outside. Amazingly, we made it safely to the castle, a little late, but alive. The journey back to our hotel was quite painless after drinking copious mugs of Mead in a fully serviceable bus and with a replacement driver.

Our planned destination for the following day was Zurich in Switzerland. I'm not entirely sure why, except there was a first-class aviation maintenance company based there servicing Swearingen Metros for the Swiss commuter airline Crossair, and we had a nose gear steering problem that they could quickly fix. However, to reach Zurich, we needed to refuel in Cardiff, which became our first stop for the day. The airport officials at Cardiff were lovely, helpful people, except when the immigration officer looked at our passports: Two Australian, one American, and one New Zealander.

With a twinkle in his eye, he said to me, "You've come for the game, boyo?"

When I replied, "What game?"

Somewhat bewildered, he said, "The All Blacks; they're playing at Cardiff Arms today. You must know that, boyo?"

The last thing in my complex globe-trotting program was keeping track of international rugby, so I flippantly answered that I'd only just arrived from America, and was aware that the Dallas Cowboys were playing the Pittsburg Steelers today, and did he happen to have the results? The outcome of this exchange was complementary tea and biscuits for Colin, Judy, and Marilyn, but none for me. The good news was they did give us fuel, but probably not on my account. They saw my three passengers as victims, traveling with a worthless New Zealander.

Our arrival at Zurich Airport was through dense clouds, snow showers, and piss-poor visibility. No sign of the beautiful Swiss Alps, and thank you, you hotshot instrument pilot for not running into any of those granite-filled clouds. Jet Aviation, the company in Zurich that handled us and fixed our nose-wheel steering problem provided an excellent service, but at European elitist celebrity prices. Trying to bullshit them with my, 'I'm just a simple country boy from New Zealand' didn't do the job. The result was an expensive overnight stop with Jet Aviation, the hotel accommodation, the meals, and the transport to and from the hotel. In 40 years, I've never bothered to go back to Switzerland, despite the support from my youngest daughter-in-law, Simone, a Swiss national.

The next day, climbing rapidly out of Zurich and its miserable weather, we headed southeast to the island of Crete with its Mediterranean climate, excellent food, retsina wine, non-elitist culture ... all of it at affordable prices. We decided to spend two nights on Crete, taking a day off to visit Knossos, the Bronze Age archaeological site that had been called Europe's oldest city. Playing tourists again was strange, but the experience informative and a relaxing time away from the demands of flying small airplanes around the globe. Airborne again, we headed southeast to Dubai, a direct flight of 2,200 miles. Another comfortable stopover in Dubai, followed by the direct flight to Madras, where my dealings with the airport bureaucracy had become a routine exercise in winning the arguments. Then it was the last segment to Singapore, landing at the General Aviation Airport of Seletar, where Colin worked with our maintenance folks to make a few minor repairs to the 3B before we delivered it to Bangkok.

In the last week of October, accompanied by Colin and Judy, I flew the Merlin-3B to Bangkok, and after landing, proceeded to the Royal Thai Army parking area to be met by a large welcoming party of Thai Army pilots and maintenance personnel. What Stillwell's had failed to tell me was that Bangkok would be my home, on and off, for the next four months. The task: Type Conversion Instructor with the Merlin-3B for five Thai Army pilots, giving dual instruction on the aircraft in the local Bangkok airport area, followed by cross-country flights around the boundaries of northern Thailand, with landings at military airfields. Some of these I remembered from my Vietnam-Laos days, but others were from a list that probably only the CIA had back then. I found the experience strange because the senior Thai military personnel trusted me as an equal, and apparently, no security threat within Thailand's Defense Forces. It's quite probable they had my credentials and military service background checked through the American Embassy, including the CIA. Some of this still remains a mystery to me, but I must say I enjoyed being back in the company of soldiers.

Some wag said that nostalgia isn't what it used to be, but flying over the Thai Air Force airfield at Udorn evoked memories from my early time at this location, and in the Laotian city of Vientiane, just across the Mekong River. These places were full of bittersweet nostalgia for a moment in my history that could never return. The year was 1960 and I had recently turned 21, a significant milestone that had been spent getting drunk in Hong Kong (all costs met by my crew). One month later, as a New Zealand Air Force pilot, I was flying a mission into Vientiane, distributing schoolbooks, gifts from New Zealand to the children of Laos. Twenty years later, looking down on the Udorn airfield, which had been transformed by the US Air Force at the beginning of the Vietnam war in 1965, the memories flooded back.

Early in 1981, my pilot's logbook shows a series of Merlin 3B flights around Australia's Outback, for what purpose I don't recall. John Flynn was with me for some of the trips, and other pilot names that I don't recognize after 40 years. The flights were from Melbourne (Essendon Airport) to Mangalore, Gladstone, Morombah, Mount Isa, Birdsville, and Broken Hill. Today, I'd need an atlas to find these places on a map, let alone remember what we were doing there. The Australian Merlin-3Bs I flew, often in command, were VH registered planes, that is Australian, and I was without a pilot's license for the country, which raises the question of how I was legal to fly Thailand registered planes. I wasn't, but nobody ever asked—except for a US air traffic controller one dark night over Ohio, when operating one of the Thai Merlin 4s, which had a Thai registration callsign.

The controller asked in a curious tone, "You sound like an Aussie, so why are you flying a Thai Air Force plane over the US of A?"

My facetious response was, "It's complex, and I'm not at liberty to tell you."

He came back with an, "Okay, I understand, you're one of those." Whatever that meant.

The final act of my Stillwell years played out with a most ambitious odyssey, beginning with one last visit to San Antonio in Texas. This time to take delivery of Swearengin's latest version of the Metroliner, the Metro-3, a totally revamped design of the Metro-2. The cabin was still designed to hold 19 passengers, but a faster, higher, quieter commuter airplane in so many different ways to a Metro-2. I took delivery of an early production model for Stillwell's, with the grand plan of a demonstration tour from Burma in the west, to Taiwan in the north, Philippines and Borneo to the east, Indonesia, Australia, and New Zealand to the south, all from my home in Singapore. Because the airplane would remain in US registration for the duration of the tour, it was necessary for me and the other participating Stillwell pilot, Keith Powles, to be checked out on the Metro-3 by an approved FAA check airman. This latest version of Metroliner had been FAA certified to operate above the arbitrary takeoff weight of 12,500 pounds, therefore requiring pilots to be type-rated. Furthermore, it was not approved for single-pilot operations.

Just before taking delivery of this plane, I sat—and passed—the written test for the FAA Airline Transport Pilot (ATP) License, so to complete its issuance, I combined my Metro-3 type rating flight with an ATP check ride by a local FAA check airman. I remember the flight as demanding, with Rick the Check Airman, requiring me to perform instrument approaches at a variety of small Texas airfields: San Marcos, Braunfels, Kerrville, and Austin. When Keith arrived from Australia, Rick flew with him in our plane, before signing him off for the Type-Rating on his FAA Commercial Pilot License. With those tasks completed, Keith and I were free to leave for Singapore and Australia.

The first day got us to St. Johns, Newfoundland, with a brief stop at Buffalo for customs and immigration clearances for leaving the USA. The next day took us to Santa Maria and on to Palma Majorca in Spain. I'm vague as to why we chose Palma, but my best guess was that Bill Fuller, who was accompanied by his wife, liked the idea of this exotic location. Whatever, it was a pleasant but expensive tourist stopover. We departed Palma, flying east down the Mediterranean Sea to Iraklion on Crete, now one of my favorite stops in southern Europe. Sadly, I couldn't justify another rest day on Crete because we were running on a tight schedule to meet Stillwell's planned demo tour in Australia and New Zealand. Next was a quick refuel for the Metro-3 at Luxor, before continuing the same day to Dubai, followed by a similar one-day run to Singapore after refueling at Madras.

Given only three days of rest at my Singapore home, we headed southeast to Bali, Darwin, and Melbourne, flying day and night over 22 hours to keep the company happy. Keith and I took turns in the cockpit, with alternating break periods of sleep in the cabin. The good news was having Marilyn, my partner, on board for the duration of the tour Down Under. We had another three-day break in Melbourne before flying across the Tasman Sea to Wellington, New Zealand, to begin the tour proper. We visited many locations, giving demo flights to numerous local airlines, large and small, but the two highlights were a round trip to the Chatham Islands, and then to Rotorua, the familial town of my family, for the most essential occasion of the marriage between Marilyn and me. My mother and father were there as well as my brother and his family. A beautiful interlude in our odyssey.

Once complete in New Zealand, we took the Metro-3 back across the Tasman Sea to Australia for demonstration flights from Sydney, Brisbane, Alice Springs, and Mount Isa, before heading northwest to Singapore, via Port Headland. With my new bride safely back in our Peace Mansion home in downtown Singapore, Keith and I, accompanied by our Stillwell's sales crew, flew to Kuala Lumpur and Kota Bahru in Peninsula Malaysia. Then it was across the South China Sea to Miri and Kota Kinabalu in East Malaysia. Next on the tour list was Manila, Baguio, and Bagabag in the Philippines, quickly followed by demonstrations in Taiwan, Thailand, and finally to one of the few places in Southeast Asia I'd never been—Burma. Then there was only one thing left to do: Keith and I to fly the aircraft from Singapore back to Melbourne, where it was destined to remain. After being with this first-class aircraft that never let us down during 220 hours of flying the world over three months, it was tough to bid farewell to this loveable metal friend.

As it happened, my always exciting days flying for Stillwell's were over. They offered me a follow-up job as their sales rep in New Zealand, which I was foolish enough to accept. The only benefit that came from our six-month stay in New Zealand was the birth of our son, Jordan. He was born prematurely by many weeks, struggling to survive in an incubator for 15 days, but so blessed to be in one of the most excellent pediatric hospitals in the South Pacific.

By the end of my three-year tenure with Stillwell's, I'd accumulated 750 flight hours on Swearingen airplanes, many of those hours on extended overwater flights: the Atlantic, the Pacific, the Persian Gulf and the South China Sea. Mostly I flew as a single pilot, enjoying the freedom that gave me and being left alone to make my own en route choices. They were good years to be a professional pilot, like me, who knew what he was doing. Although being paid a small salary for these flights, I remember them as the best flying I ever did, where every mission was a challenge in planning, execution, logistics, and doing it my way.

1982: Jetting to Bougainville Island

The only difficult thing about flying a jet plane
is getting the job in the first place

~ Neddie Morris

HIGH IN THE TROPICAL RAIN FORESTS of Bougainville's Crown Prince Range, Bougainville Copper Limited (BCL) established one of the world's major open-cut mines to work the Panguna porphyry copper deposit. The mine had begun commercial production in April 1972. Massive by any standards, the mine provided 120,000 tons of ore a day for processing to copper concentrate, a premium product because of its additional gold and silver content. At its peak, the Panguna mine was one of the biggest single suppliers of copper and gold in the world.

My association with BCL began in mid-1982, hired as one of five company pilots for their Westwind corporate jet airplane. The Westwind had been delivered from Israel the year before to replace a Swearingen Merlin-3 turboprop that BCL had used for company transport between Australia and Bougainville Island. The Israeli-built Westwind was an absolute delight to fly with its two powerful turbofan engines, a cockpit full of the latest flight instrumentation, weather radar, an extended overwater navigation system, and HF long-range communication radio. Our scheduling,

224

training, and flight operations were extremely professional thanks to the leadership and organizational skills of Neil Morris, the chief pilot at BCL. Neil had come to the rescue of Marilyn and our son, Jordan, and me, providing the job with BCL, thus allowing us to escape the limitations of New Zealand aviation, miserable weather, and a general ennui with the country of my birth.

All pilots were based in the tropical Queensland city of Townsville, with aircraft maintenance handled at Kieta Airfield on the eastern coast of Bougainville Island. The Westwind was Papua New Guinea (PNG) registered, and as such, could only be flown and maintained by PNG licensed personnel. The BCL aircraft operation used a regular timetable, with the primary sector being Townsville to Kieta and return. Keita to Brisbane and return was flown with less frequency, and there was a once-weekly flight between Kieta and Port Moresby, the capital of PNG. For pilots, the regular timetable meant not being on constant call, unlike many other corporate aircraft operations. Our homes and families were based in Townsville, with the pilots requiring frequent layovers at Bougainville and Brisbane.

Unlike previous commercial aviation jobs I had suffered since leaving the Air Force, BCL paid good salaries, provided other benefits such as low-interest house purchase loans, and additional medical coverage. Essentially, this was my first real employment opportunity in the civilian world, and with the bonus of flying a high-performance jet-powered airplane. It had been 20 years since I'd last flown a turbojet, the De Havilland Vampire fighter/bomber, an experience that had been incredibly exciting, albeit short-lived. After operating propeller-driven airplanes for so long, the opportunity to fly the turbojet-powered Westwind became a window into a future that had been unattainable for 20 years. The mantra had so often been, *If you've never flown a jet, then you can't possibly do it.* As a generation of military and airline pilots learned during the 1950s–1960s, piston-engine/propeller airplanes' transition to jets was easy, stress-free, and fun.

My conversion training on the Westwind began with a classroom-centered ground school held at Essendon Airport, near Melbourne. The closest flight simulator for the Westwind was in the USA, owned by Flight Safety and located at Wilmington Airport in Delaware. Therefore, actual flight training was done on BCL's aircraft operating out of Townsville, Cairns, and Kieta airports with Dave Berry from Essendon. Handling the Westwind, its navigation systems, and the two rear-mounted turbofan engines was like a wet dream come true. I had loved flying around the world in the Merlin 3-Bs with their twin turboprop engines, but driving this powerful jet plane was a significant step toward an exciting aviation future. As it happened, only a few years later, I would be flying the big jets—the three-engine Boeing 727 and four-engine Boeing 747, both faster than the Westwind, though lacking the glamour and opulence of this brand new corporate jet.

To complete my transition to flying a PNG registered airplane, I was required to spend a week at Port Moresby, studying for and passing written exams on the PNG Civil Aviation Regulations to be granted a Senior Commercial Pilot License and Instrument Rating. I've often told an attentive audience of white-guilt woke liberal Americans in Reno that to have the PNG license issued, I was required to show up in a grass skirt, a bone through my nose, and holding a spear. Retired pilots in the audience, mostly military, thought it was a hilarious joke. Others would snigger or be appalled ... until I said, "Just joking." Oddly, a few didn't return to the next episode of my *Sixty Years of*

Living Dangerously presentations. I guess stand-up comedy was not their thing.

On the home front in Townsville, Marilyn had found a rental house for our family near the main coastal beach of Townsville. It was an old Queenslander built in the days before air-conditioning, standing on 15-foot high stilts to keep the crocodiles, snakes, and other creepy-crawlies beneath the floor during the high flood levels in the wet summers. When Little Jordan was only-two-months old we settled in Townsville with the climate pleasantly cool and the humidity low, making the next few months a comfortable environment for baby Jordan and us. After completing my conversion training, I settled into the routine of the BCL timetable: Townsville to Bougainville and return the next day; Townsville to Bougainville to Brisbane, layover, then back to Bougainville, layover, then return to Townsville. Time at home with the family alternated between two days and three-day blocks off, but workdays could fall over weekends and public holidays. For me, the most unbelievable aspect of our schedules was that each pilot had an entitlement of six weeks' annual vacation, thanks to the current Australian labor union awards. Furthermore, during those six weeks, our salaries were increased by a 17 percent bonus payment, because we were not available to bid for overtime work on vacation! I learned that being employed in Australia had unique advantages.

One year later, we had purchased our own home in the Townsville suburb of Wulguru on a road that backed up to the slopes of Mount Stuart, the highest point on the southern side of the city. To my delight, there was a rough trail that began behind our house and climbed a ridgeline to intercept the access road leading to the 1,900-feet peak of Mount Stuart. During the dry, cool season of 1983, I hiked this trail to the summit regularly, a climb of 1,800 feet and a round trip of ten miles back to the house and ran along the Ross River banks up to 15 miles per week. The Mount Stuart climbs were additional training in preparation for a planned hiking trip in Nepal, an adventure that involved a four-week trek around the 250-mile long Annapurna Circuit, taking maximum advantage of my first glorious six-week vacation from BCL.

With its tropical climate, Townsville became an ideal location for my outdoor fitness activities, particularly during the cooler months of the dry season, April to September. However, the wet season created outdoor misery with high temperatures and humidity, as well as dangers from jellyfish and crocodiles along the ocean beaches; and on land, some of the most poisonous snakes in the world, like the Coastal taipan! These deadly snakes were in the bush country throughout the year and along the trails I hiked, but during the dry season, they were easy to see moving within the dead undergrowth. Not so in the wet season; after the rains had nourished the grasses and low scrub, not only were snakes more plentiful but concealed until almost standing on them. Being that close to a taipan was not the smartest thing to do since they were aggressive when cornered and would actively defend themselves. The record of people being bitten by taipans and not receiving the appropriate antivenin in time, with few exceptions, had always resulted in death. The taipan's venom was rated at eight times more toxic than the Indian cobra.

Despite the risks posed by poisonous snakes, I continued hiking the jungle-covered hills along northern Queensland's coastal ranges. One favorite location was on the 4,000-foot peak of Mount Elliot and Alligator Creek, which flowed down a steep granite bluff on the mountain's eastern side. For our family, this creek became a fresh water sanctuary, a place to avoid the dangers of swimming at the coastal beaches, with the waters teeming with Box jellyfish during the wet season from November to May. A curtain of death dangles below the Box jellyfish, with multiple tentacles containing one of the most toxic venoms known to man. For decades along the northern Australian coasts, many people have died in agonizing pain and shock from contact with this jellyfish. Nevertheless, during the dry season, we would take Jordan, our small son, to the ocean beaches, carrying large bottles of vinegar for emergency use if any of us were stung. Attempting to pull or rub tentacles off a victim's skin increases the venom's injection into the body, but flooding the tentacles with vinegar prevents any undischarged stinging cells from releasing their poison.

With so many dangerous critters in the sea and on the land around Australia, visitors and new immigrants to the country naturally have concerns about their day-to-day survival and are curious about the longtime residents' apparent ease in this menacing environment. When first signing up for the government's medical insurance, we were issued a small booklet that described all the nasty critters in the sea and the land in tropical northern Queensland. The booklet was filled with warnings, precautions, first aid procedures, and locating the correct medical treatments. The critter list included Box jellyfish (top of the list), land and sea snakes, sharks, crocodiles, spiders, blue-ringed octopus, stone fish, cone shells, and numerous ticks, wasps, hornets, etc. A cornucopia of ways to die in the most painful circumstances. In previous years I had worked, lived, and exercised (running) in the Southeast Asian jungles of the Malayan Peninsula and Borneo, but the level of risk trying to stay fit in the outdoors around the Townsville area had notched up tenfold.

By early 1984, we had achieved harmony with the

potential hazards and settled into enjoying the pleasures of living in a semi-tropical environment. We'd installed air-conditioning throughout our pleasant three-bedroom house, drove a new Mazda air-conditioned car around town and to places like Alligator Creek, 20 miles southeast of the city. Marilyn would drop me at the airport at the beginning of a three- to five-day flight sequence in BCL's Westwind. When I returned to Townsville, I could be off for three to five days. Our crew complement was three Captains—Neil Morris, me, and Greg Cox, with two First Officers, Shaun Davis and Bruce Walker—enough combinations of two pilots to keep the Westwind flying every day of the week. We had three full-time airplane mechanics; Rick Steward was based in Townsville, with Peter Bowdery and Dan Stuart living near Kieta Airfield on Bougainville. At this airfield, BCL had its own hangar where the majority of routine maintenance on the Westwind was performed.

Unfortunately, like so many corporate flight operations around the world, when company cost-cutting was needed, the first thing to go was either pilots, the airplane, or both. In the case of BCL in late 1984, with the price of Copper dropping, the company decided to reduce the pilot numbers by March 1985. Bruce Walker and I were the two casualties of that decision. During the period of the three-month given notice, I made numerous overtures to similar corporate flight operators across Australia and a few mercenary opportunities like becoming a Singapore Air Force flight instructor, or a C-130 Hercules pilot in Nigeria. At this stage, I remained a New Zealand citizen, with my wife Marilyn a US citizen, and Jordan, a citizen of both countries.

1983: Annapurna and Beyond

I knew that people died in mountains, long before I had my
accident (Touching the Void). I sort of understood you were
playing a game for very high stakes and you might not actually
have a choice over your fate.

~ The Beckoning Silence, Joe Simpson

NEVER IN MY 25-YEAR working life did I have, or expect to
have, the freedom of six weeks paid leave in one continuous
block. So, in the last few months of 1983, the result was a
zany scheme, long overdue, to go trekking in Nepal. It
would be the fulfillment of a long-held dream that dated
back to the mid-1960s when I'd flown an Air Force plane
into Kathmandu, bringing hospital and school equipment
for Ed Hillary's Sherpa projects. In those days, trekking was
not a commercial enterprise, but rather something the
British Gurkha officers and their families did during their
assignments in Nepal. By 1983, trekking in Nepal was an
early indicator of Adventure Tourism, but fortuitously for
me, it was still in its growth stage. At that time in Australia,
only one travel company, Australian Himalayan Expeditions
(AHE), offered extreme adventure trips in Nepal. I signed
up with them for their most challenging package, the
Annapurna Circuit, a 24-day, 250-mile hike, including the
crossing of Thorong La, a 17,700-foot mountain pass.

The start date for the trek was November 8, with a completion date of December 2, beginning and ending near the city of Pokhara. The expedition package included air travel from Sydney to Kathmandu, with overnight accommodation in Bangkok and two nights on arrival in Kathmandu. During my transit stop at Sydney Airport, I met Malcolm (Mal) Hill, a retired Australian Navy veteran close to my age, traveling to Nepal for the same adventure with AHE. We had no conception that this serendipitous meeting would last a lifetime and become a mutual inspiration for every adventure we had—and there were many—for the next 30 years.

Arriving in Kathmandu, we were met, organized, and briefed by AHE personnel. I was interested to learn that there would be two AHE trekking groups on the Annapurna Circuit, comprised of 12 clients each, one AHE Guide, and a large group of Sherpas and porters. In my group, which fortunately included Mal, our guide was Janey Davis, an attractive young lady from Wales. Our sirdar (Sherpa leader) was Tundu, an excellent local guide in his early fifties, who looked and acted like a much younger man. Because of our similar ages and budding friendship, Mal and I were assigned as tent-mates for the next 24 days. The other ten clients were all Australians, mostly from professional occupations, in ages from the late twenties to early thirties. Two couples, and the rest, single men and women. Without being aware, I was considered an outlier by everybody but Mal, who told me on the quiet that the others thought me as somewhat aloof—whatever that meant. The others were interesting people, and I enjoyed their company for the many days we were together, but unlike Mal and me, both Southeast Asia War veterans, I thought they were the standoffish ones. Perhaps some of them had been anti-Vietnam War demonstrators during their university years?

We bussed from Kathmandu to Bengas Tal, a beautiful lake near Pokhara, spent two nights camped there before hiking north to intercept the Marsyandi Valley at the small village of Bhulebhule. This placed us on the main trail of the Annapurna Circuit, which we planned to hike in a counterclockwise direction. It was also here that we began to pass or be passed by other trekkers, some in groups like ours and others traveling in twos and threes. Most appeared to be from Western Europe, Australia and Israel, but surprisingly few from North America. Where were all the Yanks, we wondered? Mal made the astute observation that maybe we had left too late to be trekking in Nepal because the signs were that the world's hoi polloi had already discovered adventure tourism. Ten years later, the two of us returned to Nepal to climb the highest trekking peak, Mera, with a summit of 21,300 feet, only to realize how wrong Mal had been. By 1992, the trekking trails in Nepal were jammed with wannabe hikers and climbers. They had the money to visit and hike in Nepal, but many lacked outdoor experience or physical ability. Looking back to the Annapurna Circuit in 1983, we had been front-runners as Nepal trekkers, well ahead of the crowds that would eventually invade the place.

I remember this as a *magical mystery tour* around the Annapurna Massif; every day was different, but with the same routine, from wake-up with *bed-tea*, packing up, heading out on the trail until settling into a new campsite for dinner and a well-earned rest. Unlike today, around the Annapurna Circuit in 1983, there were no roads, no airfields, and no hotels or inns. With a few exceptions, every night of the 24 days, we lived in tents, and I can only recall two rest days, one at Manang and one at Muktinath. During the 15 days it took to navigate and climb the Marsyandi

Valley, I'd suffered a respiratory infection, possibly caused by trail dust polluted by yaks, donkeys, goats, and human excrement. The condition was exacerbated by the increasing cold environment as we ascended to the eastern Thorong La base camp of Phedi, located at 15,000 feet. On the way we passed a dead porter, surrounded by grieving friends. Cause of death—altitude?

Trying to sleep at Phedi was difficult. I'd never climbed to such a high altitude in the mountains before, and the congestion in my chest was getting worse, accompanied by wet coughing and deep down wheezing. Experience told me I had severe bronchitis that required treatment with antibiotics. Janey, our guide, carried a complete medical kit, including a variety of antibiotics, but wouldn't provide them to me in case I was actually suffering from HAPE (high altitude pulmonary edema). She explained that antibiotic treatment could mask the HAPE, which I later learned was a specious argument because she still expected me to climb another 3,000 feet over the Pass. If I did indeed have HAPE, the correct treatment would have been to descend back through the Marsyandi Valley to a lower altitude.

Tundu, our sirdar, decided our group would leave Phedi for the Thorong crossing shortly after midnight. His justification—making sure our porters, with their heavy loads, didn't take frequent rest stops in the well-below freezing conditions of the night. The warmth of the morning sun wouldn't touch them until over the Pass and on the long descent to Muktinath. This plan was not in my best interests, but I was expected to stay with the group, and unwisely didn't object, even with severe doubts on my ability to do the climb. A steep ascent during the first hour, then slackening off slightly with a series of switchbacks. Everything frozen, making the crossing of streams and

234

snow slopes hazardous. Fortunately there was sufficient moonlight to make the night travel possible, but after two hours I was suffering from the cold and extreme effort. Assisted by Tundu and Mal, I finally made the Pass after five hours of climbing, with the sun just rising, but everyone was cold and hurried into the long descent. Another five hours I arrived at Muktinath at an altitude of 12,500 feet. Once there, lying exhausted and barely alive in my tent, Janey finally agreed to give me a dose of Bactrim antibiotics. Less than 24 hours later, my congestion, coughing and wheezing had disappeared. I was aware that I'd nearly died up there on the Pass, so to this day, I remain eternally grateful to Mal and the Sherpas for keeping me alive.

The strange paradox of this near-death experience was how it most likely continued to save my life in later years. In 1983, I had been smoking cigarettes for 25 years, having started the habit at age 17 when I joined the New Zealand Air Force. During the long hike up the Marsyandi Valley, I had been smoking top quality Benson and Hedges English cigarettes, which I'd purchased duty-free at Bangkok Airport. Even as my bronchitis progressed, I continued to smoke during rest stops, envied by many of the Sherpas and porters smoking their evil-smelling local cigarettes. I possibly smoked at Phedi, and if I did, it would have been the last cigarette I ever smoked, because after surviving the climb to Thorong La, I stopped cold turkey for eternity. Perhaps the description of that near-fatal night, written in my climbing journal provides some explanation:

I realize I'm dying for the third time: The first in an out-of-control airplane where my short life was relived before impact with the ground, and the second, freefalling into the Atlantic Ocean, hundreds of miles from land. They were jarring, terrifying experiences, but strangely this third encounter with death did not frighten me.

235

Now, on a steep mountainside in Nepal, I observe segments from my nicotine-infused lungs coughed onto the moonlit snow. Although no longer a reckless flyboy, I still hold out some hope for immortality despite my body shutting down in the cold, high altitude. Realistically, I'm too knackered and too cold to honestly care.

Why am I dying in this godforsaken place on a quest to reach the 17,700-foot summit of Thorong La? In airplanes, I always retained some control over my fate, but here, the mountain is master.

All was not lost. Mal, my new hiking mate, a true-blue Aussie, arrives in time to save me, accompanied by Tundu, our trusty Sherpa guide. Mal murmurs encouragement in my frozen ears while Tundu replaces my inadequate mittens with his own. On it goes, supported by these two gems of humanity, ten steps forward, stop, hack, spit, and pause, ten steps forward ... forever, it seems.

After my amazing recovery at Muktinath, hiking down the Kali Gandaki River valley was like a dream walk. No longer suffering from respiratory problems, combined with the cessation of cigarette smoking, I felt marvelously alive on this four-day downhill section to the village of Tatopani and its hot water springs. The following two days involved a climb of 6,000 feet to the village of Ghoropani, with its stunning views of the Annapurna and Himchuli peaks. Then it was a gradual descent for the last two trail days that brought us into the town of Pokhara. We camped that night at Phewa Lake, surrounded by the white trash of travel, most of them smoking hash, doing other drugs. This pathetic, scruffy crowd of stoned Westerners, entirely blind to the majesty of the high mountains that stand north of Pokhara.

Then it was the final day of agony, a seven-hour bus ride from Pokhara to Kathmandu. Like good wine, the Nepalese don't travel well; there was projectile vomiting from one of our porters over Mal and me, so the hot showers at the Kathmandu Sheraton hotel, were not only a pleasure but a necessity. That night's cuisine was goat meat curry washed down with duty-free Scotch and Indian beer chasers, followed by sleeping in real beds. The pleasure was sublime.

The next day, before flying back to Australia, Mal and I revisited the adventure while drinking pints of beer on the hotel veranda. Because Mal had a recent background of rock climbing and I had a distant past of ice-snow climbing, he offered the crazy suggestion that the two of us return to Nepal, without a group, to climb one of the 20,000 feet, so-called trekking peaks. That did happen, but for reasons beyond our control, it was nine years before that wish came true. At that time in Kathmandu, I was 44, and Mal, 42, so we had accepted we were living on borrowed time for playing in the games of extreme adventure. However, after completing the Annapurna Circuit in fine style for older folks, Mal and I forged a partnership that would take us to places, doing dangerous things that we could never imagine in those early days. This first demanding journey we'd completed was nothing more than an easy warm-up to what would come later.

From my perspective about the journey, I'd learned some valuable lessons that would launch me into a future that would place my passion for climbing mountains on an equal footing with flying airplanes. Significantly, I had to decide whether to use, and then work with, an organized group on future adventures. If I did travel again with a large group, I would carry my own medications for altitude acclimation (Diamox), respiratory infections (antibiotics), and dysentery (Flagyl). Also, I would retain the freedom to opt-out of decisions made by a group leader that adversely affected my health or safety. After all, I was not some greenhorn urban dweller trying to fill a bucket list, seeking adventures that I never had felt a passion for; I was already the real thing. At age 19, I had been trained by New Zealand's finest alpine mountaineers in preparation for spending five months flying small ski-planes in Antarctica. I was competent on steep snow and ice, self-extraction from crevasses, building igloos, and using cross-country skis. Later, in Southeast Asia, I would experience jungle survival training, including escape and evasion from a jungle-based enemy.

Today's reality TV survivor shows are pathetic. During my years of training, the only way to be voted off the island was in a body bag, having been bitten by a cobra or a banded krait or maybe hit by a 7.62 mm bullet from a AK-47.

Annapurna had a profound influence on my life for many years after. Often, drifting into sleep back in Australia or Bougainville, I could revisit every twist and turn on that 250 miles of trail. A most evocative experience, seeing not only the trail but the people involved. Sometimes I experimented with making Nepalese food like Dhal Bhat (curried lentils and rice), curries with goat meat, and momos (meat and garlic filled dumplings). Once back home in Australia, Mal and I kept in regular contact, including meeting in Brisbane during my overnights there with the BCL Westwind. Mal worked for the British computer company, International Computers Limited (ICL), in their Australian based division, and coincidently was familiar with BCL. At the mine on Bougainville, ICL had built BCL's computer system, which Mal had often visited in the Westwind I flew. It's a small world in the South Pacific.

For the next year, until my expected six-week vacation occurred, Mal and I began plotting our next great adventure. We made a decision that before returning to Nepal for the *Big Climb*, we needed to acquire professional skills in alpine mountaineering, and the very best place to do that was back on my pre-Antarctic turf, the Mount Cook National Park in New Zealand. Our instructors were with Alpine guides based at the Mount Cook Village: three Kiwis—Don, Kevin, Paul, and one German—Erwin.

These four were top-class, hard-ass alpine climbers. After Mal and I signed up for this two-week extreme course with Alpine guides, we showed up with attitudes of natural self-confidence, despite being in our mid-forties and 20 years older than the other six clients on the course. I don't recall either us being concerned about the high level of risk involved in the training, nor did we opt out of any potentially hazardous exercises—and there were plenty of those.

The training began with a day of rock scrambling, running descents on steep scree, and abseiling exercises down a vertical cliff face. For me, the most striking aspect of the abseiling (also known as rappelling), was the dramatic advances in climbing equipment from my first alpine training 25 years before. Ropes had changed from the hawser-laid natural fiber design to Kernmantel nylon ropes, constructed with a braided sheath covering an inside core, and far superior to hawser-laid manila by having better handling and dynamic properties. The standard double-rope system for abseiling was now fed through a Figure 8 metal descender, attached to a locking karabiner, which in turn was fixed to a seat harness. This latest abseiling equipment, always a dangerous activity, had undoubtedly lowered the risk level by a large margin.

The following four days were spent on the Hooker Glacier learning the techniques of roped travel on ice and steep snow, equipped with ice-axes, crampons, alpine hammers, snow stakes, seat harnesses, karabiners, and prusik slings. Most of this equipment was familiar to me, but again, every item was of an advanced design from what I had used in 1959. The ice-ax shafts were made of aluminum and not wood (which could break), the crampons now had 12 points and not the original ten. The two additional points were at the front, which provided the ability to 'front-point' when climbing steep snow slopes or aiding self-extraction from a crevasse. The seat harness provided a fixed, non-slipping body connection for fixed belays, crevasse falls, and gear attachment. Besides, we were wearing the latest boots for ice and snow travel, made with a plastic outer and soft inner bootie with a rigid sole for front-pointing using crampons.

The ultimate new assets, so advanced from my past, was clothing: soft pullovers and long pants made of synthetic Poly-Pro that was superior to wool in retaining warmth, even when wet; wind and rainproof jackets/pants made from space-age materials like Gore-Tex that breathed, even in heavy rain or snow. During our training, it became evident that new alpine climbing techniques were being developed as a result of the latest equipment and clothing now available. Looking back at that incredible transition that Mal and I experienced in 1984, I believe I would have eschewed the climbing game forever if nothing had changed in equipment and clothing since the 1960s.

The final week of our training with Alpine guides was spent on the upper sections of the Tasman Glacier. We were flown onto the glacier by a Mount Cook Airlines ski-plane, landing within close hiking distance of the Tasman Saddle Hut, our home and refuge for the next seven days. Two of those days were spent waiting out a blizzard with 60 miles-per-hour winds. The hut was located on a small rock outcrop, sitting on the very edge of a 200-foot cliff that dropped into a jumbled mass of crevasses on the glacier below. It was secured to the rock by numerous steel cables that vibrated in the strong winds and detectably moved the hut itself. It was a scary place even without the winds, but our usually high energy mountain instructors spent most of the storm on their bunks, sleeping or reading, only surfacing for food or needing the toilet. Visiting the toilet was another death-defying act at that place. It was located even closer to the edge of the cliff than the main hut, so a climbing rope had been rigged between the hut and toilet doors, along which we were instructed to clip-in from our climbing harness with a leash. On a good weather day, sitting on the toilet with the door open presented a vertiginous but fantastic view down the length of the Tasman Glacier.

When the weather finally cleared, the instruction was all about safe travel across crevassed terrain and secured climbing and descending on steep snow. For these exercises, we were roped together in pairs, the standard arrangement for unexpected crevasse falls and subsequent self-extraction. It also provided the most straightforward and fastest movement when using fixed belays on steep snow. The warm-up training included ice-ax self-arrest techniques and holding a falling/sliding partner, either by boot-ax or snow stake fixed belay. These were all done on a steep slope with a level run-out at the base of the incline to reduce the possibility of injury from an uncontrolled fall.

The actual climbing to the icy summits of two peaks, Aylmer and Hochstetter Dome, overlooking the head of Tasman Glacier, were realistically hazardous. On these exposed slopes, a fall not arrested by ice-ax or partner's belay would be fatal. Likewise, as pairs, we were required to drop vertically into a 50-foot deep crevasse, with one's partner holding the fall without being dragged into the crevasse as well. The difficult task was for the climber hanging in the crevasse to ascend the rope using two prusik slings, hence the term 'self-extraction.'

The final test for our group was a two-day hike from the Tasman Saddle to the end of the mountain road that leads from Mount Cook Village to the edge of the Ball Glacier. We were roped in pairs while descending the snow-covered upper sections of the Tasman Glacier and then solo hiked across the open ice of the glacier, with a side trip climbing up to the Malte Brun Hut to spend our last night sheltered there. In rain and wet snow showers, the climb to the hut was perilous on steep, sodden tussock grass, with the final challenge of crossing the flood-swollen Beetham Stream by a Tri-Wire bridge to reach the shelter. Erwin, the young German instructor, guided Mal and me on this critical section. We were wet and cold, with the wind shrieking down from the peak of Malte Brun, faced with two menacing 'damned if you don't, and dead if you do' options: wade the creek or use the Tri-Wire with its three wet cables in a strong wind while wearing 60-pound packs. With some trepidation and care, Mal and I used the Tri-Wire but were surprised to see Erwin crossing the torrent, eschewing the bridge because he thought it unsafe, which seemed odd because he was an experienced and accomplished alpine climber. Among other audacious challenges, he had solo climbed the North Face of the Eiger in Switzerland. Sadly, what Mal and I observed that day became our experience of a death foretold. Two weeks later, at the same location, with three new clients he sent across the Tri-Wire bridge, at age twenty-four, Erwin died attempting to wade the stream, losing his footing, then swept downhill and drowned between the moraine wall and the glacier ice.

Twenty years later, Paul, another of our instructors, died in an avalanche on Mount Tasman while guiding a group of newbie climbers. So much for risk management in alpine climbing. I used to think that my two passions, flying and mountaineering, needed similar talents—a strong sense of adventure and enhanced self-confidence. Yet I seemed to be one of the few pilots who possessed the level of stupidity to climb as well as fly. During my pre-Antarctic training in 1959, my first association with mountaineers left me in no doubt as to their view of flying. *Bloody dangerous contraptions; did you ever see the body parts around a mountain crash site? Well, we have, Mate! That's why they make you wear those string vests. Real handy—all the body fluids drip through—we just tie the ends together and pack out the solid remains. No weight problem!* This from a bunch of crazy mountain men who were lucky to see two climbing seasons without being buried in an avalanche, launched into space by a rockfall, or plunged into the cold blue hell of a deep crevasse.

On the last day with Alpine guides, we left the protection of Malte Brun Hut, descended to the hard exposed ice of Tasman Glacier, walked downhill to the rock-strewn moraine, and climbed up its wall to the Ball Glacier Road. There, we were met by guides from the village and driven down the road to civilization, imbibing from proffered bottles of dark rum. What a way to finish two weeks of alpine climbing Boot Camp. Mal and I left Mount Cook with confidence that in the future, we were prepared to deal with challenging alpine climbs in Nepal and elsewhere. By the end of the training with Alpine guides, at age 45, I was hooked and inspired to get out there and climb potentially dangerous mountains for as long as we could. That inspiration and passion lasted me until age 72, when my knees finally failed with advanced arthritis. In 2009, Mal at age 68 and me at age 70, successfully summited Mount Shasta (14,200 feet) in California, without using the tourist route on the south side, but the technical face on the west flank of the peak. We had been well trained, and by the end of our long, but unscathed climbing career, we were good examples of oldies with cojones.

Winging our way home to Australia, Mal to Brisbane and me to Townsville, both elated at our fitness and achievement in our mid-forties, we had no conception that we were approaching another pivotal point in our individual lives. Changes not only in our employment but where we would live in the next few years. We would not be climbing in Nepal for many years, but in the meantime I would have unlimited access to the mountains of North America, and Mal to the peaks of Europe.

1985: Finding a New Life in the USA

I felt lucky to be an alien: I could possess the country,
but the country could never possess me.

~ *The Mission Song,* John Le Carré

IN MARCH OF 1985, I had begun the process of emigrating from Australia to the United States. During the preceding three years, my American wife, Marilyn, and our infant son, Jordan, had lived contentedly in Townsville, a coastal city in Northern Queensland. We'd moved there from Singapore for employment with Bougainville Copper Ltd (BCL) as a pilot for their corporate jet aircraft.

I was out on the street without a suitable replacement flying job, but under the Australian unemployment rules of that time, the family was eligible for generous support with monthly welfare payments and continued medical coverage. I did receive one offer from New Zealand to be the chief pilot for Air Albatross at Nelson airport, but possibilities for similar employment in Australia were not forthcoming. Unfortunately, New Zealand was not a choice for me any longer. I'd left there in 1979 with no plans or desire to return.

During my 20 years' service in the New Zealand Air Force, I'd happily been stationed overseas, away from the country of my birth for seven years, then followed by six years as a civilian in Singapore and Australia. New Zealand, with its small population, unpleasant weather, parochial attitudes, and 1984 election of a contemptuous socialist prime minister, made it a place for me to avoid. The combination of his "nuclear free zone" stand—no more than an anti-USA political stunt—and his public hostility to the 'geriatric generals' (my fellow military officers) got my attention. I was aware that left-wing politics had dominated my homeland from the time David Lange came to power. He had attended Otahuhu College two years behind me and all he had going for him was a mealy-mouthed speaker and son of Communist parents. So, it was not exactly a case of *you can never go home again*, but instead I didn't recognize the country as my home anymore.

Left without any close-to-home employment options, I decided to attempt the unthinkable: a move to the United States seeking a flying job within the large corporate jet fraternity. I still retained contacts at two Flight Safety operations: the Fairchild Merlin and Metro training facility at San Antonio in Texas, and the IAI Westwind training facility at Wilmington in Delaware. My wife was not averse to returning permanently to the USA after five years absence from her family in Fort Wayne, Indiana, so the concept of leaving Australia and New Zealand had merit, assuming I could find a satisfactory flying job. The first hurdle to overcome was my lack of permanent residency in the USA. My New Zealand passport contained a multiple entry business visa for the USA, but I needed to obtain the so-called Green Card to be employed there, and would not be hired without it. Married to a US citizen for the previous four years, I had been eligible for Green Card status since the date of our marriage but had never seriously considered residing in the United States.

With Marilyn acting as sponsor, I began the tedious

task of completing the paperwork for a Green Card application, a process which could only be finalized by United States representatives in Australia. In the meantime, I flew to Los Angeles and then to Fort Wayne to take up temporary residence with Marilyn's mother, Loretta Hudson, and her two uncles. Arriving shortly before Easter, my first impression of early Spring weather in the upper Midwest was an unpleasant surprise after years of living in the tropical climes of Singapore, Queensland, and Bougainville Island. Concerned that I was probably on a wild goose chase whittling away our limited financial resources with international airfares between Australia and the USA became a constant companion, giving rise to some depression about what I hoped to achieve. Fortunately, Loretta and the two uncles at the Fort Wayne house made me feel very welcome and were most supportive of my job-hunting goals.

The first option for employment was a natural choice. With a simple phone call, Dick Kimm, the manager of the Flight Safety training facility at Wilmington, Delaware, invited me for an interview. He remembered me as an excellent student from April 1983, attending a requalification course on flying BCL's Westwind airplane. So I took an airline flight from Fort Wayne to Philadelphia, then a bus shuttle to Wilmington for the interview. Dick Kimm was most decisive in offering me a job with Flight Safety. I would be employed as both a flight and simulator instructor on the Westwind, and provide liaison with Flight Safety's international Westwind customers. At the time, I held a unique combination of pilot licenses: airline transport pilot for both New Zealand and the United States; senior commercial pilot for both Australia and Papua New Guinea. Also, as a permanent resident of the USA, and a New Zealand passport holder, I would have easy access in and out of countries in Australasia and Western Europe. The offer included a starting salary of US $30,000 per annum, medical insurance, retirement package (401K) and two weeks' vacation, which I assumed was for the first year, only to have it explained by Dick that the two weeks' would apply for the first five years of my employment! This was my awakening to one of the inconsistencies from my past when working in the USA. The employment package flying the Westwind for BCL had provided six weeks' vacation per year, beginning with the first year.

Overall, the offer to work for Flight Safety was attractive and immediately available to an out-of-work foreign misfit like me. Early acceptance would mean no more job hunting in this unfamiliar environment, and relief for my family back in Australia. I gave Dick Kimm my tentative acceptance, dependent on being issued the Green Card, that required me visiting the US Consulate in Sydney back in Australia. I did my best to sound excited by the offer, but when settled on the flight back to Fort Wayne from Philadelphia I began having misgivings about working anywhere in the USA; because of the ridiculously limited vacation package.

The critical turning point occurred on the flight back to Australia. A pilot friend flying for Qantas had suggested I meet with his American friend, Lee Manelski, who was a pilot with Trans World Airways (TWA) and a professional civilian aerobatic flier. At the time, Lee was living above his private hangar at Santa Paula Airport near Ventura, California. With a two-day stopover in Los Angeles on my journey back to Australia, I reluctantly made an effort to drive from Marina Del Rey, where I was staying, north to Highway 101, then northwest to Ventura and northeast on Hwy 126 to Santa Paula.

When I explained to Lee what I had hoped to achieve

from my US aviation search, he asked the question as to why I hadn't considered the airlines, and in particular the night freight operators, to solve my American vacation conundrum. He patiently explained that although the two-week vacation limit would still apply for initial employment with an airline, the standard crew scheduling system was often based on 'two weeks on–two weeks off.' Therefore, when bidding for specific scheduled work lines, all that was needed for a six-week vacation was to bracket your two-week vacation with a 'two week off' period at each end.

Furthermore, Lee would put me touch with a management pilot at Orion Air, based in Raleigh, North Carolina. Orion operated a fleet of B-747s, DC-8s, B-727s, and DC-9s, all in the night freight business. Orion, with its airline certificate, was a pilot and maintenance contractor, operating fleets of freight aircraft owned by United Parcel Service (UPS), Emery Worldwide, and Purolator Courier.

Before departing Los Angeles, I mailed a copy of my latest aviation resume to Lee's close friend at Orion Air. He was Fred Peters, retired US Navy pilot and past member of the Blue Angels Navy aerobatic display team. Lee and Fred had been fellow members of the USA Aerobatic (civilian) Team. Lee had information that Orion Air was actively hiring during that summer of 1985, so he recommended I make haste in finalizing my Green Card and be back in the USA as soon as possible for an interview. By early June, with my Legal Alien status approved, I arrived back in Fort Wayne in time for a scheduled appearance in Raleigh, North Carolina for an interview with Orion Air. Lee Manelski and Fred Peters had made it happen. It's not what you know, but who you know!

I decided my future employment situation made it safe to purchase a car—a five-year-old Chevy Impala station wagon that I would use to make my first road trip across the eastern states of the country from Fort Wayne, Indiana to Raleigh, North Carolina. On the way, I planned to visit Keith and Pam Hunt, an Australian couple I knew from my Bougainville days. They were living in Clarksburg, West Virginia, where Keith was a pilot for a small commuter airline. I was curious to learn why and how they'd found themselves in this rather remote part of the USA, and the background to Keith's employment with a small US airline. I spent a pleasant evening with them at their rented house while absorbing insights into surviving rural America as ex-pats from Australia and New Zealand. It turned out that they lacked permanent resident legal status in the country, and driving south the following day to North Carolina, I still wondered how they were making it work. Not long after my visit, they advised me by mail that Keith had found another commuter airline pilot job on the island of Guam. Then after a short period in Guam, they made what was to become a final move, to Rabaul in Papua New Guinea where Keith was back flying in a very familiar environment for him. He had been the chief pilot with BougAir when we'd first met on Bougainville Island in 1982. Sadly, he was killed in an aircraft accident not far from Rabaul.

Driving across country from Indiana through Ohio, then south to West Virginia, briefly through Virginia and finally into North Carolina to the city of Raleigh was an exciting and fascinating experience. It was difficult back then to comprehend that this vast eastern area of the USA would become my home territory for many years into the future. The interview process with Orion Air was well organized and in no way intimidating, perhaps because I was confident that having made it to an actual interview, I would be hired. Looking back to those two significant days, why was I so convinced of success, particularly at my age of 46 and an international pilot from New Zealand, Australia, and Papua New Guinea? From the first interview with Don McMillan, a Reserve US Air Force Officer, then with Fred Peters retired from the US Navy, and finally, with other management pilots who'd flown KC-135s with the USAF during the Vietnam War, I realized I'd found a new home. They were keen to learn of my background as a New Zealand Air Force Officer who'd spent many years over South Vietnam, including the last days in April 1975. I had no problem passing the medical exam (done by an ex-pat New Zealand doctor!), the MMPI psychological test, and providing clear evidence of my accumulated flight experience and appropriate FAA certificates, including the written test for flight engineer.

Two days later, before departing Raleigh, I was contacted by Don McMillian from the Orion Flight Crew Recruitment Department with congratulations that I'd been successful as a candidate and two offers were available: the first, to be hired as a B-727 flight engineer based out of Louisville, Kentucky and the second, to be hired as a DC-9 first officer based out of Indianapolis, Indiana. I can't recall why I chose the B-727 option, but it may have been because the training class start date was one month earlier than the DC-9 option, or perhaps the flight engineer position was suggested as a better advancement choice since most of the Orion Fleet had three-seat cockpits. The airline at that time operated six B-747s, six DC-8s, and 25 B-727s, all requiring flight engineers. The two-seat cockpit DC-9 fleet consisted of eight aircraft. Whatever the reason, and despite the hard work and lowered status of becoming a flight engineer, future events at Orion Air showed that my decision had been the smartest choice.

Orion's quoted pay, benefits, seniority system, and scheduling were not exactly enticing, particularly during the first year on probation, and I should have guessed:

vacation was locked into 14 days per year until after five years' service, when it increased to 21 days. My pay for the first year would be $18,000 and increase to $23,000 in the second year if I remained a flight engineer. If I could ever upgrade to first officer, my annual salary would max out at $30,000, or as captain, $42,000. With the bitter reality of these numbers, I'm still surprised I didn't run back to Flight Safety in Wilmington to accept Dick Kimm's offer, which was still open. However, there were other factors involved in my decision. Back in Australia, with my go-ahead, Marilyn was burning our Townsville bridges by selling the house, car, and household devices that were not compatible with the US electrical voltage, so the die was cast. I had to lock in guaranteed employment and a residential location without further delay. Furthermore, acquiring a flight engineer type rating and experience on the B-727 would be useful when seeking other airline jobs if Orion employment proved unsatisfactory.

Between the time of my successful interview at Orion Air and reporting for the training class, I drove my large V8 powered Chevy Wagon north from Raleigh on I-95 to Boston to meet with my brother-in-law, Roger Hudson (for the first time), and his girlfriend, Lucy Seger. My image as a Kiwi amateur mountaineer had forced me into a crazy-ass, 21-mile, one-day hike, along the Presidential Traverse of the White Mountains in New Hampshire with Lucy Seger and her group of Boston hikers. Footsore, bug bitten, and exhausted from an extreme hike I had not volunteered for, I arrived back in Boston to find an invite to East Hampton on Long Island, New York. Lee Manelski advised that his father, Frank, who had a large house on the beach at the Hamptons, would like me to visit and stay a few days before my class date with Orion Air in North Carolina.

So I was off on another geographic adventure in the

country I was soon going to call home. Roger Hudson outlined a driving shortcut from Boston to the eastern end of Long Island, accompanying me on a direct route through Connecticut to its southern coastline at New London and Groton. Then it was on a ferry across Long Island Sound to Orient Point. From there, two more short ferry rides over Shelter Island, all an easy and picturesque drive to the Hamptons. Frank's mansion was right on the beach at East Hampton and meeting him was a pleasure. Then retired, Frank had been one of the early pilots at TWA, flying Lockheed Constellations across the Atlantic to Europe, then later the Boeing 707s and 747s. We hit it off, talking airplanes and pilots. He was pleased that his son Lee had been instrumental in getting me hired at Orion Air.

My training class with Orion Air began on July 8, 1985, with basic indoctrination held during five days at Raleigh. There were a total of seven B-727 flight engineer new hires in this class ranging in age from 26 through to me, at 46. Three were ex-military; me from the RNZAF, John from the US Army Rangers, and one from the RAF. Our youngest member, Jeff, had been in training as a flight engineer with United Airlines at the time of the Pilots' Union Strike at that airline, and had resisted the temptation to become an interim scab. Toward the end of our training at Orion, the strike was over and Jeff was recalled to United having maintained a clean image with the Union. I seem to recall that John had been flying a corporate jet somewhere in North Carolina. The others had come from commuter airlines. One of that group was Jim Keogh, who had been a training captain on Swearingen Metros at Wings West Airline, based out of San Lois Obispo on the central coast of California. The two of us had much in common. He was from England, had served in the RAF like his father and brother, and like me, had spent considerable time at the

Flight Safety Training Center in San Antonio, using the Metro/Merlin simulator at that facility.

After completing the basic indoctrination, our class was shuttled across the state to the city of Winston Salem, home of cigarettes, tobacco, and Piedmont Air, the iconic North Carolina airline that had been contracted to train us as B-727 flight engineers. One of the euphemistic images of Piedmont Air was that you couldn't expect to be hired as a pilot unless you showed up for the interview in a rusty pickup truck with a shotgun on the rack and a bunch of baying hound-dogs in the back. It was apparent during our two weeks of the Piedmont Ground School that they were a happy bunch of good old southern boys, but very professional with their training regimen. The most memorable instructor was Captain KVAR *(Kilo Volt Ampere Reactive)*, who taught us everything we needed to know about the B-727 electrical system, and many things we could have got by without knowing, like every relay and hidden circuit in the airplane. Captain Kvar was a Vietnam Veteran, and had been a senior NCO mechanic on large helicopters.

The lectures, the home study, and the exams were tough going for all of us. I suspect that part of Orion Air's contract terms with Piedmont was not to make the training too easy. Despite the hard work, our class still managed to a have a good time on days off. Also staying at the Ramada Inn was a new hire class of Piedmont flight attendants who assumed we were pilots in training for their airline.

After a few social gatherings with these great looking southern belles, sounding like extras from *Gone With The Wind*, they figured out who we really were: "Y'all been fooling us; we thought you were Piedmont pilots, but you nothing but little ole Night Freight Dogs."

Nevertheless, at least three of our unmarried pilots got latched onto by some of these girls, including one from

Deliverance mountain country who, for a price, would bring us mason jars of White Lightning for party time. Jim's girlfriend (blond hair, blue eyes) was from Lexington, Kentucky, close to Louisville, where we expected to be based after graduation.

On completing the ground school it was time for flight engineer training in the Piedmont B-727 simulator. I was paired with Jim for this phase, and John Ingram was our instructor. John was a line captain on the B-727 in Louisville, the city he'd grown up in, and therefore was able to give us useful information on the best places to live and the work routine at the UPS base at Standiford Airfield. I was particularly interested in what my family and I could expect in Louisville.

On the home front in Australia, Marilyn was finalizing the sale of our house and car, with packers arriving to prepare the household goods for shipment to the USA. Bougainville Copper, my previous employer, had offered to move our goods to the San Francisco port onboard their company-owned ship. It would be our responsibility to clear our goods through customs at the port, then arrange and pay for onward travel to Kentucky. Marilyn and Jordan were planning to arrive in Fort Wayne, Indiana in late August, by which time I would have completed my type rating as a flight engineer on the B-727.

In the meantime, still a resident in North Carolina, it was a FAA check ride in the Piedmont simulator, followed by the real thing in an Orion operated B-727 in the colors of Emery Worldwide, flown from the Raleigh airport in a quick circuit around the patch. Although not permitted to pilot the aircraft, it was still exciting to have the B-727 endorsement on our flight engineer certificates. The final training phase was IOE (Initial Operating Experience) followed by a line check, operating the third seat and its associated tasks on revenue flights for United Parcel Service (UPS) mostly at night!

So it began: months, that became years, of operating airfreight planes mostly at night, across all the lower 48 states of America. It was a steep learning curve, understanding and doing what pilots required of a flight engineer, particularly on multiple short sectors that demanded quick turnarounds at each airfield. Maintaining paperwork, whether it was takeoff/landing performance data, load sheets or maintenance logbook entries required learning work flows to get it done in time. I felt like a one-armed paper-hanger; stick a broomstick up my butt and I'll sweep the floor at the same time! Fortunately, my IOE instructor, Gary Scholder, a pilot the age of my older son, came to the rescue in my earliest flights.

In the B-727, all three crew members were on tight operating timetables, ruthlessly demanded by our main clients. Often, the flight engineer was the weakest link in getting an airplane off the blocks, particularly since many were new hires without experience of how vital the schedules were to the clients. In this regard, UPS was by far the hardest taskmaster in the business, which made flying for them challenging. Sadly, if assigned to the Louisville domicile, as I was, you only flew UPS airplanes. All pilots hired at Orion for the B-727s, B-747s, or DC-8s fleets were initially assigned flight engineer positions, and at the bottom of the seniority lists. It didn't matter where you'd come from, or what you'd flown, you started as a flight engineer in the backseat. Welcome to your new life, Flyboy, overworked and underpaid, a stranger in a strange land.

As it turned out, some help was at hand when I was granted a re-assignment to Orion's San Francisco domicile on Purolator Courier's B-727 fleet. After only two months flying UPS airplanes from the Louisville Base on low flight time night operations and a grand total of 40 hours actual time in the engineer's seat, I would be flying from one coast to the other, part night, part day for increased pay per month. However, there was a catch: my family was now resident in a Louisville apartment complex, so I'd become a long distance commuter between home and San Francisco for the foreseeable future.

My temporary accommodation was in a downtown private apartment owned by Chris Linwell, an old school friend of Marilyn's, originally from Fort Wayne. Chris had me bunk down on a futon in a corner of his living room using a sleeping bag for a minimal room charge. I probably used that bed no more than four times a month because I was either spending nights on layovers with Orion, or back in Louisville with the family. I've remained forever grateful to Chris for this special arrangement at a time when Marilyn and I were struggling to get on our feet financially in the USA. My 2,500-mile commute between Louisville and San Francisco was accomplished by jump-seating (no cost) between Oakland and Louisville airports on UPS DC-8 flights.

Thankfully, flight operations with Purolator were more relaxed than UPS, on schedules that had long flight times between airports. An example was San Francisco to Denver, to Indianapolis to Newark, a total flight time of eight hours, with a daytime layover in New Jersey of 14 hours. The return to San Francisco was via the same airports, mostly night, but with a daytime arrival. Orion Air maintained an apartment and crew car in New Jersey, close to Newark airport, but not always easy to find in such a heavily populated area. In those days without GPS driving guidance, finding the apartment after being awake all night could be chancy business using only a paper map. Finding the car at the airport was also difficult if the last crew had not parked it in the expected location. The assigned cars and apartments were a distinctive Orion Air arrangement, with keys for both, left in the cars. Thankfully, the majority of the apartment locations were in the eastern states, so it became a pleasure to have stopovers in western cities where hotels and limo service to and from were arranged.

The constant night operations, particularly in winter, were challenging. Many of the airports we flew to lacked 24-hour Tower Control and therefore no information on current runway surface conditions, including snow cover and braking effectiveness. Arrival and departure at these airports required communication with the nearest FSS (Flight Service Station) and frequencies for local air traffic coordination. Fortunately, most of the Orion crew members were competent at handling these difficult operating conditions, despite being treated by 'real' airline pilots as not good enough to be hired by the major carriers. We lacked the square jaw, straight teeth, crooked smile, and in many cases the right (if any) college degree! There should be no surprise that I was proud to belong to this gang of misfits who really knew how to fly airplanes with little help from operations and administrative staff. Also, the small group who ran the airline were good managers, leaving us alone at the sharp end to fly our nightly missions.

From the beginning of November 1985 to the end of March 1986 I flew the Purolator operations based out of San Francisco, and then re-assigned to a new domicile with Purolator at Indianapolis, an airport only two hours' drive from my home in Louisville. Life in the USA began to look very good, no longer a long distance commuter, and flying a blend of night/day flights between Los Angeles and Boston, with a few stops at Indianapolis. Even more exciting, I'd been accepted as a flight engineer instructor for Orion Air on a fixed annual salary of $37,000 beginning in

June 1986, permanently domiciled in Louisville. This was the first positive indication that my wild-ass gamble of moving to America was coming true.

As an instructor, my primary function was teaching B-727 new hires the fine art of simulation, initially using flight simulators belonging to USAir, located in Pittsburg. Within a few months of becoming a permanent FE instructor, Orion Air established its own training center in Louisville, that included B-727 and DC-8 simulators. On occasion, I was still required to fly the line, mostly to perform IOE instruction, but my normal work schedule was now confined to a short drive from home to the Orion Training Center. What a relief to often be working daytime hours, returning to the family each evening like normal people did.

By November of 1986 I was able to upgrade to a first officer position, flying the right seat of the B-727, initially on UPS operations from Louisville, but that would change early the following year, flying for a new Orion Air contract with Consolidated Freight based out of Indianapolis. During this transition I remained employed as an FE instructor at the training center until leaving this position in March 1987, and returning to flying the line as a full-fledged first officer on Consolidated Freight B-727 operations from Indianapolis. For me, the main attractions of this new operation was the mixed day/night flying to many destinations west of Louisville, in particular to locations north of California: Portland in Oregon, Seattle in Washington, Boise in Idaho, Salt Lake in Utah, and Reno in Nevada. From these flights I began to acquire a completely different perception of the United States than what I'd experienced over the previous two years in the Midwest, New England, the Carolinas, and various deep southern States. As a recently born-again alpine mountaineer from New Zealand in 1984, and trekker from Nepal in 1983, I'd

259

already been thrilled by visits along the Appalachian Trail in the White Mountains of New Hampshire, and through the Great Smoky National Park that borders Tennessee and North Carolina; but seeing the awesome mountain ranges of the real American West for the first time was mind-blowing. I knew that somewhere out there was going to be my future life.

1986: False Elitism of International Airline Pilots

I FIRST MET ROB while flying Cessna 402s for James Air, a small commuter airline based in Nelson. At that time I remember Rob was seeking pilot employment with Air New Zealand, and like me, without success. According to Jeff, a fellow new hire of mine at Orion Air in 1985, Rob had moved to Alaska in 1982, found a flying job there with a Bush operator, and subsequently married an American. Then, once equipped with Immigration Green Card status, Rob and his family made their way south to Billings, Montana, with him hired as a pilot with Big Sky Airlines. In early 1985 Rob was interviewed by Orion Air, offered a position as Flight Engineer on B-727 freight airplanes, but turned it down in favor of finally being accepted for training at Air New Zealand.

Jeff, who had flown with Rob at Big Sky, told me that Rob was delighted to be hired by Air New Zealand because he had found the American aviation way of doing things not up to his professional standards—in particular radio procedures. He returned to New Zealand after spurning the US aviation scene, leaving his wife and children in America. Apparently, they had no desire to live in New Zealand. It amazed me that Rob, 20 years younger than me, with so many more opportunities in the American airline scene than he could ever hope for in the small aviation world of New

261

Zealand, would run back home to fly as a junior pilot with
Air New Zealand, as a big frog in a little pond, and create
the beginning of final separation from the USA and his
family.

To be fair, at the time Rob was seeking a job with the
major airlines in the USA, there was a low period in pilot
hiring, numerous crew member strikes, layoffs, and general
turmoil in the industry. However, like me, he could have
hired on at Orion Air with the assistance of Jeff's sponsor,
possibly two months ahead of me. Although hard to call at
the time, within five years he would have enjoyed the huge
advancement in the air-freight business, that put me in the
captain's seat of a B-747, earning big money, paying far less
tax than New Zealand, and enjoying the great American
dream. Perhaps Rob thought that being a flight engineer
would be humiliating, instead of wisely accepting it as a
stepping stone to the front seats. At the time, many
American passenger-carrying pilots believed *Night Freight
Dogs* were an inferior class of pilots. Rob and other
passenger-carrying glamour pilots should have studied the
success of Federal Express (FedEx), who in 1985 were
already demonstrating an unbelievable future for UPS,
Amazon, and Supply Chain Logistics with their overnight
delivery operations.

For the next 15 years that I progressed upward at Orion
Air and United Parcel Service as a pilot, I kept thinking of
Rob's thoughtless dismissal of US airline pilots as not being
real professionals. Call them whatever nomenclature you
think, but from my extensive experience with American
pilots, they were very good in handling complex day and
night operations in wild winter weather, in the most
crowded air traffic sky in the world, and over a country of
extreme varied terrain with 14,000-foot mountain ranges,
and high elevation city airports. I had determined that only

a handful of New Zealand airline pilots would be able to handle flight operations in this demanding environment. They had already demonstrated their cold-weather incompetence in Antarctica in 1979 in conditions US pilots face every northern winter.

In 1970, while still serving in the New Zealand Air Force, I studied and passed the most demanding written test papers for the New Zealand Civil Aviation Airline Transport Pilot License (ATPL). The tests required very detailed study on each subject, and many of the questions had to be answered in essay form. There were no true/false or multi-choice questions in these papers, unlike the American FAA tests for similar qualifications. As a result, there was an obvious lack of objectiveness in how these tests were evaluated. I recall sitting in the ATPL exam room with two long-time First Officers from Air New Zealand, who for three years had been attempting to pass all the tests so they could qualify for captain upgrade. So, why had the tests been made so difficult?

My best guess was that in the post WW2 world of New Zealand aviation, being a pilot with one of the two airlines in the country was considered a unique and special privilege, reserved for only a special few. Therefore, the examiners of Civil Aviation New Zealand had constructed tests that contained esoteric skills and knowledge that would sort the chosen ones from the clueless. *If you couldn't explain in a one hundred word essay why the sun comes up in the east and descends in the west, you shouldn't be flying airplanes.* After flying with US airlines for a few years, I was often reminded that in the British Commonwealth—Britain, Australia, and New Zealand—many of their airline pilots considered themselves a clique of elites.

How very different in America, the country of the most airlines, the most pilots, and the largest movement of air traffic day and night. Here, the written exams for FAA Flight Certificates: Private Pilot, Commercial Pilot, Instrument Rating, Flight Engineer, and Airline Transport Pilot are a series of questions, either multi-choice or true/false. To pass those exams, one only needed to study the really important information about airplane flying that had been determined by the FAA and their regulations. There was no need to understand how to design or build an airplane, or know the physics of the atmosphere at the level of a PhD graduate.

Demonstrating one's ability in flying and operating an airplane has not changed since Orville and Wilbur. You can either do it or you can't. The world is covered in airplane wrecks flown by people who couldn't. In professional aviation, whether military or commercial, check-rides with qualified instructors or CAA/FAA Check Airman in actual airplanes (not flight simulators) cannot hide inadequacies or incompetence of the pilot being checked. In a cockpit of two or more pilots, everyone is an open book on how they control and operate the airplane. It's easy to cheat on written aviation exams, either the straightforward stuff of the USA, or the esoteric inquisition of the British Commonwealth. However, you can't fool other pilots in the cockpit in the Wild Blue Yonder—unless it's in a Third World airline where its pilots are protected by political correctness, and their handbook should be called *Flying for Dummies*.

1986: Flying with the Glorious Misfits

Strange Stories from Orion Air

THE CREW MEMBERS OF ORION AIR from 1985 to 1987 were an eclectic group, made up of ex-military pilots: US Air Force, US Navy and Marine aviators, US Army, a few RAF, and one RNZAF (me). Except for the RAF guys, most were veterans of Vietnam, which was a definite plus, and possibly one of the reasons I was hired. The non-military pilots included a large group of younger men and women from US commuter airlines, scud-running night freight operators, and corporate pilots. There was also a small group of internationals: Norwegians, Swedish, Iranians, British, Afghans, a Pakistani, a Vietnamese, and me.

All pilots hired at Orion for the B-727s, B-747s, or DC-8s fleets were initially assigned flight engineer positions and placed at the bottom of seniority lists. It didn't matter whether you'd been in the military flying SR-71s, F-117s, B-52s, or Air Force One. You began as a Bog-Rat engineer in the backseat. One exception to this rule was a small group of pilots flying two-seat crewed DC-9s for Purolator Courier based out of Indianapolis. The other exception was the surprise introduction of previously qualified B-727 captains inserted into our ranks in early 1987. They'd been hired off the street and positioned out of seniority to meet an

265

immediate pilot shortage because of new contracts with Flying Tigers DC-8s and Consolidated Freights B-727s.

We had no union representation at Orion, but management tried to placate full-time crew members with the promise of upgrading First Officers like me within six months, at a time when they expected to have the manpower to do the training. It was all very disappointing for this to happen, but it was either resign or go with the flow, and as a First Officer and FE simulator instructor, I was now earning close to $40,000 annually, enough for our family to survive in rural Kentucky. I did get the upgrade to captain at the end of six months and had my annual pay rise to $55,000, a princely sum compared with what I'd expected back in 1985.

In the meantime, as a First Officer, I had the pleasure of flying with a small number of these temporary captains, who definitely belonged in the misfit category. Most had been strikers at Continental Airlines in 1983, a strike that ultimately failed because many 'scab' Continental pilots and new hires crossed the picket lines. These strikers had the integrity not to give in to Continental's new management, moonlighting with different airlines like Orion to stay current and financially viable. The captains I flew with had the common courtesy to understand their intrusion into full-time Orion pilots' upward mobility. Personally, I gained valuable experience and knowledge from these old-hand airline pilots, providing assurance that my future flying in the USA and international skies would be highly professional.

My number-one pilot from this group was Jim Weed, tall, very fit, jogged faster than me, and five years my senior. Jim was ex-US Navy and had flown F-8 Crusaders off Carriers during the Vietnam war, a background that placed him in hero status for me. As an unofficial tutor, Jim showed me so much more than his expertise in flying the B-727. He provided arcane information on how the interstates were numbered and how to understand the mileage markers along the side. In-flight, on clear nights, I learned where to find Polaris and other notable northern hemisphere stars and why our radar would indicate strange patterns in the ground-mapping mode over the plains of the Midwest.

In Portland, Oregon, he introduced me to the pleasures of eating Cinnabon fat-pills at the malls, and fresh strawberry frappes for breakfast at Denny's restaurants. Then in the evenings, it was baked Alaskan Halibut and King Salmon, washed down with draught Alaskan amber beer. In Philadelphia, it was how to find the best Philly Cheese hoagies, washed down with Rolling Rock beer. The important stuff I learned from Jim was how to maximize income in the United States, the primary logic being: it's not how much you earn, it's how much you get to keep. That was and still is finding ways to minimize the amount of federal and state tax we paid. As I discovered, one solution to that problem was very close to Portland by residing in Vancouver, Washington (no state income tax!) immediately across the Columbia River, and using Portland airport for jump-seating to work in Louisville, Kentucky. This was an option I ultimately chose in 1995.

Pat Stewart was another of these ex-Continental pilots I enjoyed flying with. Pat had been a senior pilot on the DC-10s, regularly flying to New Zealand and Australia from Los Angeles, and had flown numerous military charters into Vietnam during the war. Like Jim Weed, he was very familiar with northern Oregon and Portland, so on the same Portland layover, when Pat joined me on a Mount Jefferson climb, we used the rental car for a full-day touring the coastal sections of northern Oregon and southern parts of Washington State. This included visiting the unique town of Astoria, Cape Disappointment State Park, Fort Canby, and the US Coast Guard Station on the Cape.

I believe it was Pat who suddenly leaped out of the left seat on a B-727, throwing himself across the center console onto my lap, just after parking on the ramp and shutting down the engines. It was daytime at an airfield I can't recall—it may have been Portland—but it was a Consolidated Freight airplane. Pat and I were good friends, but not that friendly. It scared the heck out of me, and I noted that Pat was also terrified, so I looked across his body and out through the left cockpit window and saw a large K-Loader driving straight into the nose where Pat had been sitting. Initially, there was no sign of a driver in the seat until shortly before it made contact, when a pair of startled eyes and flailing hands appeared above the control panel, shutting down the engine before it would have caused severe damage. The impact was noticeable in the cockpit, with the nose lurching to the right. Most surprising was the lack of damage to the skin of the fuselage. We had a mechanic check for internal issues, and he found nothing to ground the plane, so off we went to the next sector. The young kid driving the K-Loader had fallen back off the driver's seat with sudden acceleration and had to claw his way back up to reach the control panel.

Incidents like this, including inflight problems with the Boeing 727, were rare in my experience, despite the intense nature of the flight operations required of us. I believe the three-man cockpit had much to do with limiting pilot errors, dealing with failed components, and vastly improved crew awareness from three sets of eyes and three sets of hands. Another significant safety feature was the three-engine configuration, engines all situated close to the aircraft centerline. The two incidents when I had to shut down an engine on the B-727 were no big deal with minimal asymmetry to keep the aircraft straight and still flying with 65% thrust from two remaining live engines.

One of the strangest flight sequences I did in early 1987 was flying with a captain who had only one eye. Tim was one of the temporary pilots, like Jim Weed and Pat Stewart, but I don't remember him being ex-Continental. He explained during our pre-flight briefing that he was missing an eye, a limitation I found hard to believe. How could the FAA give such a waiver on a First Class Medical Certificate that was required to operate the pilot seats of a B-727? Having assumed that other pilots had already flown with him at Orion, I reluctantly went along with the night's mission, although in retrospect, I should have declined the flight. The required schedule was from Louisville to Cedar Rapids and return.

The weather forecast for our arrival at Cedar Rapids was marginal, with low cloud, poor visibility in blowing snow, and a ten-knot crosswind component. There was no tower control as usual—closed for the night!—so when overhead the airport, we had to rely on the most recent report from another aircraft, a scud-runner, that had departed ten minutes before. The weather was as forecast, but the good news was that snow accumulation on the runway was minimal and braking action probably fair to good. Tim was the pilot flying, and briefed for the ILS (Instrument Landing System) approach and down we went to the Decision Height (200 feet above the runway) without seeing the approach (lead-in) lights and a brief glimpse of the runway edge lights as we began a missed approach climb out.

During the approach, I'd been concerned about how good Tim's peripheral vision was, a concern raised by his question as to what the engine gauges were reading. I think he may have asked me ... "to keep an eye" outside for the runway, or perhaps that had been me saying, "you need to keep an eye" on the glideslope. Whatever was going on in the cockpit during that approach, I was so discombobulated by Tim's possible vision limitations that I'd forgotten to remotely activate the runway approach lights using the dedicated VHF radiofrequency. I explained to Tim what I'd screwed up and suggested we return for another approach, which we did successfully, now having the approach lights bright and shiny, showing through the blowing snow. Luckily, I never flew with Tim again, nor did I hear from other pilots who had ever flown with him, so I began to wonder whether he really existed in the flesh. Perhaps that night I'd stepped into the Twilight Zone with Tim, a casualty that hadn't survived the air war over Vietnam. Spooky nights with the misfits!

Now for a few funny stories about cultural differences, including words being lost in translation. First, my lack of interest in American 'games.' Ernest Hemingway once said: auto racing, bullfighting, and mountain climbing are the only real sports—all others are games. I can agree with that, having been a mountaineer and a kid running away from bulls while crossing New Zealand farm country on the way to school. In my early days as a flight engineer with Orion Air I was flying with Ron Peterson and Tony Delduco on a Manchester, New Hampshire overnight. In the morning we had breakfast at the hotel, and on the way out I grabbed a complimentary copy of the *USA Today* newspaper for reading on the flight back to Louisville.

After reaching cruise altitude, Ron turned to me requesting the publication, and I handed it over to him. For the next five minutes, Ron kept shuffling through the various sections of the paper, eventually asking me about the missing Sports section. In reality I'd dumped it, and the Business section, in a trash bin outside the hotel. Ron couldn't believe what I'd done because he'd been so looking forward to reading the latest results from the NFL, NBA, and whatever other alphabet soup names of American sports teams that I knew nothing of and had zero interest in. To make matters worse I told him that because there was no rugby or cricket news in the paper I had every justification in tossing the Sports section away. He was so disgusted with my ignorance of American 'games,' I don't recall Ron ever flying with me again.

During the time I spent as a flight engineer simulator instructor for Orion Air, I had the enjoyment and occasional amusement of working with a mixed bag of pilots who were joining the airline to be B-727 guys and gals in the back seat. Two of my most memorable students were Bob Estus and Jim Cooper, both ex-Air Force B-52 pilots. Bob was from somewhere in New England with a mid-Atlantic accent I could easily understand and be understood. However, Jim was from Texas, with a twang that was sometimes unintelligible to me, and vice versa. During our lesson briefings before entering the simulator, we all seemed to understand each other, but once inside the Box, under the stress of handling a complicated procedure, there would often be a breakdown in translation between Jim and me. For example, I would instruct Jim to follow a set pattern of actions on the engineer panel, and Jim's response was to shrug his shoulders, look at me, and mouth some words in Texas Speak. Neither of us had any idea of what the other was saying, so Bob, sitting in one of the front seats, would come to the rescue by doing the translation. "Jim, what Peter just said was to do the following ...."

Bob would listen to Jim's garble and explain, "What Jim just said was get stuffed, he's had enough for the day!" Just kidding, but you get the drift of these fun times in the Box.

Another classic lost in translation event in the Box was

between a young pilot from Lexington, and me. Jeff Judy was an excellent student, and we didn't have accent problems, but on this occasion we did have a total idiomatic breakdown. It happened on Jeff's final check-ride with an FAA inspector who would sign him off as an approved flight engineer. Everything went well until it was time for Jeff to get out of his seat and move it away from the floor panel that housed the screw release for lowering the landing gear manually. Jeff opened the panel, had the manual crank device in his hands, but kept fumbling about trying to connect the crank with the fitting under the floor. As was usual in the Box, it was nighttime, with only minimal cockpit lighting illuminating the area Jeff was kneeling on.

In frustration with his delay I shouted at him, "Get your bloody torch so you can see what you're doing!"

His response was a look of total confusion until one of the pilots said, "Jeff, what Peter means is get out your flashlight." And so, his check-ride concluded with a solid approval by the FAA inspector and a few laughs about our misunderstanding.

In the debrief, Jeff said to me, "Peter, when you said the word—torch—I imagined witches carrying burning torches, and what would I be doing in the cockpit of a 727 with one of those?"

As the years go by, still relating this story, it's possible that I actually shouted, "Get your flaming torch so you can see what you're doing." From the world I grew up in, the use of 'bloody' and 'flaming' were interchangeable expletives. Sadly, I'm unable to check with Jeff because he passed away in 2018. I miss you, Jeff; you were wonderful to fly with.

My next story about language involves telling an Englishman to keep his mouth shut in an IRA hangout in Boston. This was not for Individual Retirement Accounts, but rather a place where Retirement with Extreme Prejudice could have happened that night to my flight engineer trainee. The backstory to this hazardous event began in Los Angeles the day before. I'd been assigned to provide Initial Operating Experience (IOE) to a newly hired flight engineer on the B-727. His name was Tony Dawson, born in London to quintessential English parents, and a distant associate of Margaret Thatcher. He was with me for seven days and nights, flying between Los Angeles and Boston, with stops at Indianapolis, Phoenix, and Rochester. The final schedule had us laying over in Boston for a long weekend, with accommodations at a hotel close to downtown. After living and surviving in America, often forced into drinking local beer, best described by Monty Python as "Like making love in a canoe; that is … f***ing close to water," I'd discovered the joys of Irish pubs. These pubs, mostly located in northeastern states, served on-tap real beer from Ireland, England, Germany, Belgium, and Holland. So my plan for our first night in Boston was to visit a typical Irish pub, and our local guide would be Lucy Seger, a student at UMass and friend of my American family. Lucy collected us in her small pickup truck and drove us through the labyrinth of Boston streets, under fire on all sides by crazy Boston drivers. It was scary stuff until we had many drinks under the belt.

On Lucy's advice the best of Irish pubs in town was the Black Rose, situated down on the docks, with a brief comment that it was frequented by members of the Provincial Irish Republican Army (IRA) and by their American supporters, so we could expect the Guinness to be served perfectly. Sounded good to me until inside with our first drinks in hand, there was an announcement the band was about to play with a lead singer called Sands, either John or Sean. Whoever, in 1981, only a few years before, Bobby Sands of the IRA had starved himself to death in Her Majesty's Prison Maze (thank you, Margaret Thatcher), and I'd just brought a hated Englishmen into a lair of his enemy! Lucy and I were safe—she was a Connecticut Yankee, and I was an Australian speaking Kiwi—but it was imperative that we keep Tony from talking to other patrons with his snobbish British accent. I recall telling the barman that Tony was a mute, so could only order more Guinness with hand signals. To put the three of us in a positive light I went up to the band's low platform, introduced myself as an Australian, and requested they play "The Wild Colonial Boy," and the crowd loved it! After that, we made a strategic retreat from the Black Rose, making sure that Tony continued to play a mute until we were safely back in Lucy's vehicle. Forty-five years later, the three of us are still alive; Tony, a close friend residing nearby in Reno, Lucy living with me after 24 years of marriage; and me, who recently found out I'm actually a descendant of an actual Wild Colonial Boy ... an Irish dissident, shipped out in chains from Britain on a convict ship to Australia in 1823.

The beginning of saving fellow crew members from termination happened on a layover in Sacramento. It was a Emery Worldwide B-727 schedule where I was the Captain, Rick was First Officer, and Dan was Flight Engineer. Both Rick and Dan lived in California, so they went home for the weekend and I went climbing in Yosemite. On the Monday evening I showed up—still in one piece—Rick was there, but no Dan. I was about to advise Orion Scheduling with the information of requiring a replacement engineer after Dan had called from his home in Grass City—blocked roads. Just then, I noticed Jan, a B-727 captain relaxing in a corner. Jan was booked as a jump-seater to Dayton, Ohio, positioning for work. So now I had three pilots for the flight:

Rick would become the Flight Engineer, Jan would be the First Officer, and me the Captain.

Was it too good to work? I could avoid telling Scheduling and the company management that Dan had failed to show up. Nobody at Emery or Orion would ever know the truth! All seemed well until I asked Rick for the takeoff performance data and he responded that all the books that flight engineers carried were missing. We quickly realized that Dan had taken them home with him. Easy decision— screw the books, we know we'll get off the ground, and away we went, hurtling into the dark night totally relaxed, feeling good about saving Dan's butt. We were not flying direct to Dayton, but making a stop at Albuquerque, New Mexico, and once airborne I became concerned that if we had a surprise FAA inspection on the ramp, they would discover we were without the required flight manuals. After sweating the 40 minutes we spent on the ground at Albuquerque, there was no sign of the FAA. So, it all ended well for us and Dan.

Flying at night with or without the Devil? This was a decision forced on me one evening in Louisville at the beginning of a routine UPS B-727 schedule. I was the First Officer flying with Captain Bob, whom I knew well and respected. We'd been paired together on many occasions and I was aware of his wartime experiences flying the AC-47 'Spooky' gunships, raining down massive firepower on Viet Cong and NLF forces in South Vietnam. I also knew that he'd become a practicing Evangelical and follower of Jimmy Lee Swaggart, but had never pushed his strong religious beliefs on me, so this action to save us from the Devil was a surprise. It happened when I contacted Louisville Control for our departure clearance. The Controller came back with a standard clearance, that included the four numeral Transponder code, which in this case was 3666.

While reading the clearance back to the Controller, Bob interrupted me; "We can't accept that code. Have him change it."

I looked across at Bob in bewilderment until I realized what his issue was, and told him, "I'm not going to make a laughing stock of myself. You call him back and explain your problem, because it sure ain't mine!"

That didn't work with Bob; he reminded me that he was the designated pilot flying and I was the designated radio operator, so in the interests of getting underway I called Control with the request for a different code. The initial response was silence, then followed by a 'say again' query, and finally a new code given, with a slight snigger in the Controller's voice. Since that night, I've often wondered if we had got airborne with the 3666 code would we have been struck by lightning or perhaps had the plane ripped apart in a tornado funnel? Sure were strange times at Orion Air.

1987: Climbing and Flying with Orion Air

*The obsession of climbing: It's about having fun and about living
to the full. We thought it was worth risking everything, all the
rest of your life, every happiness you ever could have had.
Mountains change who you are, and they mold who you are. It
becomes something that's life-enhancing and life-defining.*
~ *The Beckoning Silence*, Joe Simpson

IN THE SPRING OF 1987, I began to blend mountain
climbing with flying, carrying my full alpine kit on the
cargo floor of my Boeing 727 to Portland in Oregon, first to
climb the 11,200-foot peak of Mount Hood, then the 12,300-
foot summit of Mount Adams, during long weekend
layovers that were a convenient feature of being a Night
Freight Dog pilot. The numerous volcanic peaks of Washington
State beckoned, but most were too far from Portland to be
attempted during a weekend and would have to wait for
later. Adams had been the exception, a peak that had
required an earlier weekend layover to survey the road and
trail accesses to the usual climb route trailhead at Cold
Springs.

For that survey, I'd hired a rental car to make the drive
from Portland along the I-80 Interstate, 60 miles through the
majestic Columbia Gorge to the town of Hood River, then a
left turn over the Columbia River on the Singing Bridge to

the Washington State town of White Salmon. From there, another 40 miles north to the settlement of Trout Lake and the Mount Adams Ranger Station. The station provided detailed information about the climbing routes on the mountain and directions to the forestry roads leading the way to the Cold Springs trailhead at an elevation of 6,000 feet. On this beautiful rain-free day in the Northwest, I had a companion who'd acted as an unofficial guide from Portland to Hood River, a section of road he knew well. However, like me, he was now in uncharted territory but enjoyed the sights, sounds, and smells of the prolific conifer forest surrounding us.

In his early sixties, Roy Hopper was overweight, not very fit, and a chow-hound of the first order. He was a crew member with Orion Air, not a qualified pilot but a PFE (Professional Flight Engineer) who'd flown into Portland with me and layover at the company hotel. I'd discovered him that morning, making the most of the complimentary breakfast, settling in for the day watching television, and planning his lunch and dinner. Roy was not popular with other crew members, possibly because of his image as an outlier from the rest of us and his constant eating during flight, consuming food that he carried in numerous loose bags. On this beautiful Sunday morning, feeling a little sorry for him, I asked if he was interested in joining me on my Mount Adams survey. He jumped at the chance, saying that he knew the Columbia Gorge very well and would show me the way from the hotel to Interstate 84. We went off with Roy's first important stop at a 7-11 store to purchase drinks and snacks for the long journey ahead. At least a dozen Pepsi cans with a pile of chips and dips was his comfort food, while mine was a simple six-pack of beer.

I was surprised to find Roy very engaging, well-read, with an in-depth knowledge of British and European history. I don't believe many of our crew members even bothered to listen to Roy, which was a pity since he had much to offer. Anyway, after the excellent guided tour he provided on our drive upriver through the Columbia Gorge, I was pleased to have brought him with me. On the last stage of our journey, following an ascending series of roads through the forest, ways that became rougher and narrower the higher we got, I decided to call a halt at a nasty switchback that led to a steep one-way section of road. I'd realized that my two-wheel-drive rental car wasn't ideally suited to go any farther, but I'd seen enough until the day of my actual attempt on the mountain when I would accept the chance of damaging a rental car by driving the additional one mile to the trailhead. At our turn-around location, there was a small creek running beside the road. Roy took off his shoes and socks and paddled in the stream's deeper pools with great delight. I got the impression that he'd never been in such a mountain wilderness before because he was so enchanted and excited about the experience.

Then it was time to return to civilization, taking great care descending the narrow rough roads to Trout Lake and back to White Salmon, where Roy suggested we return to Portland via the route on the northern side of the Columbia River, Washington's Highway 40. This was a narrow two-way road that took some care in negotiating, but well worth the extra time because of its tunnels, the closeness to the riverbank, small towns, leaning cliff faces, and impressive views of the massive Bonneville Dam. When we arrived back at the hotel, Roy offered to buy me dinner at his favorite Mexican restaurant, which he said was only a short drive away. There must have been good Mexican restaurants on every city block in Portland, but one hour later, driving in the heavy evening traffic, Roy finally said we'd arrived. To this day, I don't know what the attraction of this particular restaurant was, although I do recall Roy scooping up salsa with the complimentary tortilla chips like a starving Mexican peasant, muttering through the falling crumbs how great the chips and salsa were at this place. So came the end of a rather strange day in my new life.

On Monday night, as scheduled, we flew back to Indianapolis, where I was re-scheduled to continue on to Philadelphia for a layover the following day. As it happened, the word was out about my weekend trip to Mount Adams, and in the relative quiet of the crew breakroom at Indianapolis, Wayne Shaffer called everybody to attention with the hilarious comment, "Over the weekend, Pete Tremayne took Roy into the forests of southern Washington, and now the bears are hanging their food in the trees!" Sadly, that great comedian and wonderful person, Wayne, whom I'd flown with often in my first year at Orion Air, passed away at a young age.

Two weeks later, I was back in Portland for another long weekend layover, this time to actually attempt a summit climb of Mount Adams. With my new knowledge of the roads to the mountain base, I drove from Portland across the Columbia River to Vancouver in Washington. Then it was east along Highway 40 to White Salmon and Trout Lake, where I lodged a climbing plan with the ranger station and headed up the mountain to Cold Springs to camp the first night. My front-wheel drive rental car handled the last section of the road without a problem. The second night on the mountain, I made early camp at 9,000 feet in blizzard conditions but woke the next morning to clear weather. I reached the 12,300-foot summit by midday and descended back to Cold Springs without seeing other climbers. My guess was the previous day's blizzard had deterred anybody else from pushing through the weather and solid cloud cover that existed below my high camp.

This was the first of 30 ascents I would eventually make on Mount Adams.

After the success on Adams, I continued to bid for flights with weekend layovers in Portland, with climbing plans to attempt Mount Jefferson, a 10,500-foot volcanic peak in Oregon. Getting there from Portland required a lengthy drive and a long hike to the base of the mountain. The northern face route I took was a most unwise choice. The experience was summed up in a journal entry at the time: *A day of exposure with extreme prejudice. I must never try a route like this again without a partner and rope!* I returned to the mountain three weeks later, but this time to a safer route on the peak's southern face. On this adventure, I was accompanied by Pat Stewart, my Orion Captain, for the weekend. His interest was trout fishing, which he could do at Pamelia and Hank Lakes located below the southern climbing route. We were in constant rain for the first day and night, followed by snow and whiteouts during my failed attempt to reach the summit the second day. After retreating to our camp, Pat and I decided on bailing out in the rain and dark to the Pamelia Lake trailhead. That became my last layover in Portland until the next year.

By the end of August 1987, I was in upgrade training for a captain's position on the B-727 based out of Dayton, Ohio, flying for our client Emery Worldwide. My FAA check-ride in the left seat of a B-727 was done at Grand Rapids with Frank Hemko in late September, followed in early October with my first revenue flight as a captain with Emery. This revenue flight was from Dayton to Syracuse to Burlington in Vermont and a long weekend layover there. This became an opportunity to climb the highest point in the State of New York, Mount Marcy, with an elevation of 5,344 feet, a pimple compared with the Northwest peaks I'd become used to. Two weeks later, I was back in Burlington for another weekend layover, this time to climb the highest point in Vermont, the 4393-foot Mount Masefield. Nothing inspiring about this climb, except a near-miss of being killed by falling spears of ice shedding from tall antennas near the summit. I was stupidly standing beneath the towers, wondering what had caused the big holes in the soft snow, when a 100-pound lump of ice hit the snow within three feet of me. Then I knew.

In the meantime, I had the opportunity to do my first big climb in Yosemite National Park, the 12,900-foot Koip Peak, located on the eastern boundary of the park. This was made possible by a weekend layover at Sacramento in mid-October. I camped the first night at Crane Flat in a reserved campsite. Gary, the reservation guy, showed up after dark and was kind enough to let me stay in my tent while he slept in his car. Over the years I've said you meet outstanding people in the mountains, and Gary was my first best example. The next day I drove up to Tuolumne Meadows Ranger Station to obtain a wilderness permit for entry at the Mono/Parker Pass trailhead. Because the listing was for the next day, I planned to sleep in my rental car at the trailhead parking, only to be chased off by a ranger. "No camping closer than four miles beyond any trailhead." These were my early days of learning the strict rules of American national parks, policed and enforced along the heavily traveled roads, viewing trails and park-run campgrounds, where probably 99 percent of visitors existed. If you wished to be away from the crowds and pesky officialdom, I learned you should hike out beyond the four-mile limit.

So, after a night sleeping in my car outside the Tioga Pass entry gates, I returned to the trailhead and hiked out four miles to camp at the miners' ghost town near Mono Pass. There I met with two experienced Sierra Club ladies who were camped nearby and had hiked in to climb Koip

Peak located beyond Parker Pass, another five miles from where we were camped. The next morning the three of us set off on the trail to Parker Pass, then up a spectacular series of switchbacks to a steep scree ridge called Koip Peak Pass at 12,300 feet. From there, it was a scramble on sloping loose talus to the Koip Peak summit at 12,900 feet. Great views of the valleys and peaks covering the eastern side of Yosemite, including the highest point in the Park—Mount Lyell—and the two high mountains of Banner and Ritter to the south of the park boundary Donohue Pass. All these peaks I would climb in the years ahead.

1988: Flying the Boeing 727 for UPS

IN LATE 1987, flying as a B-727 captain for Orion Air, a Black Swan event was on the horizon, an occurrence that none of our crew members could have predicted. In December of 1987, I was given the opportunity by Tom Keeting, the manager of flight training at Orion Air, to apply for a pilot position with the newly formed United Parcel Service (UPS) airline. The result: I was hired with the first 50 crew members for the airline as a B-727 First Officer, but not as a Captain. This downgrade was a letdown, both in the loss of status and, importantly, a significant drop in income for the first year on probation. However, remaining with Orion Air was not an option because its future was now in jeopardy with the loss of its major contract with UPS.

As a former employee of Orion Air, I had no illusions that the marriage of a highly specialized aviation personnel group to the conservative and egalitarian UPS would be easy. Both parties would be in conflict for some time until an acceptable middle ground could be determined. UPS exacerbated the situation by hiring airline management personnel, who had neither the experience nor expertise to direct and lead the air operation into a bright future that was clearly attainable. The rumor was that some of these management pilots had been scabs at other airlines, and if so, we believed UPS had intentionally sought out these losers.

From the earliest days of the operation in 1988, this management group displayed an almost total lack of respect or concern for the pilots being hired into UPS. Was this attitude by a deliberate directive from Head Office, or did it merely develop unchecked in Louisville? Whatever the reason, the result was the same: a complete loss of credibility in the airline management by the crew members and a resort to grievance procedures to have even the most basic terms of our initial contract followed.

Among the crew members hired in that first year, there existed the collective wisdom of years of airline management, operations, and scheduling of the very same airplanes that UPS was now controlling less efficiently than before. Also, under the management structure peculiar to UPS, these experienced pilots were considered nothing more than 'hourly wage workers,' so their opinions and knowledge were inadmissible. However, on the credit side, the isolation created by this antiquated philosophy and hostile management environment forged the one thousand plus members into one of the most effective pilot unions in the USA—the Independent Pilots Association (IPA). With the IPA's help, we established quality leadership, credibility, mutual trust, and the ability to make the operation really work. The rest is history.

In January 1988, joining the first class of crew members for the B-727, I was with established friends from Orion Air. Although bumped back to the right seat, I was happy to fly with captains I knew and respected. In turn, they valued me as a highly qualified asset from Orion and a fellow Vietnam veteran. Again, I was on hallowed ground with my brothers-in-arms. As the months progressed, so did the crew member buildup, primarily with pilots from the four contractors: Orion Air, Ryan Air, Evergreen, and Interstate. Interacting with the other contract airline pilots went smoothly because their flight operations had been similar, hauling freight and mutually known as 'night freight dogs' by the 'real' airline pilots. Unfortunately, because of UPS's hiring protocol, we were soon invaded by many of these 'real' pilots, who were hired as captains. To us, they were known as 'boat people,' a reluctant bunch of refugees from failed or failing passenger-carrying airlines.

Many of these refugees understood that any airline flying job was better than no job, but their loss of dignity and elite airline status on being forced into flying night freight was apparent. At that time in aviation history, few passenger airline pilots had any conception of what UPS Airlines could become. If they'd studied the rise and success of Federal Express (FedEx), the future of stable, guaranteed employment for pilots was a recession-proof, pandemic-proof industry. Forget the passenger business. After all, the flight attendants were no longer young and glamorous (unless they were male?), and the passengers down the back were now mostly hoi polloi.

It's been years since my hiring with UPS and the disappointment I'd felt on being mistreated with a demotion to First Officer. So I don't intend to revisit my failed negotiations with the incompetent airline management pilots that UPS had hired or with the corrupt Teamster Union representatives. Back then, I decided to go with the flow, accepting that as a Legal Alien (Green Card holder) at age 47, I had been in the right place at the right time, and darn lucky to be hired by a company such as UPS. In the meantime, waiting for an upgrade to captain, the good news was being part of a multi-billion dollar company and sitting at the top of the First Officer seniority list, a situation that allowed me to bid for layovers in the mountain-filled states and achieve the long vacations that Lee Manelski had promoted two years before. I would continue to have only two weeks per year for the next five years but could bid scheduled lines of two weeks off, before and after the vacation period. This became the chance to regain the six-week vacations I'd enjoyed with Bougainville Copper in Australia and realized the need to make the most of it before upgrading to captain and once again become a bottom feeder on that seniority list.

With winter arriving in the northern states, my mountaineering activities were on hold for the season. During November, December, and January1989, I had the privilege of flying with the same crew: Captain George Gillette, ex-Chief Pilot at Braniff International Airlines, and Engineer Wayne Cunningham, ex-Air Force pilot. George knew a great deal about flying the B-727-200 (Dash-200), the later version of the original B-727-100 (Dash-100), and it was our good fortune to operate this Boeing model most of those three months. UPS possessed a fleet of eight of these airplanes, which had been used by the contractor, Ryan Air, until September 1988. I found the move to this stretched version of the Dash-100 I'd been flying for almost four years an exciting challenge. It looked almost identical on the exterior, but with a 20 feet longer fuselage (ten feet in front of the wing and ten feet behind) and a circular intake on the center engine instead of the oval intake of the Dash-100. The cockpit was the same, but with upgraded avionics, including such niceties as auto brakes and auto thrust-levers. The cabin was 20 feet longer—more passengers for the people carriers or considerably more cargo in our operation. The other significant difference was the power output of the three engines, with up to 20 percent more thrust than the Dash-100, providing a much-increased power to weight ratio.

With occasional advice from George, I was thrilled with the handling of the Dash-200. It seemed to fly better and quieter than its smaller counterpart, and it was easy to make smoother landings using a simple technique. My experience from many landings in the Dash-100 had been tarnished by occasional hard touchdowns when operating at light weights—no cargo and low fuel. With the Dash-200, when close to touchdown, after slowing the descent rate, the trick was to push the nose down a tad before the main wheels met the runway. For aerodynamic reasons, I can't remember, the result was always a gentle landing. Who knows, maybe I was finally becoming a talented pilot?

My plan to be on the expedition to Denali from late May into June of 1989, an expected period of five to six weeks, would be possible by sandwiching my pitiful two-week annual vacation between scheduled time off at both ends. Again, this was achievable because of my senior status, a position that wasn't to last much longer, because I had been promised an upgrade to captain in late July. That promotion would move my seniority from the top of one list to the bottom of another, but I would be well compensated with increased income and greater self-esteem in the process.

Being back in the captain's seat of the B-727 was a great feeling. It had been one and a half years since my last position with Orion Air, operating as a captain for Emery Worldwide out of Dayton, Ohio. This promotion within UPS was well-timed, with significant advances in pay and conditions, recently fought for, and won by our new pilots union, the IPA. For the next one and a half years, I flew the line in B-727s, and unlike my time with Orion, there were more flights during the daytime, a pleasant change. Our trips zigzagged across all of the Lower 48 States and Alaska, Canada, and Mexico. Uniquely, many of the cities we visited happened at night, and I never ventured far from the air-conditioned comfort and safety of the B-727 cockpit.

After all, who wants to be a sightseer in Newark, Detroit, Oakland, Chicago, Birmingham, or Philadelphia in the middle of the night? As an illustration, one night in downtown Oakland, California, after an evening meal at a Thai restaurant, my young First Officer walked back to our hotel when a police officer in a cruiser stopped him and asked whether he was carrying (a gun).

Thinking he was in trouble, the kid said, "No, of course not."

The officer responded, "Well, son, you shouldn't be in this part of town; climb in, and I'll drive you back to your hotel."

As a new captain at UPS, I had the enjoyable experience of flying with new hires, first officers and engineers, who joined the company from 1989 through 1991. Unlike the retreads from failed airlines hired by necessity in 1988, the newcomers were mostly young and enthusiastic about flying for a freight airline. They were knowledgeable about Federal Express's success and understood that getting in with UPS at the beginning would be a winner. They were right: 30 years later, these excellent young men and women I flew with during those early days at UPS are just now retiring at age 65, after brilliant aviation careers and with bountiful retirement benefits.

A significant aspect of these new hires was their eclectic composition. Like me, some were recent immigrants to the United States. I was the sole New Zealander, no one from Australia, two women from Holland, one woman from Columbia, three men from South Africa, four men from Norway, three women from Sweden, one woman from Finland, three men from Canada, and three men from the United Kingdom—to name just a few. In the larger crowd of US-born pilots, UPS had hired a wide range of ethnic groups, including African, Hispanic, and Asian Americans.

My first international flights with UPS began with schedules into Mexico, originating in Dallas Fort Worth to Ellington Field near Houston, across the border to Monterrey, then to Toluca (southwest of Mexico City), with the last stop and overnight at Guadalajara. Followed the next day by a return back to Fort Worth via the same airports in Mexico. I found these trips exciting, flying into a country I had never been to before, and so much fun with my Spanish-speaking Engineer, Johnny Zuniga, from Costa Rico. He was invaluable in the air for translating Spanish radio transmissions between local pilots and Air Traffic Control. The controllers were required to communicate with us in English, but it was good to know what the local flights were doing and where they were in the sky. As valuable as Johnny was in the air, he became a trouble-making pest on the ground during our layovers at Guadalajara. In the evenings, at our favorite restaurant, he would instruct the waiters to play "falling over" games with myself and First Officer Randy Forbes, while we became inebriated on margaritas – and the other diners would have a great laugh at our expense.

An interesting aviation experience from the Mexico trips was flying into Toluca, its airport located at an elevation of 8,500 feet above sea level, close to the FAA maximum limit for takeoff and landing the B-727. The Toluca runway length was 13,000 feet, but a large segment of that runway was needed for takeoffs and the landing roll-out even at regular operating weights. At that elevation, with high Mexico temperatures, the actual speed (TAS) was 20–30 mph faster than indicated in the cockpit. It was a challenging airport, not just because of the high altitude, but was surrounded by high volcanic mountains, notably the 15,500-foot Nevado De Toluca, 20 miles southwest of the airport.

Johnny Zuniga was a perfect example of the young new hires who joined UPS in late 1989. He was my engineer on the series of flights to Mexico in April and May of 1990, then one year later, he was back as my First Officer for two months on the B-727; fortunately, not to Mexico! So, very rapid promotions for his new hires group, most of whom I considered excellent pilots. In April and May of 1991, flying with Johnny in the right seat and Engineer Mark Hedrick in the back was the highpoint of my B-727 flying. I had just been awarded a captain's position on the Boeing 747, with conversion training to begin in late May.

Strangely, although excited about my B-747 future, I experienced bittersweet moments during these last flights in the B-727. The three of us had been awarded an uncomplicated schedule, with short flight times and long rest periods between flights. Every night, except weekends, we flew from Knoxville, Tennessee, to the UPS hub at Louisville, Kentucky, arriving around midnight, then returning to Knoxville at 5 a.m. Our hotel accommodation was at the Knoxville airport, so in bed by 6 a.m., sleep until 3 p.m., have dinner, and relax until departing for Louisville at 11 p.m. Repeat the schedule until the long weekend layovers, which found me day-hiking the Smoky Mountains National Park, a short drive from Knoxville.

Knoxville and Louisville's air distance was only 200 miles, with many of the flights flown in a Dash-200, with light fuel loads and an arched vertical profile. Twenty minutes climb to 35,000 feet, power off, and 20 minutes descent to the destination. It was great fun and too easy, so to add some challenge during the flights, Johnny and I competed with, "Who can do the smoothest landings?" Mark kept the book on the nightly results, and I became frustrated that this young lad from Costa Rico was almost as good a pilot as me! How could that be? Whatever, the two months with Johnny and Mark had been a wonderful experience and a perfect finish to my B-727 days. From 1985 with Orion Air until moving to the B-747, I flew 2,100 hours in this classic three-engine airplane: 1,600 as pilot and 500 as flight engineer.

1988: Climbing and Flying with UPS Airlines

IN THE SPRING OF 1988, my status at the top of the UPS First Officer seniority list for the next 20 months gave me a choice to fly with only senior captains from the contractor group—pilots I knew, liked, and respected. This selection process had to take into account the weekend layover destinations because of my increased interest in mountaineering. Initially, UPS schedules did not include layovers in Oregon and Washington states. Those schedules were still being operated by the contractor, Evergreen Airlines. So my ambitions to continue climbing in the Northwest were on hold until mid-summer. In the meantime, I researched other mountain locations that were within easy driving distance of current UPS scheduled layovers.

My first selection was to operate from Ontario in Southern California into its major airport between Los Angeles and San Bernardino. For the next three months, my chosen crew was Captain Ed Burton, ex-Air Force and avid golfer, and Flight Engineer Lloyd Jenny, also ex-Air Force with his residence in Riverside. During our many long layovers in Ontario, from very early on Saturday mornings to late Monday afternoons, Ed played golf, Lloyd went home, and I went mountaineering. Even now, I contemplate how I chose the peaks to climb, where they were, and how

293

difficult the challenge. The first part was easy; I studied the Rand McNally Road Atlas for the United States with its paper maps that showed not only roads but significant features like peaks and their elevations. The second part was mostly unknown because I lacked written route guides and there was no internet, therefore no climbing guides, but the results were always an unexpected adventure. Flying had become comfortable and safe, but my part-time passion led me further into a high-risk lifestyle, one I would survive for the next 30 years.

According to the road atlas, San Bernardino was surrounded by high mountains, including two peaks above 11,000 feet: San Jacinto and San Gorgonio. Access trails to both peaks were only a short drive from the Ontario hotel used for crew layovers, but I decided to leave these climbs for the future. My impassioned interest was Mount Whitney, 14,495 feet, listed in the atlas as the highest point in the USA's Lower 48 States. Reaching this peak began with a 200-mile drive from Ontario to a small town in the Owens Valley called Lone Pine. Most of the journey was along California Highway 395, a road that years later I would refer to as 'the highway to the danger zone' because that same 395 kept bringing me to perilous adventures on the high places of the Sierra Nevada mountains—and still does.

From that earliest road trip along 395 from Southern California, I've been fascinated by the interconnection between its aviation history, the high desert, the Mojave, and the peaks of the High Sierra. Just north of the San Bernardino Mountains is the city of Palmdale, home of Lockheed's Skunk Works and other aviation manufacturers. In the desert north of there is Edwards Air Force Base from where in 1948, Chuck Yeager broke the sound barrier, and the Mojave Air and Space Port littered with unused commercial jets. To the northeast, between Mojave and the

Owens Valley entrance is the Naval Air Weapons Station at China Lake. To the west of China Lake rises the southern terminus of the High Sierra mountain range, which runs northwest for three hundred miles of many granite peaks above 13,000 feet, with 14 peaks above 14,000 feet, of which Mount Whitney is the highest. The sky above the southern peaks of the High Sierra is filled with the noise of fast moving Navy jet fighters, the Top Gun MOA (Military Operation Area). In 1988 they were F-14 Tomcats; now they're F-18 Hornets and F-35 Lightning fighters.

I had been told a well-formed trail of 11 miles led from a trailhead (known as Whitney Portal) at 8,400 feet elevation to the Whitney summit, a 6,000-foot climb and descent, often done in one day by super fit hikers! However, there was a catch; the trail was only completely snow-free between late June to early October, and my first attempt was on April 30th. Whitney Portal was a short drive uphill from Lone Pine, the small town on Hwy 395, at 4,000 feet elevation. Having driven through the night from Ontario, I arrived at the Portal at 4 a.m. and was on the trail by first light. The path was easy to negotiate until reaching 9,000 feet and the first snow cover. From that point on, the trail was difficult to follow, with soft snow becoming deeper as the elevation increased.

After a full day slogging upward in directions that were nowhere close to the trail, I set up camp on an area of level snow in blizzard conditions at an elevation of 11,800 feet. After resting in the tent for a few hours, I began suffering from altitude symptoms: hard to breathe, headache, and respiratory congestion. Despite periodic snow showers, I decided to bail out and descend in a partial moonlight nightscape. From subsequent climbs and descents without snow on the Whitney Trail, I learned that my descent that first night on the mountain was extremely perilous;

295

slipping, falling, tumbling down granite slabs, sometimes buried in small snow avalanches.

What naivety on my part. Although I had the right equipment for big snow climbs—ice axe, crampons, heavy leather boots, windproof clothing—I lacked snowshoes (or cross-country skis) to handle the deep powder snow of the Sierra Nevada. Then, what stupidity on my part to consider coming back to the same mountain the following weekend, but I did just that. After returning to Ontario to fly with Ed and Lloyd during the week, I was back on Hwy 395, heading north to Lone Pine and Whitney Portal the next Saturday. This weekend adventure on Whitney was more successful; still not reaching the summit, but teaming up with another climber who was familiar with the trail, thereby enabling us to follow the safest climbing route despite the snow cover. We camped for two nights at the 12,000 feet Trail Camp, the last level location below the 14,495-foot summit. From Trail Camp I had my first view of the 1,700-foot rock face that reaches up to Trail Crest, with its 100 switch-backed pathway cut into granite slabs and steep scree slopes. Unfortunately, in this second week of May, the switchbacks were filled with snow and ice.

My newfound climbing buddy, Jeff, had been there before at this time of year, and pointed out the winter climbing route to bypass the switchbacks—a long steep snow slope to the right of the switchbacks and to the left of a vertical rockface reaching toward the summit of Mount Muir. The snow slope was clear of protruding rock up until near Trail Crest, so it was a straightforward climb using boot crampons and ice axe. I don't recall whether Jeff and I roped together for the ascent, but on many times I returned to this slope, I always felt safe climbing and descending without rope protection. Bizarrely, that first morning as Jeff and I traversed beneath the lower switchbacks, en route to the base of the slope, we witnessed a falling climber accident. A scream of terror turned out to be from a woman sliding down an ice covered granite slab, having slipped from a notched rock section of the switchbacks. She plunged into a steep cone of soft snow that slowed her fall until she stopped on almost level ground.

We were too far away to be of immediate assistance, but her two companions eventually reached her. They had been following her on the dangerous icy trail, and like her, without crampons or ice axes. Amazingly, she had suffered only bruising and abrasions. Nothing was broken, but she certainly suffered from shock. Her companions gave us a thumbs-up and shouted that they would get her back to their tents at Trail Camp. This incident was my introduction to the presence of novice climbers and hikers, with limited experience, inadequately prepared and poorly equipped, that I would continue witnessing in the mountains of North America. To be fair, I was also a novice, not in alpine mountain training, experience, and having the right equipment, but lacking knowledge of the Sierra Nevada environment.

The primary lesson I learned from those early climbs in the Whitney area was that April and May was too soon to make fast ascents before the snow would either melt or consolidate. Oddly enough, unlike the climbing I'd done the previous year on the Northwest Cascade volcanic mountains, the Sierra Nevada peaks lacked glaciers, and therefore no crevasses to fall into or avoid. The tradeoff was post-holing, often waste deep, in soft powder snow, commonly known as *corn snow*, unconsolidated granular snow that has gone through a short freeze-and-thaw process. It rarely firms up, simply sublimating (changing from snow crystals to water vapor) during the spring and summer heat of California.

297

On the morning of the accident, Jeff and I made hard work whacking through the steep snow slope, finally reaching Trail Crest before turning back, running out of time to get back down, pack up tents and reach Whitney Portal before dark. Jeff was on Whitney so early in the season because he was training for a guided climb of Denali (20,300-foot Mount McKinley in Alaska) the following month. We agreed to keep in touch, a fateful decision that would lead me to climbing and barely surviving Denali with Jeff one year later.

Three weeks after my second attempt at Whitney, I was back on Hwy 395, driving north from Ontario to attempt someplace different until the time when snow cover on the Whitney route had dramatically decreased. This latest adventure coincided with Memorial weekend, the annual start date for summer fun in the mountains, but often the last days of extreme winter weather. As I was about to discover, this was one of those occasions. I had been studying area maps and getting visuals of a parallel valley to the one that contained the Whitney Trail. In this valley, immediately to the south, a trail climbed up to Meysan Lake situated at 11,600 feet, with a headwall above and a snow-filled chute that provided a climbing route to Green Pass at 13,200 feet. South of this pass lay Mount LeConte (13,960 feet) and to the north, Mount Mallory (13,850 feet). Aptly, close by, was Mount Irvine (13,800 feet). As a British Empire climber and occasional friend of Ed Hillary, I wanted to be up there with the earliest heroes of Everest.

This long weekend gave me three days to play in the mountains, and as happened, I needed every moment to achieve some satisfaction for my efforts. The Meysan Lake Trail was impossible to follow because of snow cover, which resulted in battling deep snow on the south side of the valley. Two weeks later, in the same valley, with visibly less snow and following the actual trail, it was evident my first route, on the south side, had been crossing snow-covered talus (jumbled large granite rocks). This earliest attempt to reach Meysan Lake took 11 hours to climb 3,000 feet over five miles, with many unsafe falls taken through the soft snow into the talus jumble beneath, often requiring release of my 60-pound pack to enable extraction. My struggles that day were to live on as a lasting lesson in what terrain and snow conditions to avoid in the High Sierra mountains.

I spent two nights camped by the still-frozen lake, the first night in blizzard conditions, mostly awake, holding down my inadequate tent from coming apart in horrendous wind gusts. This was another lesson to remember for climbs in the High Sierra during late spring/early summer. After the terrible night, and the wind finally stopped, I succumbed to a most needed sleep until midday. Then, in the afternoon I climbed the steep snow chute, using crampons and ice axe up to the plateau of Green Pass. It was a pleasant and easy exercise, not carrying the heavy pack, and moving on firm snow. I spent no more than 30 minutes at the Pass because of the need to return to my tent before dark. It was enough time to discover why I had come into the Meysan Valley: An optional route to Trail Camp on the Mount Whitney trail, and noticing that climbing Mount Mallory from the Pass would be straightforward. The second night by the lake was calm and cold with some snowfall, but followed by a clear morning and a relatively easy trip down the valley on its northern side. Then, the now-familiar drive south on Hwy 395 to Ontario ... and back to my job in the sky!

Two weeks later I was back in Ontario, this time as a passenger on a UPS scheduled flight. I had planned a four-day adventure on what I called 'Peter's Grand Traverse.'

This involved a return to camp one night at Meysan Lake, the next day climb the snow chute to Green Pass, summiting Mounts Mallory and Irvine, then descend into the valley that leads to Arc Pass, crossing that, for descent to the 12,000-foot Whitney Trail Camp for two nights. The third day would be my third attempt at reaching Whitney's summit, then back to my tent for another night, and hike out to Whitney Portal on the fourth day. As it happened, I was able to follow the Meysan Trail to the lake, which was still partly frozen.

The next day I made it all the way to Trail Camp, but climbed only Mount Mallory on the way. Access to the base of Mount Irvine was a little more complex, so it had to wait for another visit. What a difference two weeks of snow-melt had made in both valleys. The lower sections of the trails were completely clear of snow up to 11,000 feet, and above that, only scattered patches, until reaching the slopes leading up to Trail Crest on the Whitney Trail. The 100 switchbacks to the Crest were still impacted with snow and ice, so I used the parallel slope with crampons and ice axe, accompanied by three other climbers, similarly equipped.

The continuation of the trail from Trail Crest to the Whitney summit was most impressive, an incredible engineering feat, cut through sheer rock, steep talus, and around rock pinnacles. I was destined to walk this trail many times in the future. The first occasion was overwhelming, but I never ceased to be awed by the journey along this rock highway above 14,000 feet. The summit was a surprise—a large sloping plateau with the highest point at 14,495 feet, then dropping down a vertical face to nothingness, and with a splendid view. I was introduced to marmots for the first time. These furry little critters came out from under the summit rocks, looking for handouts from early season climbers. I wondered how they made it through the winter months, because there was no sign of plants on this barren landscape. I thought them very friendly after giving them an occasional treat, very cute and photogenic until I returned to my tent at Trail Camp. Two of them had dug underneath the sides of the tent and were busy tearing apart the food bag I'd left, peeing and pooping on my sleeping bag, and when surprised by my arrival, ripped a hole in the side of the tent to escape.

So, another important lesson for camping in the High Sierra. Though there were no trees at Trail Camp, there were enormous boulders I later learned to use by rigging a sling from the top of a vertical face, keeping the food bag well clear from the ground and the top. One behavior of marmots I noticed was their disappearance when the sun went down, and not appearing again until the morning sun was on the rocks. Keeping food in the tent at night was not a problem with marmots, but definitely a problem with bears. In those long-ago days, to prevent bears from tearing one's tent— and maybe you—apart, food bags had to be hung in tall trees, and if not done well, the bears would get your food. Fifteen years later, the food-stealing problem from bears, marmots, and other small critters was solved with the compulsory introduction of bear-proof cannisters in the High Sierra. At night, all food items, including trash and toothpaste, are placed in the cannister, which is then placed some distance from the tent. Despite the effectiveness of the cannisters, I've seen backpacks torn apart by bears when the victim has inadvertently left some small food item, an energy bar or even its wrapper, in one of the pack pockets.

With most of my last night's meal eaten or contaminated by marmots, it was fortunate I was returning to civilization the next day. Breakfast consisted of un-creamed, unsweetened coffee and a last energy bar left over from the Whitney summit climb. The descent to Whitney Portal was a delight, with the trail mostly clear of snow and returning as a conquering hero (in my own mind) of the highest point in the Lower 48 States. I'm not sure whether I experienced an epiphany from this adventure, and for the future implications that linked me to the High Sierra, but I was certainly addicted to the environment and elated at what I'd achieved.

By mid-summer 1988 I was crewed with Captain Paul Darby, a British ex-pat who had served in Vietnam with US Forces, and Flight Engineer Dick Phillips, ex-Air Force. We had weekend layovers in Portland, so I was back to climb Mount Jefferson in Oregon, followed by layovers in Salt Lake City, an opportunity to explore the High Uinta Wilderness in northern Utah, including a dicey free-solo rock ascent of the 12,500-foot Mount Hayden.

Then, during a long weekend (Labor Day) layover in Oakland, California, I drove over Sonora Pass on Highway 108 in the middle of the night to enter Yosemite National Park from its eastern entrance. This bizarre journey was for a summit attempt on Mount Lyell (13,100 feet), the highest point in Yosemite. The road trip from and back to Oakland was hazardous, and my failed climb to within 200 feet of the summit was high risk. I would need crampons, ice axe, and a roped partner. Many years later I did reach the summit of Mount Lyell using crampons and ice axe, but free-solo. The key was having the knowledge of exactly where to step off the glacier onto the steep rockface that leads to the summit ridge.

In early January of 1989, I was invited by Jeff, the climber from Palmdale I had met on Mount Whitney the previous May, to join him on a climb of the 20,320-foot Mount McKinley (Denali) during May and June. As preparation for this extreme mountaineering expedition in

Alaska, I was asked to do winter climbs of San Gorgonio, the 11,500-foot mountain, ninety miles east of Los Angeles and close to San Bernardino. We would be an expedition of four: Jeff, his wife, Kim, friend Bryan—all aged 40, and me—aged 50. On the San Gorgonio climbs, I would meet and work with the other three, learn to travel on snowshoes, and practice moving as a roped team. Thanks to my senior First Officer status with UPS, I had no difficulty scheduling layovers at Ontario, from where it was a short drive to the base of San Gorgonio.

For reasons I don't recall, I made a shift from layovers in Ontario to Denver, Colorado. After checking out the Rand McNally Road Atlas, I had discovered Longs Peak, a 14,200-foot mountain within an easy drive from Denver. As a result, I flew with Captain Jack Mahall and Engineer Steve Drake throughout April into May's first two weeks. The schedules were an appealing change, mainly daytime flying from Denver to Billings to Des Moines—for a long lunch break and short sleep—then back to Denver for the night. On long weekends, I went mountaineering on Longs Peak— three hazardous climbs. Jack went on long-distance cycling rides and Steve jump-seated home to Los Angeles. During our daily rest periods at Des Moines, Jack went off riding his bike (carried in the plane), leaving Steve and me sleeping for a few hours after lunch. One afternoon as we three came together for the flight back to Denver, Jack hobbled into the briefing room with a sprained ankle having taken a fall from his bike. Jack could have put me in the left seat where the nosewheel steering yoke was located, but instead, insisted on still playing captain, though unable to use the rudder pedals or brakes. He had me do the flying, but we needed a workaround for ground handling. The fix was Jack did the nosewheel steering, and I footed the brakes before takeoff and after landing.

From mid-May until the end of June, I was in Alaska for the Denali expedition. When I returned home to Louisville, Kentucky, I was reassigned to the UPS ground school and simulator for upgrade training to B-727 captain, which culminated with a line-check in September. Then finally, I was flying schedules as a captain from the beginning of October. However, as expected, my days of climbing on the company's time were over because my new junior status did not allow me to win schedules with long layovers in the desired mountain locations.

Soon winter was on its way, affecting the mountains in the northern States, and additionally, I suffered a fitness limitation that forced me to stop running and jogging. The irony was, after returning from three weeks climbing, mostly above 17,000 feet on Denali, I felt super fit at the lower elevations. One consequence was speeding up my running, including sprinting around school tracks and golf courses, finally resulting in a pinched sacroiliac nerve. The lower back pain was so severe that I had to give up running, tennis, racquetball, squash rackets, and even kicking soccer balls with my youngest son. The good news from my newfound chiropractor was I could continue to climb mountains with heavy backpacks, ride bikes, and still have sex. So that's what I practiced for the next 30 years, but strangely, I never rode bikes!

1989: Surviving Denali

"Without the possibility of death, adventure is not possible."

Reinhold Messner after his solo ascent of Everest in 1980

WAS JUNE 17, 1989, a day to remember or forget? It depended on the particular perspective I was able to focus on the event. We made the decision to turn back 600 feet below the summit of Denali, after voting for survival and not victory. If we had continued in a last desperate effort to grab the 20,320-foot prize, our chances of surviving the descent to the High Camp were extremely limited. At best, we would have suffered severe frostbite. At worst, death. So go the hard decisions of mountaineering. Three weeks of struggle, exposure, and ordeal moving slowly upward on the massive ice slopes of Denali, North America's highest peak, now seemed a futile gesture—all for nothing. Or was it? I look back over the scrawled notes of my Denali journal in an attempt to find justification for this extreme and apparently useless effort.

Our plan was to fly into the Kahiltna Base Camp, at an elevation of 7,500 feet on May 29th, and hope for three weeks of good weather during the month of June. At Base Camp, numerous climbing parties were returning from unsuccessful attempts on the summit, now waiting to be flown out. It was reported that conditions had been unsafe for climbing for most of the past three weeks. Three British climbers had fallen to their deaths. Another group had their tents and two clients blown off the 3,000 feet headwall below High Camp at 17,200 feet. Two Japanese climbers died in their tent at Denali Pass, 18,200 feet. Was it hypothermia, carbon monoxide poisoning, or high altitude pulmonary edema? No one seemed to know. What was certain, the weather had been extreme for the time of year, so we hoped that conditions would improve for our attempt during the next three weeks. The odds could well be in our favor.

After a week on the mountain we had a problem—morning procrastination. Jeff and his wife were reluctant to get up early enough for a full day's climbing. On June 7, although not the best weather conditions, but with other groups moving past our camp, we were not packed up until two in the afternoon. Then it became a slow march, with long breaks in the extreme cold conditions for repairs to Bryan's crampons. We circumnavigated Windy Corner in icy conditions for the longest, coldest 13 hours off climbing I had ever experienced, stumbling into the 14,200-foot High Base camp at three in the morning, with the temperature at minus-10° F. My feet were near freezing, and upper body close to hypothermia, thinking I would never be warm again. Kim and Bryan seemed much worse than me.

There was no discussion on either the cold or our choice of moving so late and for so long, all because of indecision by our leader. After that terrible day, I decided we would never make the summit if Jeff's vacillation continued, but despite numerous clear and constructive references to this problem, nothing changed. I gave us the name *Jeff's Midnight Wanderers*. After three days of rest and warmth at the High Base camp, we were blessed with a good weather day for climbing the Headwall to the Notch at 16,200-feet.

306

We made a carry of four days' food and fuel that we cached at the Notch. Predictably, we began the climb late, at 2:30 p.m., and didn't reach the Notch until 8.30 p.m. Fortunately, the weather remained excellent with great views on both sides of the West Buttress. The climb and descent of the headwall was protected by fixed ropes, which were difficult to use, particularly on the descent. We returned to a very cold camp in the early hours of the morning.

On June 12, as expected, another late start, and no excuse! The weather was perfect with a morning temperature around minus-2 F. With heavier loads we staggered up to the Notch again, not arriving until 9 p.m. Jeff then decided that because of the late hour we'd remain and camp at the Notch instead of continuing to the 17,200-foot High Camp. It was not a popular decision. Snow blocks and walls had to be constructed in very hard snow on a steep exposed slope, a place where climbers had fallen stepping out of their tents to pee without crampons on their boots. It was midnight before the work was complete. Then, very cold and exhausted, we cooked in our individual tents.

On such an exposed high ridge, with a beautiful clear day, Bryan and I expected we would be on our way to the much safer location of the High Camp, but it didn't happen until 6 p.m.—another wasted opportunity. We traveled along the superb ridge of the West Buttress for approximately 1.5 miles and a climb of 1,000 feet, but it took until midnight with our heavy loads, cold wind, and Kim's now noticeable distress. Once there, it was a hasty thrown-up camp and time for one hot drink. Early the next morning, Bryan and I build snow block walls to protect our tent against the wind, which continued unabated throughout the day. Jeff and Kim didn't make an appearance, so I assumed they were peeing and pooping in their tent.

That next night, sleeping at 17,200 feet, I suffered from

periodic breathing (Cheyne-Stokes Respiration), which made sleeping almost impossible. Every time I dropped off to sleep, I would gasp for breath, needing to force myself to stay awake. After taking a Diamox tablet, and with increased ventilation in the tent, the symptoms diminished before dawn. I also began to suspect that continuing to cook in the tent vestibule was giving both Bryan and me a dose of carbon monoxide poisoning, something easy to do at that altitude, where only 50 percent normal oxygen is available.

On June 15, at High Camp, with the wind undiminished, but the sun shining through a thin layer of cloud, five other climbing groups were camped nearby, but nobody moved, all hoping for a good summit climb the next day. If not then, for us, our last day for a summit attempt would be the following day (June 17). Either way, we needed to start a descent by June 18 at the latest in order to reach Anchorage in time for flights home. The constantly bad weather on Denali had made the expedition most disagreeable, with its constant cold and high winds and dangerous living conditions. Midnight temperatures were minus-40° F, and minus-20°F at midday.

The next day we began preparations early, and in exceptionally cold conditions. The sky was mostly clear with some wind and snow pluming over the summit. All climbing teams held off moving until 10 a.m., when Brian Okonek of Denali Guides began a carry-up to Denali Pass. Mugstump and his team of three left for the summit. Others, like ourselves, postponed until finally by mid-afternoon, the conditions had noticeably improved, but then it was too late to move according to Jeff. *He opined that we should have tried this morning and ignore the conditions.* At last! He realized that constant procrastination leads to failure, and we may have thrown away our last chance for a successful summit climb. So his Plan B was to leave at 7 a.m. the next morning, regardless of conditions.

The Genet team decided to make a last attempt that afternoon, but the Chilean Women's team was still waiting like us. Frustratingly, the afternoon was the most settled we'd experienced for many days, with a warm sun and no wind. It became obvious that most teams having left that morning would reach the summit and return to High Camp in pleasant conditions. Bryan and I couldn't help feeling we had blown our last chance by not leaving that afternoon, but we hoped good fortune would smile on us the next day. If so, then Jeff could take all the credit for his wise decisions. Astoundingly, early that morning he was considering giving up altogether and descending to the 14,200-foot Base Camp. He'd been displaying very erratic judgement in recent days.

At 9:45 a.m. on June 17, we left for the summit in perfect conditions, although some snow pluming was obvious along the summit ridge. We hoped this wind would reduce by late afternoon, our estimate for reaching the summit. We made good time to Denali Pass, with a wind howling in from the east. Then it was a slow climb up the ridge to the football field, with the summit knoll just ahead, maybe two hours to go. We reached 19,700 feet at the same time as a cloud bank rolled in from the west, driven by gale force winds. The summit knoll rapidly became obscured by the clouds and the general consensus from ourselves and other climbing parties in the vicinity was for a hasty retreat to the High Camp before the weather situation deteriorated further, limiting our chances of a safe return. The static temperature was minus 20° F and dropping. The decision to turn back, so close below the summit, was heartbreaking, in the realization that was our last chance at a summit attempt, but the decision to retreat was the only choice if we were to survive Denali.

Our descent to High Camp was extremely hazardous, with gale force winds, exhaustion, frozen drinking water, and demoralized. We took special care from Denali Pass to the High Camp, because there had been numerous fatal accidents on this section of the descent. Finally, at 10 p.m., we arrived at our tents and gratefully crawled into sleeping bags to endure the noise of ever increasing wind gusts as the night progressed. Bryan was really depressed because of our failure. My reaction would come later, but I knew that had the fine weather held, I would have made the summit, so for the moment I was content. At least we were all still alive and without frostbite. The Genet team that returned from the summit early this morning had suffered a number of frostbite casualties. That would have been tough—no summit and no toes!

That night, I slept well for the first time at the high altitude, despite a roaring storm throughout the night and morning. While waiting for the wind to drop, we packed up camp, and then decided to descend down the Rescue Gully, which was a straight shot of 3,000 feet to the High Base camp at 14,200 feet. This decision was based on a move by the Genet and RMI groups to do the same because they considered the West Buttress route too exposed with the prevailing wind. This descent on fixed ropes took forever, but absolutely necessary on the steep exposed slope and imbedded crevasses.

On June 19, we began a night journey down from 11,000 feet to the Kahiltna Base Camp carried out in beautiful conditions. There was no wind, not particular cold, with firm snow underfoot. We arrived at the Base Camp in early morning and erected our tents for the last time on this abominable mountain. Bryan and I had a celebration with many mugs of essential hot fluids before being flown out to the town of Talkeetna by Jay and Cliff Hudson at midday on the June 20, after 22 days on the mountain.

My final assessment: Overall, it was a great disappointment. The combination of bad decisions and constant extreme weather had made our expedition a hazardous mountain experience. But I couldn't complain too much, because I had gone into this climb with my eyes open, guessing something like this would occur. At least we all survived, returning to the flat plains below with no injuries or frostbite!

1992: Mera Peak, The Last Great Adventure

A MASSIVE WHITE RAMP towered over me, reaching endlessly to where the deep indigo sky met the rim of the world. Thin banners of snow streamed downwind off the slopes above, obscuring any possible view of the summit ridge. Mingma was up ahead, waiting patiently, as he had for the last six hours since we left High Camp at 19,000 feet. I marveled at his ability to climb so effortlessly in this thin air and envied his Sherpa genes and his youth for the hundredth time.

On leaving High Camp, I counted 50 paces between rests; then I was down to 15. Mingma Sherpa, lifeguard and guide, must have considered me the slowest client he'd had on a mountain. He was undoubtedly aware that the day was passing and our progress toward the summit was painfully slow. I needed an excuse to stop the agony and retreat without too much loss of face, convinced my 52-year-old body would no longer survive the effort or altitude. We've passed 20,500 feet—taller than Denali and the highest I'd climbed. Indeed, this was enough ... call it a day. It wasn't really giving up. It was the sensible thing to do, the responsible decision to make. I gestured at Mingma to wait up and slowly climbed to where he was leaning on his ice axe, braced against the constant wind.

312

I expressed doubt as to my ability to continue climbing. Mingma suggested we rest awhile and have something to eat, then perhaps climb to within sight of the summit ridge. I slumped into the snow, looking downslope and toward the north. If for no other reason, the view was worth the climb. The massive black rock faces of Everest and Lhotse towered above us to the north. East to northeast was Kanchenjunga, Chamlang, Makalu, and Baruntse. To the west were the peaks of Ama Dablam, Cho Oyu, and Kangtega. Six of the highest peaks of the world were in view from this vantage point. Should I have been satisfied with this achievement? Mingma was silent. We were temporarily sheltered from the wind, and in the quiet, I pondered my motives for being there: Mera Peak, 21,500 feet, Kingdom of Nepal, March 27, 1992.

It began in 1983. I had signed up for a strenuous five-week high-altitude trek in the Himalayas. It was a 250-mile ramble over some of the highest mountain passes and through the world's deepest valleys. My traveling companion was Mal Hill, a 42-year-old Aussie from Brisbane, and I had recently reached the age of 44. Both of us had some limited climbing experience; Mal on rock faces and me with alpine mountaineering. We coughed, hacked, and stumbled our way around this Himalayan marathon to keep up with the other, much younger expedition members. Surprisingly, after four weeks on the trail, we both returned to civilization in good shape. We had pitted ourselves well against the fierce opposition of youth. We re-entered Kathmandu victoriously, and two days later, rested, feasted, and downing a few pints of good beer, decided that despite our aging bodies, we could easily knock off a Himalayan 20,000 footer. So the journey to Mera Peak began.

The demands of the real world were to interfere with our climbing goals and desires. My corporate pilot position in Australia went away, and I moved with my Alaskan-born wife to the United States. Mal also had a job change and moved to Manchester, England. The Himalayan mountains became a fanciful dream. Both of us continued to climb, albeit modestly. Me in California, Oregon, and Alaska; Mal in the United Kingdom and Switzerland. But the dream remained despite the passing years.

Eventually, it was 1991, and the game was afoot. We had the time, the means, and the motivation still intact. However, the sobering reality was that we'd been pushing the limit back in our forties. Eight years later, in our early fifties, we had to be mad to contemplate a 20,000 footer, never mind Mera Peak with a summit of 21,500 feet. Yet our confidence overrode commonsense, so we planned our venture in the spring of 1992. With the assistance of Wilderness Expeditions in Sydney, Mal put together a small team of climbers for Mera with a start date ex-Kathmandu of March 8.

I left Louisville on March 5, loaded with 90 pounds of equipment, including UPS baseball hats, tee-shirts, and the UPS flag I'd carried to 19,600 feet on Denali in 1989. I meet Mal in Bangkok; the old firm was together again, wanting to make the most of every precious day ahead. Already I saw the trip over before it had begun, a measure of the intense anticipation such an adventure engenders.

I was introduced to Pete Trethewey, the sole member of the original Aussie team that Mal put together. Pete, a 35 year-old from Melbourne, was in the computer business with Mal. He had climbed in Australia and appeared to be a vital asset to our team. The remainder of Mal's team had bailed out of the project for various reasons. But that was okay. This was always intended to be a very personal climb.

However, on March 7, we learned that our Nepal support organization, In–Wilderness, had fielded two more climbers on arrival in Kathmandu. Both were Australians who originally had planned for a high-altitude trek in the Everest area. Martin Shaw, 43, lived in Sydney and did tax business for the federal government. Born in Zimbabwe, Martin had traveled extensively in Africa and Asia. He also had the distinction of climbing Mount Kenya and several volcanoes in Indonesia. Our fifth member was Russell Harvey, 27, the youngest of the team, from Sydney and equipped with valuable expedition skills. He worked as an ambulance officer and para-medic in Sydney, and his Sherpa name would be Doctor. Russell had more energy than the rest of us put together and spoke passable Nepali, learned during a previous trip to Nepal.

The return to Kathmandu was spellbinding. The air, the smells, the people, and the high snow peaks towered above the green hills to the north of the city. All were so familiar and delightfully exotic. We were driven through the narrow, noisy streets to take up residence in the 'Summit.' Hotels in Kathmandu have wonderfully evocative names: Everest, Annapurna, Yak & Yeti, and naturally, the Summit. What could be more appropriate for a group of intrepid mountaineers? At the hotel, we met our expedition leader for the first time. Mingma Dorje Sherpa looked 30 but could be older or younger with an easy smile and relaxed manner. Mingma was a qualified high altitude guide and member of the Nepal Mountaineering Association. He had been on Everest three times, once reaching 28,000 feet. Another attempt involved an avalanche at 24,500 feet on the West Ridge. Mingma escaped with frostbite but left behind a close friend, who died in the wreckage of their tent.

There was little time to enjoy the sights and sounds of Kathmandu. The following morning was spent finalizing climbing permits, equipment, and packing. By 2 p.m., we were on a bus for a seven-hour journey to the jump-off town of Jiri. Mera Peak is in the Khumbu region of Nepal, situated to the east of Kathmandu. It's the home of the Sherpas and Sagamatha, Mother of the Universe. That's Mount Everest to us outsiders. There are two methods of reaching the Khumbu: One can fly by Twin Otter from Kathmandu airport to the 9,200-foot high Lukla airstrip in 45 minutes, or one can bus to Jiri and then walk for seven days to reach the same location. Tourists take the airplane; climbers normally walk. For climbers, the walk from Jiri has two distinct advantages: altitude acclimation and fitness training. The cumulative distance is close to 100 miles with a series of ascents that total 25,000 feet. Also, the walk from Jiri encompasses much of the traditional route from Kathmandu to the Base Camp of Everest, travelled by the great Himalayan mountaineers of the past. We would literally walk in the footsteps of Eric Shipton, Sir Edmund Hillary, and lesser known masters of the Himalaya.

I have never enjoyed bus trips in Nepal, the journey from Kathmandu to Jiri being no exception. The road is rough, narrow and snakes up and down Himalayan 'foothills' that would be classified as alpine peaks in any other country. The bus suffered two tire blowouts and other mysterious breakdowns. The other climbers and I were kept out of the loop and had no idea what was going on. Welcome back to Nepal! I needed to remember to relax. Despite the apparent confusion, the Nepalese have a happy knack of sorting things out … it just takes time! The journey was not without interest. The punctured tires were repaired at a roadside workshop by a young boy, the size of my 10 year-old son, while the adults sat and watched. We commented on the usefulness of bringing up Western children in the same way.

Around 11 p.m. we stopped at a roadside inn for steaming plates of rice and curried lentils, washed down with copious draughts of hot sweet tea. This supper break gave all of us—Sherpas, porters, and clients, an opportunity to observe and chat with each other. We were a self-contained expedition. That is, we, the clients were supported by Sherpa climbing guides, a cook team and numerous Nepalese porters. The porters carried the group camping gear, bulk food, and also much of our personal equipment. For the initial stage of the expedition, to Lukla, we were supported by a group of 20, Mingma being the overall leader and organizer. His assistant, Nema Dorje Tamang, although not a Sherpa, was an experienced high altitude climber and guide. Nema was an ethnic Tamang, a hill people like the Sherpa with a common Tibetan and Buddhist heritage. Pasang Sherpa was the cook, assisted by Vishnu, Hari, and Kooma. In addition, we had Karma Sherpa, an experienced trekking guide who assisted Nema in the day-to-day direction of the porters.

It was 2 a.m. before we eventually reached Jiri. We'd been on the road 12 hours and not seven, as originally suggested by Mingma. It was as black as the inside of a cow ... and cold. The village dogs howled and barked at our arrival. We stumbled around in the darkness, getting feeling back into stiff limbs and numbly watched the Sherpas erecting tents in a small field. Sleeping bags were found in the jumble of equipment and we collapsed into grateful sleep for the few remaining hours before daylight. The climb couldn't possibly be any worse than the bus journey we'd just experienced!

Dawn in a Nepalese village—the dogs stopped barking, finally exhausted, and the cocks started crowing. It was 6 a.m. 'Bed Tea'! We were awakened by Vishnu unzipping the tent door and thrusting large mugs of hot tea into our protesting hands. Ten minutes later he was back with hot washing water. *Shave that face! Brush those teeth!*

Stuff this sleeping bag! Roll that mattress! Pack up, and get the hell out of the tent before 6:30 or it will be folded around your ears!

Ah! I remembered this routine so well—and hated it with a vengeance. Mal had shared cramped tents with me for years and knew my reaction to this custom. He quickly packed and left the tent to me and my constant bitching. I was out of the tent with my bags just as the first pegs were pulled and the fly was dragged off the poles. I muttered curses at the Sherpas and porters, who simply smiled engagingly and wished me good morning as they folded the tent and whisked away my equipment bag.

Breakfast was ready—a large pot of hot cereal, fried eggs, and chapattis, followed by more tea, hot chocolate, and even instant coffee! My choice in the mountains is always the tea. This is a land of tea drinkers and it comes first class, embellished with a wonderful wood smoke flavor. It was now 7 a.m. The porters had already left on the first day's march. It was our turn to get underway. A subtle air of excitement was evident in the group. The sky was clear and the day was beginning to warm with the first touch of sun on the campsite. A number of village kids milled around looking for handouts, and laugh with us when we tried to scold them in broken Nepali. Nepalese parents are normally ashamed to learn their children have been begging, and we attempted to reinforce the lesson. We left the campsite behind, walking through the main street of Jiri to the road head, where the trail to the Khumbu and Sagamatha begins.

The main street of Jiri was alive with activity; even at this early hour of 7 a.m. the roadside stalls were open and busy. Groups of porters with loads resting on stone benches were preparing to move off. There were other groups of foreigners up and about. Perhaps they were trekkers or maybe climbers like us? I was sure we'd meet some of them along the trail. At the end of the street was a bridge over a somewhat polluted stream. Beyond, a turning area for large vehicles and the beginning of the trail to the Solu Khumbu. No signs, just a wide untidy path heading off into the hills. We joked and laughed with the local kids who'd been following our small party as if we were the Pied Piper. Photos were taken and we were on the way. What expectations we had! After months of preparation, anticipation, and the unrelenting hassle of getting to this place, I finally began to believe I would reach Mera Peak.

We were assured by Mingma that the day's walk was no more than four hours, climbing from Jiri at 6,000 feet to cross Kharubas Pass at 9,000 feet, then steeply descending to the village of Shivalaya, to return to an elevation of 6,000 feet. This pattern of climb and descent continued throughout the approach walk. Each day we ascended 3,000 to 5,000 feet, then gave up much of the height gain by late afternoon. As the days progressed the campsite locations became higher as we moved toward the Solu Khumbu and Mera.

The first day's walk was glorious. It was spring, and the rhododendrons were in full bloom. Their magnificent scarlet blossoms covered the hillsides. I was finally walking in the Himalayas at the right time of year to witness this spectacle. It was obvious Mal and the others were also enchanted by our surroundings and we chattered and laughed like a bunch of kids out of school for the summer. The Nepalese we passed on the trail were friendly and talkative. The use of English was common. Many pressed their hands together and said Namaste, the traditional greeting. For those of us who had been here before, we returned the greeting in kind. Our newcomers soon learned that this social custom was genuine and not just a display for tourists.

The sun was warm; there was little wind and we

traveled comfortably in shorts and tee shirts. I'd handed out the UPS baseball hats and tee shirts (compliments of UPS Personnel in Louisville) to the four Aussies, Mingma, Nema, and Pasang. The color black looked good on the Sherpas and for all of us was most practical; it didn't show dirt. The baseball hats were well received by the Sherpas and became a status symbol. In the weeks that followed it was rare to see either Mingma or Nema without the hats, and I suspect they even slept with them on.

During that first day I mistakenly gave Nema Dorje Tamang the name of 'Dozzie,' which stuck for the remainder of the expedition. Walking with Mingma, I attempted to determine the names and pecking order of the various Sherpas who accompanied us. Mingma patiently and repeatedly verbalized Nema's full name to me. I failed to understand, and settled for 'Dozzie' as my best interpretation of Dorje. It would have been so much easier to call him Nema. 'Dozzie' he became, the finest of travelling companions—quiet, strong, resilient, and ready with a smile and helping hand. While Mingma traveled ahead of the group, Dozzie acted as sweeper, waiting patiently while one or more of his clients dallied on the trail, perhaps for a photographic moment, the call of nature, or out of sheer exhaustion.

We paused for a lazy lunch below Kharubas Pass. Good views and great weather. Pasang and his team provided a cooked lunch, washed down with hot lemonade and tea. I knew I was truly back in Nepal, and enjoyed every moment. We relaxed in the sun and began to learn about our fellow travelers. The afternoon's walk would be easy—all downhill to Shivalaya.

I invited an African trekker to join us for lunch. Esa was a young man from the Ivory Coast travelling alone and supposedly on his way to Beijing, presumably after he'd returned to Kathmandu. He was somewhat of an enigma, surrounded by an aura of mystery and adventure, as are most foreigners one meets in the high mountain trails of Nepal. Lunch finished, we trekked downhill to Shivalaya, a tidy little village sitting on the eastern bank of the Khimti River, a narrow strip of level ground between steep valley walls. Our trail winded down to a suspension bridge that spans the Khimti River, leading directly into the village.

Sitting huddled under the bridge supports was a scarecrow figure dressed in filthy rags. The man's face was almost European, but very dark. At first glance, I believed him to be a remnant of that sad tribe of Western hippies who drifted into Nepal during the 70s. Their quest was for Eastern enlightenment, but all too often cheap drugs and relaxed law enforcement offered the less determined a quick path to 'Clear Light.' They eventually became an embarrassment to the Nepalese government and were encouraged to go elsewhere. The man, or this remnant of a man, appeared lost to his own family and culture, a cruel ending to an 'alternative lifestyle.' Whatever he was, our Sherpas and porters treated him as an outcast.

Later that evening we saw him stumbling downriver on his stick legs, pursued by large dogs from the village snarling and barking in their fury. He barely kept them at bay with the help of a long stick. At some territorial boundary known to the dogs, they halted their chase and returned to the village. The ragged figure disappeared into the evening mist rising off the river. Perhaps this was rough justice at work, karma meted out to a thief, a hardened criminal. Nevertheless, we were saddened by the event, witness to a life without dignity. But this was neither our country nor our rules. We could not interfere.

The river was clean and swift. Martin, Russell and I took the opportunity to wash clothes and bodies in this very cold water. I recall from previous trips that this was a luxury we'd lose as we climbed to higher elevations. The closer we approached the multitude of glaciers that feed the rivers and streams of Nepal, the colder and more unbearable washing would become. Even there, at Shivalaya, under a near tropical sun and at relatively low elevation, the bathing experience was decidedly unpleasant. Mal was no fool! He was quite content sitting on the riverbank washing feet and socks only. Young Pete was lying down in his tent, our first victim of Kathmandu Quickstep, a.k.a. 'the runs.'

Dinner, this first night on the trail, was delicious. Pasang and his cook boys gave us a taste of their very best outdoor cuisine. Young Pete stuck his head into the mess tent, took one sniff, gagged, withdrew quickly, and staggered off into the night. The rest of us spared a few words of sympathy and then returned to eating with a vengeance. It was just a matter of time before each and every one of us would suffer the same fate.

During the course of this dinner we were introduced to the Kerosene Lamp ceremony, a pseudo religious event conducted by Dozzie. The object of worship was a very sad excuse for a kerosene pressure lantern. It had no glass and no pump handle. During the day it was transported on Dozzie's backpack, the delicate mantle exposed to wind, dust, rain, and snow. As evening approached, Dozzie reverently knelt to light this most temperamental contraption. Yards of flame leaped into the darkening sky before it was brought under some semblance of control. A pump handle was borrowed from another lantern we never saw, and was rarely available for any of us Sahibs to use. While eating dinner by the light of this magical device, massive flare-ups, almost to the tent roof, were common. We learned not to touch it; instead, shouted for Dozzie. It seems he was the only one who had the power to control this wondrous thing.

Dinner in the mess tent was the center of our social life during the expedition. Dynamic conversation on a wide range of subjects became the order of each evening. Mingma appeared briefly for an informal planning conference, seeking our concurrence for the following day's activity. After that first day, we were known to Sherpas and porters by assigned nicknames: I was Pilot, Mal was Grandfather, Russell was Doctor, Martin was Marty, and Peter was Young Pete.

The rest at Shivalaya was wonderful. I slept soundly for ten hours, making up some of the sleep deficit from the previous few days. Bed tea at 6 a.m., and another day began.

The memories of Jiri, warmth, and the excitement of that first day on the trail were blown away by the deathly cold wind of Mera. I studied the broken brown shell peeled from Pasang's hardboiled egg lying on the snow between my cramponed boots. In the misery of imminent failure I attempted to divine a pattern of fate in the pieces of shell, as if they were prophetic leaves in a teacup.

Dejectedly, I ask Mingma to take photographs that I'd planned for the Summit, and from my pack pulled the string of flags prepared at Base Camp. At the top, Australia, then New Zealand, Old Glory, and finally the UPS banner. For Mingma, I was ashamed I did not have the flag of Nepal in the cluster; a planning oversight on my part. I faced upslope, Everest at my back, while Mingma took a series of shots. With the photos complete, Mingma handed back the camera, threw on his pack, turned, and headed off up the slope without a word. I felt obliged to follow. Wearily, I put on my pack, picked up the ice axe and set off in Mingma's trail. I couldn't believe I was actually moving uphill again, albeit slowly. Ten paces, rest; nine paces, rest; eight paces, rest … as I ran down to a maximum of five on the now much steeper slope.

Mingma had psyched me into this. I reflected back to the many times I'd climbed solo, when my mental strength determined the outcome of the climb—not the physical. I'd learned that there are always more reasons for turning back than continuing to a summit and can recall retreating off more mountains than I've successfully climbed. But then, I was still alive for this climb! My mental excuse that day was respiratory disorder: chest cold, bronchitis, possible pneumonia, or even the dreaded HAPE (High Altitude Pulmonary Edema). The chest cold was genuine, the first symptoms at Tangnang four days earlier. I was convinced that the exertion and extreme altitude would quickly progress the common cold to something more serious; that's what all the books on mountain medicine say.

Mal believed I'd been reading too much on the subject and talking myself out of the climb. It looked as if he might have been right. However, despite Mal's astute perception and my mental justification for quitting, there was something seriously wrong in my chest. My lungs were burning with every gasped breath and a deep seated pain was a constant companion. So, I followed Mingma in the knowledge that I'd possibly be carried off this mountain severely disabled. My mind turned inward, ignoring the wind, the pain, and the agony of each step.

Mingma disappeared over the skyline, and it seemed I was totally alone on the mountain. The snow was hard and the slope was steep. Despite terrible tiredness, I had to concentrate on each step: *Take great care. For God's sake, keep those crampon spikes on the surface; use the ice axe correctly. If you slip now, you'll have a nasty little fall. About 2000 feet, give or take a few!*

I'd climbed so much alone in recent years that this experience on Mera felt normal. The tough part was the sure knowledge that one careless step would result in a fall, probably with fatal consequences. No rope, no belays, and no immediate rescue. Such is the lot of the solo climber. Yet many venture into the mountains alone, either out of circumstance or personal choice. The risks are high, but the experience of being alone on high peaks is a very special gift and always I've felt privileged to have the opportunity.

The slope began to ease off and Mingma's head and shoulders appeared above the ridgeline. But what was this? He was not alone! Dozzie was with him, and Mal, Pete, and Russell. They were all grinning like Cheshire cats from beneath goggles and hoods. They'd been to the Summit and were on their way down. It was a moment for celebration, my pain and despair temporarily forgotten. I felt great joy in their victory and clasped each gloved hand in turn. I was particularly elated at Mal's success; he wanted this so badly. Dozzie and Russell appeared to be in good shape but the strain and tiredness was evident on the faces of Mal and Pete.

We had little time to talk. Standing in that wind chilled our bodies—we needed to move on. I briefly explained my chest problems to the others. They responded—no worries, the Summit could be seen from just over the next ridge. Go for it! Mal, God bless him, said he'd climb with me and Mingma until we saw the summit cone. Now, there was no choice; I had to continue until I dropped or reached the Summit, whichever came first.

Since returning from Mera I've often wondered how Mal found the resources, physical and mental, to climb back up the slope again. *Old climbing buddy—I owe you one.*

Back on the mountain, we climbed slowly in Mingma's footsteps. The slope was finally easing off, and with Mal pacing alongside, the effort and agony during the previous hours was almost forgotten. Mingma stopped, waiting for us. He pointed upslope, smiling. Then I saw it—the summit cone. At long last! It was still some distance off, but the slope looked relatively easy, and for the first time since leaving High Camp I believed I'd make it. Any thoughts of irreparable damage to my chest were put aside. Damn the consequences! I was so high then, a few more hundred feet wouldn't make any difference.

Mal and Mingma stood huddled against the wind, looking toward me expectantly. I tried to smile, and asked Mingma whether he'd put up with me for a few more tedious hours of climbing; he nodded. I shook Mal's hand and set off in the direction of the Summit. Mingma saw Mal safely on his way down to join the others, then quickly caught up with me, passed, and moved strongly up the slope. He made no effort to wait for me. Later, I realized his priority was to find a way over the crevasse that circled the higher slopes of the summit cone. Dozzie and his team had some difficulty getting across the large crack in the ice slope, and Mingma was concerned that our final ascent of the Summit might not possible.

The last snow slopes beneath the summit cone were almost level, but it still required a tremendous effort to move one foot in front of the other. Despite the chest pain and the agony of physical movement, I marveled at my mental lucidity: well above 21,000 feet, without supplemental oxygen, seeing and feeling things quite clearly. Blast the common cold and subsequent bronchitis—this would be a day to remember, a truly great summit day though I felt like what I really was, a middle-aged man stumbling about in places I had no right to be! I recall my discussion with Sir Edmund Hillary on the airstrip at Lukla, just eight days before. I had opined that I was getting too old for climbing and Mera would definitely be the Last Great Adventure.

His response was typical: "Don't be ridiculous—you're never too old to climb."

Well, Sir Ed, right now, I'd make you eat those words! I was ashamed of my performance in front of Mingma, and could only hope to finish with some dignity intact. Crawling on all fours up the summit cone would not be appropriate.

For the moment, we were the only two people on the mountain, the others far below, already at High Camp, or even lower. I read somewhere that those who live among, or at the foot of mountains see them as bridges between the human world and the dominion of the gods.

It was during one of my numerous rests beneath the summit that I tried to relate my perceptions to those of Mingma's. What did he see and feel up there—was it the same as me? Certainly, I was in awe of these massive piles of stone and ice, and we were insignificant specks on this huge tilted landscape of Mera. But I could not perceive this as a religious experience. Rather as an affirmation of faith: in my friends, the dream to climb, in Mingma, Dozzie and in myself. Perhaps, hidden beneath the pain and agony of each step was a feeling of transcendence, a knowledge that the future direction of my life would be changed on the Summit of Mera. With these thoughts, I shuffled slowly upward to where Mingma waited—between heaven and earth.

The wind had dropped to a light breeze and the cobalt blue sky was almost clear of clouds as I began the ascent of the summit cone. Mingma was sitting patiently on the down slope lip of the crevasse where the others crossed, if the tracks were any indication. I felt relaxed knowing that the ordeal was almost over and smiled happily at Mingma as I moved up the crevasse edge to where he waited. His news was not good. The small protruding nose of ice on the upslope lip that enabled Dozzie and team to cross had broken away. We were faced with a yawning gap over which some serious mountain gymnastics would be necessary to reach the upper slope of the summit cone.

Furthermore, we had no protection against a fall—no rope or belay devices.

I looked up to the summit proper. It was a mere 50 feet above where we stood. One thing was certain; I did not climb 21,500 feet only to fall unroped into a deep crevasse! For me, this was the Summit. Enough was enough. I advised Mingma of my final decision: "Let's get down off this mountain before we do something stupid." We descended 150 feet to a relatively flat area below the summit cone for a short photo session. Everest was in the background, clouds streaming eastwards off its black granite peak. What a wonderful view and feeling of achievement. But like most big climbs, the joy was short-lived. We still had to descend safely, many thousands of feet to the Base Camp at Khare.

It was 2 p.m. We'd been climbing since 5 a.m. and could not expect to reach the camp for at least another six hours. Time enough to celebrate on the long walk out to the airstrip at Lukla, and later, in the bars of Kathmandu. For the moment, the two of us were faced with a lonely descent of steep snow slopes and the heavily crevassed lower glaciers which were bad enough that morning. With bodies and minds numb from exhaustion, we had a daunting task ahead. My only comfort was Mingma. If anyone could get me down off that mountain alive, he was the man. On the other hand, I doubted whether I could be of any worthwhile assistance to him.

We descended the first 2000 feet rapidly, with only a few short breaks. Below, the mountain was obscured by swirling cloud, and darkness was fast approaching. I saw a figure moving quickly up the slope toward us. Another guardian angel? As he drew closer, I recognized Karma Sherpa, all smiles, climbing the steep hard snow without the aid of crampons—bloody amazing! From beneath the folds of his jacket Karma produced a bottle of heated orange juice, complete with drinking mugs for Mingma and me. This was surely the finest drink I'd ever had. *Thank you, Karma. For this, I shall never forget you.*

With only feeble protests from me, Mingma took my pack and placed it on Karma's shoulders. I was really being pampered ... and enjoying every minute. No doubt in Mingma's estimation, the only way they'd get me down to Base Camp that night was to provide every assistance. He was probably correct. Without further delay we were on our way again, with a quick stop at the High Camp location to uplift the remaining equipment. Karma's ability to remain upright on the steep ice of the lower glacier, without crampons, continued to astound me. I joked with Mingma that Karma, on receiving his first pair of crampons, would be unable to stand on steep ice and snow. Like a goat, he was a natural sure-footed animal without the need of artificial climbing devices.

We were now moving in the cloud, with night so close the visibility was extremely limited. It was time to get off the glacier ice and onto the rocks below. We reached the edge of the glacier just as night finally arrived. Crampons and plastic boots were quickly removed, headlamps were donned and switched on for the final descent in total darkness.

What followed was a true mountain nightmare: the rock was steep and loose underfoot. We were all tired beyond normal limits and the light from our lamps was totally inadequate. Mingma did the route finding out front. Karma moved slightly ahead of me, checking my every step, ensuring I didn't take a fall. There were moments when it seemed we had been travelling in this void for eternity and that it would never end. I kept drifting into partial sleep, suddenly coming awake with a sharp cry from Karma as he saw me stumble over some obstruction on the trail. I had been there before, but never so tired or at such high altitude. Time and distance appeared to pass so very slowly when walking the mountains by night.

With great relief, we reached Base Camp at 8 p.m. We'd been out and about for 16 hours; time to stop. The camp was strangely quiet. It seemed my climbing buddies had all passed out with exhaustion. Mal was barely awake and had left a lamp on in our tent. He muttered a few congratulatory remarks, then promptly fell asleep. Apart from the Sherpas and a number of porters warming themselves by the fire, Russell was the only other person up. The cook team provided hot drinks and food. I wolfed down quantities of soup and hot tea, talked with Russell and Mingma until much of my outward tiredness dissipated. Oddly enough, after all the extremes of the past 24 hours, I was beginning to feel almost normal. But during the night I began coughing, a terrible hacking, retching session that woke the camp from its post adventure stupor. By morning, much of my chest congestion had gone and the day's walk down the Hinku valley into the forest was relatively easy.

Shortly after leaving Base Camp we passed another climbing group moving up from Tangnang. Mal and I stopped to talk with a middle-aged Sherpa travelling with the group. When we explained we'd summited Mera Peak, he was visibly moved. I guess our age was showing after the ordeal of the past few weeks. With a broad smile and much hand shaking, he kept repeating 'namaste.' To be blessed by this mature man of the mountains was praise indeed and made all the effort and agony worthwhile. I turned away, tears brimming, and moved off quickly down the trail.

A few days later we met an old woman travelling with Yak herders, who grasped Mal's arm with dirty, withered hands of steel. He was terrified she would either tear out his heart or hurl him into the fiery pit. Instead, she kept repeating 'namaste', shaking his hand with incredible vigor. It would appear that the old greybeard climbers had achieved a state of grace in the eyes of some Sherpas. There again, they could be cursing us for the foolish foreign devils that we were?

That night, resting comfortably in our forest camp, I quietly discussed with Mal where we had been, what it meant to us, and speculated on future climbs. Was this the 'Last Great Adventure,' or as before, a prelude to something far more grand and ambitious? To climb higher would take more than motivation and physical ability. On Mera we reached our limit, dictated by the worldly demands of time and money.

1993: The Presidents in Winter

Thus would I have it.
Time enough to learn that the mountain is a lie,
that the best climb hopefully towards nothing,
and yearn for summits that are bare.
Why not return to the fat plains below? It is too late.

~ *The Climber,* Alistair Te Ariki Campbell

IN THE QUICKLY GROWING DUSK of evening, I was treated to the incredible sight of my tent floating free in the wind one hundred feet above the snow-covered ridge. The suddenness of the event left me paralyzed, utterly helpless. A strong slap of wind tore the newly erected tent from my hands and lifted it high overhead within seconds. Then came the immediate realization of a night lying curled in the snow, without shelter, exposed to the severe winter cold and high winds. It would be a night of significant discomfort at best, of pure survival at worst.

On Sunday, March 7, 1993, my precarious perch was high on Mount Madison of the Presidential Range, New Hampshire. My first day out on a solo attempt of the Winter Traverse of the Presidents. What a great start. Not only would I have to abandon the adventure, but I'd be damn lucky to see out the night.

I watched the tent's graceful movements in the wind, almost with detachment. It danced like a giant box kite, still directly overhead, and I expected it to move away rapidly at any moment. It rolled and twisted in the currents of air, then with great speed slid to my right and slammed back to earth, tangling in the branches of the small scrubby trees.

My immobility changed to sudden movement, crashing through the trees and snow toward the shelter I'd given up for lost, but I moved as in a nightmare, unable to make any headway. The tent flapped violently in the gusts of wind, threatening to come free. I was not going to make it. *Oh God, give me strength!* The nightmare was absolute: I was sinking waist-deep in the soft powder snow, my snowshoes removed before erecting the tent.

I must wear snowshoes, find my headlamp, and secure the other equipment before going after the tent. Quick, quick. But be smart, be careful, don't jeopardize my survival even more by a hasty dash into the gloom of evening and blowing snow. The adrenalin rush was taking effect. I did what had to be done and moved off on snowshoes toward the tent—but it was gone ... blown away during the few minutes of preparation. I quickly determined a few prominent features to mark the campsite location and mush across the slope to where the tent last lay. But where the hell was it now? Which way to search—up, down, or traverse the hillside? Did it really make any difference? It was probably half a mile away by now! I chose down. It was the easiest, and a rise in the slope below obscures the view.

I moved down 50 yards—and bingo! It was actually there, hanging up in the trees again, 20 yards farther on. I ran, stumbled and slid—and pounced. Got it! Hard to believe. Then to get this wild critter back to the campsite, wherever that was! It was almost dark. I clipped on the headlamp and started back up the slope with the tent flapping madly in the wind. I should have collapsed it again, but didn't dare. The very reason I lost it was the difficulty of solo assembly in such conditions. So I dragged, yanked, and pulled this out-of-control monster through the trees and snow, sobbing with exertion and frustration. A snowshoe came loose; I tripped and fell into two feet of soft snow. Shit, shit, shit! There was a metallic crack, easily audible over the screaming wind, as one of the high-stress tent poles gave way. Drat and double drat.

333

Finally, I was back at the tent site I'd so laboriously carved into the snowbank. Tied this bloody thing down, ice axe one end, a two-foot snow stake the other. Dark by then, but I had to check the damage. The pole had broken at a joint, but it hung together by jamming. The bug screen on the roof of the tent was torn—but who cared about bugs?

Typically, living in tents on mountains in these conditions (I've done it more than once), I rest badly, kept awake by buffeting wind and concern that the tent will not last out the hours of darkness. I knew that night would be different. Just having a tent was a bloody miracle. The 'Mountain Gods' had smiled down kindly in response to my stupidity. I was one lucky climber—for the moment, at least.

Out of the wind and blowing snow, I was back in the Human Race. A tribe of one seeking shelter from a very hostile world. Fire was the next priority. Out with my trusty gasoline stove, which had never let me down, even on the high Arctic slopes of Denali. But that night it refused to burn at full pressure. I was on full survival alert again. I needed fluid—cold would do, but preferably hot—and only the stove could melt the snow to produce the necessary.

The temperature had dropped to plus 10°F. I climbed into the sleeping bag and worked on the stove. Repair kit out, reading glasses on, but they kept fogging up. And then my headlamp went dim and quit. Great, what a trip! *First things first: reading glasses and new batteries inside my vest to warm up. Replace the batteries in the headlamp by feel. Don't get them mixed. Then, glasses on, light working again, and attend to the stove repair—a simple fix.* The pump assembly had frozen with the cold. Free it up, grease the plunger diaphragm with a slice of salami and reassemble. It worked just fine. Excellent—I was back with the living again! The hot drinks and dehydrated dinner were lovely—what a great meal after such a miserable day. And finally to rest. Tomorrow couldn't be half as bad as today.

The following day, in the same general location, I climbed in a total whiteout. There were no footprints, no shadows, and only the occasional glimpse of black rocks floating in the void. The visibility sucked as I was feeling my way between one stone cairn and the next, angling up along the northern flank of Mount Adams. The stone trail markers, although commendably large, were covered with wind-impacted snow and not easy to see.

This was fun: the surface snow was too soft for crampons but too icy beneath for snowshoes' safe use. I finally settled for crampons. I'd rather wade through knee-deep snow than risk sliding down some unseen ice slope. The crampon spikes kept catching on hidden rocks, threatening to tip my seventy-pound pack and me over in a floundering heap. It happened, each event requiring a tremendous effort to get right-side up again. The large cairn at Thunderbolt Junction loomed into view. I was making progress, but the visibility had deteriorated to where it was impossible to see the next trail marker from the last.

I should have gotten out the compass to get a feel for direction, but I'd been there before—three times in summer. It sure looked different now. I had to find a place out of the howling gale. That was the ticket. But where? I could only see 50 feet at the most. I left the trail line at right angles, climbed up a slope, dropped my backpack (including the compass) and continued straight up to a ridgeline. I looked back downslope as the pack disappeared in the void. That was okay; I knew where it was!

There was a deep snowbank protected by rocks on the other side of the ridgeline. It would have to do. I'd dig in well. Back the way I came. Fantastic, there was my pack. *No problem, Peter, you've got this landscape scoped.* I returned to the chosen spot, staggering under the weight of a snow-covered bag. What was this? I dimly saw larger rocks farther down the opposite slope. Even better—a well-protected enclave of rock and drifted snow. Some digging would be required, but the effort would be worth it; protection from the relentless wind and blowing snow.

It was 3 p.m. Plenty of daylight left to make a bombproof shelter, unlike the evening below Madison. And so it began—one to two hours of battling the snow, wind, and tent. I made a temporary repair on the fractured pole—another small step in the game of survival. One thing fixed, another broken, the ice axe shaft snow shovel proved incompatible with my large axe. I'd left the more suitable ice tool behind as a compromise on weight. The shovel fitting bent out of shape, and I was reduced to using the damn thing like a tiny tot's sand spade. The conditions were sure taking a toll on my equipment and well-being.

At last, it was still daylight, and I was inside a firmly fixed shelter. Dry clothes on, inside the sleeping bag, with the stove burning hot and well. Ah! This was good living. The only remaining doubt was how the heck I'd find my way back to the trail if the visibility remained as bad. Oh well, it must be clear tomorrow—no sweat; a cakewalk! In the worst case, I'd run a few compass bearings—not that I really knew where to start. Never mind, I'd worry about that in the morning.

In the meantime, I lay back and relaxed—warm, dry, well-fed—and reflected on the reasons for being on this crazy venture. I'd invited up to five others to join me on a Winter Traverse of the Presidential Range, generally touted as The Greatest Adventure in the Northeast United States. For one reason or another, each probable starter became no-shows: George had leg problems, Emil won a top contract, Leigh went skiing in Switzerland, John had his arm in a sling from shoveling snow, and Glenn chose Colorado instead. So there I was, solo climbing again. I had time off, and nothing would deter me from going for it. Until then, of course. I had doubts of even reaching Mount Washington in these conditions, which was another four miles along the main ridge. I could handle the deep powder snow, the broken equipment, and even the gale force winds, but 50-foot visibility was something else. There were too many unseen rock faces to fall off.

As evening approached, the wind abated somewhat, and large snowflakes began falling. With a start, I awoke from a doze to the sound of voices. Good grief—other crazies were out there? I quickly stuck my head out of the tent flap but saw nothing except falling snow. It sounded like they were digging in at the first location I'd selected for myself. Their voices indicated an organization of purpose, battling the elements to get their tent sheltered from the wind and securely tied down. Since they were okay, I did not make my presence known. *See you in the morning, guys.* I was snug and warm and had no intention of venturing out until the next day, self-contained inside the tent, with a pee-bottle, stove, and plenty of snow to convert into hot liquid.

I slept well, only faintly aware of the reduction in wind strength and the pitter-patter of heavy snow falling throughout the night. It was morning but dark in the tent from layers of snow against the walls. Some digging was required to clear the doorway, only to find the visibility little changed from yesterday. But what a dramatic difference in the landscape! At least 18 inches of fresh snow had fallen during the night and the whiteout situation was extreme. This really was a setback. Some serious decisions needed to be made within the next few hours. Would I sit out another day up there or retrace my route down past Madison to Randolph and the rental car? Perhaps even the latter choice would be difficult to execute safely in these appalling conditions. One thing was sure: if the snow kept falling, it might not be possible to move at all for many days. Better to bail out before it was too late.

I started by having a leisurely and substantial breakfast. I never knew when I'd get the opportunity to eat the next hot meal. I pulled out the compass, saw which way, degree-wise, that I needed to intercept the trail from the campsite. That was odd. The darn compass must have been on the fritz, perhaps too close to crampons or ice axe. Why the hell was it showing the tent alignment 180 degrees from where I knew it was? Maybe a look outside would clear up the mystery. The visibility was still terrible, but I could see the vague outlines of rock cairns not far from the tent. What the ding-dong were they doing in that direction? And what trail was this that I'd camped by? Just then, through a slight clearing of the swirling mists, I saw what could only be the large cairn of Thunderbolt Junction—in the reverse direction and considerably closer from where I thought I'd camped. My God! I walked in a complete circle yesterday afternoon before setting up camp!

I was totally floored by this revelation. How the hell did I ever find my all-important pack again amid such confusion? Another gift from the 'Mountain Gods.' It was definitely time to get off this rock while I was still ahead. I couldn't afford any more mistakes, or for sure, it would be the death of me.

There was a temporary improvement in the visibility, and once again, I was stunned. The other climbers' tent came into view, high on an open snow slope, nowhere near the location I thought them to be. Time to say hello, but to be safe, I took a compass bearing between the two tents as I went. Sure enough, halfway over, both tents disappeared in enveloping mist, and I was forced to walk the remaining distance on the compass bearing. I blundered into their camp, falling over the tent tie-downs. *Where the hell did you guys come from? Oh, just passing by, smelt the tea, and dropped in for a cuppa.* Ha ha. There were two of them, experienced climbers with good gear, and the three of us were probably the only humans alive on that accursed range.

Their story of the previous afternoon was similar to mine. They reached the large cairn at Thunderbolt Junction and then got disoriented, found a slope, dug in, and there we all were, happy little campers on one of the worst mountain ranges in North America for extreme weather. The highest wind ever recorded in the USA—230 mph, was on Mount Washington, just along the ridge from there. I asked the lads what they planned to do? They had five more free days and vehicles at both ends of the range. The best of luck! I was outta there, heading back to my car at Randolph, God willing, and a fair breeze!

Easier said than done. The visibility was so bad, I was forced to walk a compass bearing to find each cairn stumbling, falling, and sliding in the deep snow and underlying ice. I looked forward to the Valley Way trail, down through the trees using just snowshoes in the soft powder. Surprise, surprise, the newly fallen snow slid down the route in mini-avalanches, exposing the hard-packed surface beneath. There were four torturous miles of exhausting, sometimes dangerous descent to the trailhead, but finally, I was there. Oh, joy, it wasn't yet dark, the car hadn't been stolen, and the Sam Adams beer in the trunk was still unfrozen. Two of these little numbers, and who cared a fat-rat's bum about climbing in winter. It was really very easy, but please don't ask me back!

To the others who missed out on this great adventure, what can I say? I know you'll be green with envy when you realize what a fun time you could've had. Next winter, when I'm looking for volunteers, I can expect a total turnout ... *not!*

But of course the adventure didn't really finish like that. I had two beautiful days left in the White Mountains. A major winter storm warning was in effect, the sky dark and threatening, the snow still falling, and so it was back into the hills to have some fun. *That's the spirit. Don't let on you're a quitter.*

After an overly comfortable night in the Nereledge Inn, it was up Route 16 again to the Pinkham Notch trailhead. I figured that a two-day attack on Mount Washington should be entirely possible via the shortest route—and very straightforward after the Madison-Adams affair. I planned for an easy walk to the Hermit Lake shelters, spend the night, and in the morning make a fast ascent up Lion Head trail to the summit. All going well; I should make it back to Manchester by the next evening in position for the flight to Louisville the following day.

With minimum equipment and a hard-packed trail, Hermit Lake's journey is easy, but once again, it was snowing in 'them there mountains.' Tuckerman's Ravine view was a big fat zero, totally obscured by clouds and blowing snow. Not to worry; the following morning was sure to be okay, particularly with a winter storm in the offing.

The night in the shelter was bitterly cold, and I longed for the flimsy but warm comfort of my tent. It was like an icebox there, and I remained buried in my sleeping bag from dusk to dawn, trying to stay warm. But then it was 6 a.m. Out of the bag, I lit up the stove and prepared for a quick departure. It had snowed heavily during the night, at least a foot of fresh powder. I waded through the drifts to the 'off-season' toilet, a two-berth affair that was half-covered with snow. I forced the inward opening door against the packed snow, got inside, and kicked the door closed. Big mistake! I was trapped in this evil-smelling place, unable to pull the door open! Besides the embarrassment of being locked in this shit-house, I was frustrated with the delay getting starting on the trail. I banged on the walls and shouted in the knowledge that there was no one in the area, particularly at that time of day. Miraculously, the door suddenly came free, and gratefully, I exited the building, half expecting to hear hoots of laughter from a gathered crowd. As it happened, I was still alone in the softly falling snow.

With snowshoe conditions I moved off to the base of the Lion Head trail, sinking deeply into the top layers of new snow and dislodging large dollops of the white stuff from the overhanging trees. *Oh joy, here we go again.* Within a few hundred yards, the trail angled up steeply, and I could no longer maintain traction with the snowshoes. It was crampon-time, and what a battle to put them on in the deep snow! I wrestled with the straps for at least 20 minutes, during which time another climber passed by. Without the benefit of skis or snowshoes, Pierre, a native of Quebec, had been gratefully following in my tracks.

Ahead, Pierre fought his way up the steep slope, and I was the grateful one. He'd been there before, in summer, and was not deterred by the ever-increasing incline as I would've been on my own. The top layers of snow slid down in a fast-moving river from Pierre's footsteps as we began front-pointing with our crampons on the hard ice beneath. If it weren't for the stunted pines on either side, giving a false sense of security, this would be an exposed and hazardous climb. One section was particularly nasty, and I tried not to think about coming back down. Pierre kept pushing; we'd make the summit and be off that mountain in superb style!

We topped the steep slopes near the rock outcrop known as Lion Head one hour and eight hundred feet higher. The wind hit face-on with hurricane force, and the surface visibility dropped to less than 30 feet in blowing snow. We encountered waist-deep drifts on the lee side of the rocks, floundered around, making little headway, and then Pierre decided he'd had enough. Without snowshoes, he wouldn't make his way along the next section of the trail. We bid each other Godspeed, and he was quickly lost in the swirling snow beneath Lion Head. Alone on the mountain again, I felt some trepidation about continuing in what now appeared to be a full-blown storm. But what the heck, I've been in worse—the Antarctic, Denali, or Mera Peak!

Out of the crampons and into snowshoes once more, which was much better. No improvement in the weather, but at least I was making headway through the drifts. Moving faster toward the heart of the storm and farther away from the sanctuary of Hermit Lake. But damn it, I did really want to reach the summit!

I was surprised by the sudden easing of the gradient. Moving along the rim of Tuckerman's Ravine, it was almost flat ground, and I was able to quickly traverse between each successive trail marker with a slightly improved visibility. I felt sad for Pierre. If he'd struggled on for another hundred yards, he could also be running free, with the chance of victory close at hand. The excitement was with me now. I knew the summit was near, even if it was not visible, and the thought of winning a solo prize in such appalling winter conditions was sweet indeed.

However, as I moved up onto the summit cone, it became increasingly evident that I'd need some improvement in the visibility before committing to a summit bid. I resorted to running compass bearings as I angled toward the summit and continued pushing uphill with some guarantee I'd eventually reach the top. The problem would be getting back down to this location to intercept the reverse bearing back to the trail markers on the rim of Tuckerman's Ravine. One tiny error in direction or distance would probably result in becoming lost or stumbling blindly over the edge of a high rock outcrop.

It was a bitter blow: so close, with victory a life-or-death decision. I was vividly reminded of the heartbreaking turn back below the summit of Denali in 1989. The scenario was similar, but I was aware that Mount Washington could be visited anytime with relative ease, so give it away. *Don't be a fool—you've already lost a goodly number of your nine lives during the past few days.* I agonized over the decision for ten minutes, leaning into the howling wind, staring into the void above, and chilled to the core of my soul. I'd failed again, below another summit. At times like this, it was impossible to reconcile the conflict between doing what you know to be safe and the resolve to push on against impossible odds. And all for what? Some trivial pile of rock in a faraway corner of North America. Who will care if I win, lose or die in the attempt? Family and friends will undoubtedly grieve, but this is no Everest, and the general public couldn't care less. So what's the point? The point was it mattered to me, and it's always tough to turn back.

So, with a heavy heart, I retraced my steps along the reverse, compass bearing, in extreme blizzard conditions, but not really noticing in the frustration of defeat. I slowly became aware that I'd need all my concentration and limited expertise to make it down in one piece. At Lion Head rock, I couldn't see anything down the steep slope where the dangerous section of the trail began. I was acutely aware that I had to start at the correct position as the slope tipped over into the near-vertical, or I'd end up perched on the lip of some precarious clifftop. I fought to swap snowshoes for crampons, hopefully for the last time that day, and then moved off from the shelter of the rocks down into a white world.

Unbelievably, two ghostly figures were moving up toward me. Their clothes and faces were thick with impacted snow, their heads bent against the wind; they didn't see me until I was almost on top of them. They reeled back, almost in horror, not expecting to see another living soul on the mountain. I guess I look like hell. I'd been out in this for many hours, wearing a ski mask and white from head to toe. We shouted a few pleasantries to each other before they moved on very slowly, weighed down with heavy packs. Their plan was to traverse Mt. Washington and then along the ridge toward Adams. *Good luck, guys; believe me, you'll need it.* As it turned out, they didn't last much longer. Like Pierre battling the drifts without snowshoes and with their heavy loads, they decided to turn back shortly after our meeting.

At least I had a fix on the trail over the lip of the lower slope. Initially, it was easy, sliding in a mini-avalanche through the gap in the trees and moving farther out of the wind. I reached the steep section, neglecting to turn face-in to the slope, and came off in a tumbling, falling mess, ending suspended head-down in a small tree 30 feet below. This really pissed me off. I should never have allowed that to happen, and furthermore, I was damn lucky not to have driven the ice axe pick through my skull. The tip was perched a couple of inches from my face! So the *Great International Mountaineer* carefully extricated himself from the tree, thanking God no one was around to see and slinked off down the remainder of the trail to the Hermit Lake shelters. Enough was enough. I was outta there—this time for good. I finally admitted defeat against the Presidents in Winter.

1993: Flying the Boeing 747 for UPS

If it's not a Boeing, I'm not Going

GROUND SCHOOL FOR THE B-747 was done at the UPS Training Center at Louisville, followed by flight simulator training at Dallas Fort Worth. On June 19, 1991, I was signed off by an FAA Check Airman—with the B-747 Type added to my American Airline transport license. What an achievement for a simple country boy from New Zealand, establishing his place in the world's largest airline industry … and giving the finger to that small arrogant group of Air New Zealand pilots who considered themselves elitists in the airline piloting business and far superior to American aviators.

Becoming a B-747 captain was the ultimate achievement of my piloting career: Moving up from the piece of British junk—the Bristol Freighter, to the War Machine, the C-130 Hercules—to luxury corporate jets, to the B-727, then finally to the Queen of the Skies.

UPS's first B-747s were Dash-100s and Dash-200s, the so-called 'classics' that had come from PAN AM and TWA, converted from passenger to cargo configuration. An early B-747 pilot had told me the most challenging thing about flying the B-747 was getting the job in the first place. He was right; the B-747 was fun to fly, easy to handle, super-fast at

345

Mach.86 in cruise, and with excellent redundancy from its four engines and multiple backup systems. These days, as a passenger, do I feel totally safe crossing the Pacific for 12 hours in a two-engined Boeing 777? The simple answer is no. My long experience of flying two-engined propeller airplanes over the oceans had provided first-hand knowledge of possible descent into the deep dark sea following an engine failure. Sadly, one day it will happen to a modern two-engined jet airliner. When today's international airlines praise the safety of their two-engined planes, ask them the question: "If they're so safe, why does the US president's Air Force One still have four engines?"

I commanded UPS B-747s for 4,200 hours, always feeling safe, fortunate, and totally in control, including operations in and out of short snow-covered runways in the northern winters. The shift from flying B-727s, mostly within the Lower 48 States at night, to operating the B-747 on daytime operations coast to coast across the USA and internationally to Europe and Asia, was energizing and exciting. Because employment with UPS had become the security I'd been searching for since retirement from the New Zealand Air Force, combined with flying commercial jets that were predictable and stress-free, my best memories from that time are not about airplanes, but about the unique pilots I'd shared cockpits with for 12 years.

My first hands-on piloting of an actual B-747 happened on a scheduled revenue flight from Louisville, Kentucky to Ontario, California with Captain Tom Gummer riding shotgun in the right seat and Lee Bowden in the engineer's position. Thanks, guys, for your kind support on that first day of July 1991. Amazingly, this massive airplane was easy to handle in flight, but moving around on the ground needed practice. The sight image from the cockpit of taxiways, parking spots, and taxiing speed were all deceptive because of the high pilot eye level and the main landing gear situated 100 feet behind the cockpit. Not a problem. I had to be a fast learner, deadheading to Montreal, Canada the next day for a contract flight for El Al, the Israeli Airline, from Montreal to Amsterdam, Holland. Tom Tarnowski, a B-747 instructor with UPS, checked me out on Long-Range Oceanic Navigation across the northern Atlantic. We returned to the USA the next day, landing at JFK, New York.

It had been ten years since my last Atlantic crossings in the much smaller twin-engined Swearingen Merlins and Metros. Those flights had been from Saint Johns in Newfoundland, Canada to Lisbon in Portugal. For long-range navigation back then, I had been using the VLF/Omega system, and now, in the B-747, I was introduced to the latest Inertial Navigation System (INS), comprised of three units that operated in Triple-Mix, each one checking the other two, thus determining the best accuracy. The other change from my many flights across the Atlantic on delivery flights was operating in the North Atlantic Minimum Navigation Performance Airspace (NAT MNPS) airspace between 27,500 feet and 40,000 feet. UPS B-747s were approved to do this based on the accuracy of the installed INS equipment. With the Merlin 3B, the small turbo-prop planes I'd delivered were capable of flying above 27,500 feet altitude, but the MNPS airspace was a no-go zone for non-approved operators which had forced me to operate those small planes no higher than 26,000 feet.

A fascinating aspect of operating in the MNPS was the shifting tracks that had to be flown precisely between North America and Europe. These tracks would be shifted north or south depending on the high altitude winds (jet streams) prevailing from the west and considered the predominant air traffic flow that changed every 12 hours. For the passenger-carrying airlines, most of the flights eastbound from North America departed at a time that would have them arriving in Europe close to dawn. Then, 12 hours later, flights westbound would leave Europe at a time that would have them landing in North America at its daybreak. Operators like UPS and FedEx, carrying only cargo, could be scheduled to cross the Atlantic any time, eastbound or westbound, which often had us operating against the primary traffic flow.

Over two months, I was route-checked to all the B-747 destinations at that time when there were only six aircraft in our B-747 fleet. The shortest flight was to Newark, New Jersey from Louisville, less than two hours each way—late afternoon, early morning, making one million dollars profit each flight—at least that was the scuttlebutt. I did flights to Honolulu and back from Ontario, loving the layovers at Waikiki, returning to a Pacific wonderland from my past. Then there were schedules from Ontario to Philadelphia, opportunities to eat Philly Cheese hoagies, washed down with Rolling Rock beer. Our most extended trip in those days was Louisville to Anchorage, Alaska, then across the North Pacific to Narita, Japan, with a return the same way. Often, we operated two round trips from Anchorage to Narita before returning to Louisville. The Pacific crossing from California to Honolulu and the North Pacific from Alaska to Asia were not as demanding as the Atlantic crossings, with its crowded skies, complex route structure, and busy radio communications.

From 1993, UPS began taking delivery of additional B-747s and as a result, we launched exciting new routes, notably daily flights to Cologne, Germany. These were flown from either Newark or Philadelphia, with one-day layovers in Cologne, a city that became the UPS freight hub for Europe. In late 1994 our North Pacific flights from

Alaska to Japan were extended to Seoul, Korea, Hong Kong, and Taipei in Taiwan. On those flights to Asian cities, it felt like I was returning home after an absence of many years. Having been based in Singapore and flown throughout the region from 1960 to 1981, the sights, people, and environment were nostalgically familiar. Even the painted checkerboard on the curving descent to land at Kai Tak airport in Hong Kong was still there; no changes from my first arrival in 1960 with a Bristol Freighter 34 years before.

As added B-747s appeared on the Louisville Ramp, another group of new hires arrived on the property, many of them ex-military, all destined for the engineer seat, regardless of their background as fighter, attack, or bomber pilots. There was also a cosmopolitan group of pilots from commuter airlines, corporate aviation, and other freight airlines. As the years rolled on, I flew hundreds of flight sectors to domestic and international airports served by UPS B-747s.

I would often be asked by these ex-military pilots (American-born) how I, a foreigner, came to be a senior pilot with this prestigious US company. What they really were asking was: why was an outsider like me occupying a seat that should be theirs? In response, I delighted in telling the story of how I had ended up flying B-747s and earning the big bucks by default, which wasn't the reason I had immigrated to the USA. Instead, I told them I had come to America to get a simple, moderate-paid job flying corporate jets, but had turned down the jobs when offered a Flight Safety position because of the pathetic two-week vacation package. Then, I would elaborate with the sad story of leaving Fort Wayne and flying back to Australia in disgust, a place where any job there would be better than any job in America! But ultimately, returning to the USA, I reluctantly accepted a flight engineer position with the Night Freight

Dogs of Kentucky, and was subsequently forced into the left seat of a B-747, because I must have been such a bloody good pilot!

Crewing with these ex-military pilots was fine by me. I liked them all, loved listening to their war stories, and believed most of them enjoyed my history as a New Zealand South Vietnam veteran pilot and the time I spent as a US Navy ski-plane aviator in Antarctica. One of the oddities with many of the UPS crew members was their total lack of reading fiction while on layovers. Instead, they read non-fiction and newspapers, or watched TV, even the incomprehensible channels in Japan and Korea. One of the few exceptions was Geary Chancy, a retired US Marine F-18 aviator still living in Jacksonville, Florida, with his wife and young daughter, Andrea, who suffered from cerebral palsy.

From my earliest flights with Geary, we were simpatico buddies because of our joint interest in reading quality fiction. Among many authors, he introduced me to Cormac McCarthy's *The Border Trilogy: All the Pretty Horses, The Crossing, Cities on the Plains.* I had flown with Geary on two schedules from Louisville to Narita, Japan, in mid-1993, with both of us looking forward to again crewing together on our first flight to Cologne, Germany. I made that flight, but Geary did not. He and his wife, Mary Jane, were killed in an unbelievable tragedy—an Amtrak train collision with a bridge that plunged into the Alabama bayou. Miraculously, Andrea was saved, possibly by Geary and Mary Jane pushing their wheelchair-bound daughter to safety, before they both perished in the wreckage. Geary was replaced on my Cologne flight by Ken Smith, a fellow student with Geary during their flight engineer training with UPS. I wasn't much of a churchgoer in those days, but I journeyed with Ken along the Rhine to light candles in the cathedrals of Mainz, Koblenz, and back at Cologne, all in memory of Geary and Mary Jane.

Another Flight Engineer I crewed with during 1993 was Monica Betor, who had come from the US Air Force, where she had been a KC-135 flight instructor and was married to one of her previous students. Along with First Officer Mike Zolke, we spent Christmas in Cologne, including attending Mass at the Dom Cathedral on Christmas Eve and lighting more candles for Geary and Mary Jane. I felt privileged to fly with other military pilots: Mark McKinnon, an F-15 Eagle fighter jock; Dean Nakayama, a US Navy A-7 Corsair aviator, Japanese American, and bit player in the movie *The Final Countdown*. He's seen taking the barrier on the carrier *Nimitz* in his A-7. Jay Laughlin, another US Navy A-7 aviator who I conned into climbing mountains in Alaska, Korea, and Taiwan; Pete Kozlowicz, Polish American and one-time US Air Force F-102 interceptor pilot; Jack Stanfield, Vietnam veteran US Marine F-4 Phantom aviator who had been shot down by enemy gunfire; and Hal Baker, US Navy A-6E Intruder aviator who had flown alongside Stephen Coonts, author of *Flight of the Intruder*.

Then there was Mike Bender, a fellow climber and hiker, married to a New Zealand Māori girl. Mike was in the first class at the US Air Force Academy in Colorado Springs before joining the Strategic Air Command (SAC) to fly the B-47 and B-52 bombers. Then, as a civilian, he flew C-130s for Continental Air Services in and out of Laos during the Vietnam War. Mike passed away in 2018. Last in line, I remember Bob Ashey, callsign *Romper*, US Air Force F-111 Fighter Bombers, and RAF Hunters and Buccaneers on exchange in England. I never flew with Bob but shared many hilarious stories over drinks at the Regal Alaskan Hotel in Anchorage. I had crewed the B-727 and B-747 with his wife, Ineke, another pilot with UPS. Bob passed away in

2019. Mike and Bob, I miss you both.

In 1995, accompanied by my new partner and wife-to-be, Lucy, I made a permanent relocation to Vancouver, located in southwest Washington State. The primary reason was the legal avoidance of state income tax, with a bonus feature of being in an area covered with big mountains. The latest international UPS schedules allowed for 12 to 15 days on duty, followed by 12 days at home, the perfect arrangement to climb mountains in Washington, Oregon, and California. The only problem was becoming a commuter, traveling to work 2,600 miles distant in Louisville, then returning home the same way. By design, I'd located within a 30-minute drive from Oregon's Portland Airport, serviced daily by UPS flights between Louisville and Portland.

The business of commuting to and from work didn't always go smoothly. There were hiccups with the flights from Portland that I relied on for jump-seating to Louisville. Because of weather or mechanical problems, aircraft delays occasionally had me arriving close to check-in time as the captain on a zero-dark-30 departure for a six-hour flight to Alaska. Still lacking sleep from the UPS DC-8 cockpit cramped-seat flight of five hours from Portland, I'd nod off during the long ride across the barren landscape of northern Canada. I have to admit, I've always had problems trying to sleep in the passenger seats of commercial airliners but found the left-hand pilot's seat of the B-747 most conducive to snoozing. This was particularly so with the shoulder harness in place to prevent slumping forward over the control wheel and dribbling onto the navigation charts. In those long dark mornings between Winnipeg and Anchorage, with the autopilot navigating from the three INS systems to great-circle the big bird to our destination, I often woke to a silent cockpit—except for the harmony of snores from my two alert crew members!

Now it's time to remember some of the non-military pilots I had the pleasure of crewing with on the Big Bird. There was The Rainbow Crew: Me, the Pakeha boy from New Zealand; Sloan Davis, the African American and ex-policeman from Florida, our First Officer; and Heidi Meyer, blond hair and blue eyes as our Flight Engineer. We flew many trips together, mostly in the Lower 48 States. Then, Vicente Orlandella from Argentina, who learned to play the violin on layovers in Cologne and Philadelphia; not pleasant to be in a hotel room next to him, but it was for a good cause. His young daughter was learning the violin, and Vicente believed it necessary to help her. From South Africa came Ivan Leibrandt, a pilot who had crewed with my New Zealand brother, David, as merchant seamen on SAF Marine Tankers out of Port Elizabeth, South Africa. Ivan had been a midshipman and David the ship's radio officer. I guess it was a smaller world in those days.

During my last year with UPS, I had a great deal of fun crewing with two young pilots, First Officer Marc Brinkman (aka Skymonkey) and Engineer Ken Lawson. In common, we were avid watchers of Cohen Brothers movies, particularly *The Big Lebowski* and the Dude's penchant for White Russian cocktails. The result was the three of us drinking 'the beverage' on layovers in Japan, Korea, Taiwan, and Hong Kong, while watching Cohen movies on VHS tapes we had rented in Anchorage, Alaska.

Some of the ex-military pilots I flew with at UPS would opine: *If you can't understand that airline flying is boring, then you've never really flown.* I began to agree with them after many years of operating the B-747. It was too easy, too safe, and not often filled with thrills, but it did pay well, and the international layovers were fun, mostly with likeable crew members. I should say I wasn't bored with the flying, but it had become monotonous. Frank Hemko, a US Marine aviator who had flown C-130s in Vietnam, would often say *when flying ceases to be fun, you should stop flying*. Since my early years at Orion Air, I had known Frank, where he had been an excellent pilot instructor on the B-727. He was so prolific when imparting airplane knowledge, it was said that taking instruction from Frank was like taking a sip of water from a fire hydrant.

Frank was right about the time to stop flying. On May 10, 1999, six days before turning age 60, I made my last landing at Louisville in a B-747-200 near midnight, a pleasingly smooth touchdown, then very carefully taxied to a tight parking spot between a pair of B-747s without hitting anything. I set the parking brake, shut down the four engines, and disembarked before the plane caught fire, saying, "If it does, I know nothing!" My eldest son, Jeremy, was on board, sitting in the cockpit. He was an airline pilot with Comair, and UPS had given him a ride to Anchorage, Alaska to be with me on this final journey. We were impressed with the send-off afforded me by the UPS folks in Alaska. There were fire trucks spraying water over the aircraft as we exited the cargo ramp for the runway, and the ATC controllers at Anchorage and Louisville made special mention of the occasion. It was very moving, even for a superior, arrogant pilot like myself! What a privilege to have worked for this unique airline, hired in their first pilot class as their token New Zealander.

In 1999, FAA regulations stipulated that airline pilots reaching the age of 60 could not continue piloting the Big Jets because they were medically unfit to do so. The age 60 rule was not based on scientific research, but rather an arbitrary figure decided between the CEOs of US airlines and the FAA during the period of transition from propeller to jet-engined airplanes. The message was: *Pilots over 60 were too old to fly the fast new jet airliners, so their FAA medical certificates would change from First Class to Second Class, but still allowed them to continue flying as flight engineers.* It was a clever deception because the real reason was to enable airlines to rid themselves of older pilots without a battle from their unions.

Approaching the day of reckoning when I would be medically unfit to pilot the Big Jets, I advised UPS that I was happy to be reassigned to the engineer position on the B-747. Frankly, I had no intention of doing that, but needed to keep my options open in case something changed. Nevertheless, it surprised the Company when I announced my intention not to be one of the pathetic old codgers who moved from the front seats to the back seat of the B-747. I became one of few pilot retirees at UPS who decided to leave forever and was awarded respect from the younger pilots; after all, my departure would move them up on the seniority list! As for the older pilots, they were curious as to why I didn't stay on as an engineer and wondered how I would survive financially in early retirement. Furthermore, as a retired airline captain, I was expected to have a captain's house, private airplane, Harley motorcycle, large boat, sportscars, and a trophy wife.

I did have a trophy wife, Lucy, 20 years my junior, known affectionately as the Child Bride by my Australian climbing friends. But the rest of the Boys Toys I did not possess, and had no intention of doing so. At the time, we owned a modest condominium in Vancouver, a cheap sedan car, and a 4WD pickup—both well used. Yet we were a classic example of the *Millionaires Next Door*: no debt, no mortgages or car payments, sizeable cash saving accounts, and an extensive investment portfolio. What baffled the older pilots was my motivation for leaving when I could have remained at UPS, still earning a six-figure income for years to come. My best explanation at that time was how I defined happiness and what I thought was materially and spiritually necessary to provide that happiness. One thing was clear to me. As we age, the reality of what we need to be happy changes dramatically in favor of good health, vitality, and physical fitness, far outweighing the need for possessions and a luxurious lifestyle. So, in retirement, I finally found myself home for the rest of my life, hard to believe it was over. No more dragging around the world, always tired, often sick, and wasting half my life away from people I cared about. The smell of freedom was sweet, and of course, the mountains beckoned.

In the 22 years since that last flight, I have not placed my hands on the controls of an airplane again, nor have I felt the impulse to do so. In the 42 years of professional flying, I had done everything a thousand times or more, those things that Pilot Officer Magee, a Canadian fighter pilot in the Royal Air Force, had illuminated in 1940:

> *Oh! I have slipped the surly bonds of earth*
> *And danced the skies on laughter-silvered wings;*
> *Sunward I've climbed, and joined the tumbling mirth*
> *of sun-split clouds – and done a hundred things*
> *You have not dreamed of – wheeled and soared and swung*
> *High in the sunlit silence.*

John Gillespie Magee was killed at the age of 19 on December 11, 1941, during a Spitfire training flight. In his brilliant poem *High Flight,* he encapsulated the calm emotions but flamboyant displays of military pilots who had the Right Stuff. To qualify for this elite honor, you needed to spend years flying upside down, looping, rolling, high-speed stalling, spinning, air combat tail chasing, and often losing control of an airplane, but surviving within seconds of touching the void. I had had the privilege to belong to that exclusive club of Sky Warriors, trained by the survivors of WW2, fighter and bomber pilots, who did their best to make me like them.

I had flown the Harvard AT-6 military trainer as a student and flight instructor. Had a brief but exciting fling with the De Havilland Vampire jet fighter and blundered over the jungles of Malaya, Borneo, and Vietnam during two wars, in the ugliest, noisiest, slowest piston-engined airplane ever designed by man. I flew ski-equipped planes above the dazzling white plains and glaciers of Antarctica, then operated the Lockheed C-130 Hercules worldwide. As a civilian, I piloted the Israeli Westwind corporate jet into primitive airstrips around Papua New Guinea. In between these exciting times, I soloed a single-engine Beechcraft Bonanza two-thirds around the globe, followed by numerous delivery flights of twin-engine turboprop planes from the United States to Southeast Asia and Australia. Finally, I had gilded the lily with 15 years flying Boeing 727s and 747s for the prestigious UPS Airline in the United States.

By the end of my aviation career, I had nothing more to prove to myself and certainly nothing to prove to others. Furthermore, I had come to understand how blessed I had been in surviving the high risk flying that was my existence before finding the shelter of operating the big commercial jets. I would forever miss performing the skills I was a master of, but as I walked away from that last flight, my thoughts had already mutated to the mountains I would climb. One passion had ended, and the other was in waiting for many years ahead.

In recent years, I was provided with the best justification for my decision I had made in 1999, and it came from a hiking friend, Big-Rob from Boston who was quoting the Dalai Lama.

When asked what surprised him the most about

humanity, the Dalai Lama answered: *Man sacrifices his health in order to make money. Then he sacrifices money to recuperate his health. And then he is so anxious about the future that he does not enjoy the present; the result being that he does not live in the present or the future; he lives as if he is never going to die, and then dies having never really lived.*

A few years on, as hoped for, but not entirely expected, retirement life looked like being the best days of my life. We had retained our Vancouver condo and purchased a beautiful beachside property in Western Australia, living the ultimate snowbird life of endless summers, jetting between the two countries six months apart. I had belatedly caught up with my Australian-based son and granddaughters and made regular visits to friends and relatives in New Zealand. I was living an unlimited, super-healthy outdoor lifestyle on Australia's beaches and in the mountains of the western United States.

2002: The Fatal Attraction of Mount Hood

(He) would be dead within the hour, and led to believe that Mount Hood was a beginner's mountain, suitable for his first climb. Unfortunately, there's no such thing as a 'beginner's mountain.' It's a concept that doesn't work, like beginner sex.

~ *Deep Survival*, Laurence Gonzales

OVER MY 42 YEARS of professional aviation, initially flying piston-propeller planes below 10,000 feet over New Zealand, Australia, Antarctica, and Southeast Asia, then flying 4-engined turboprops and ferrying small 2-engined turboprop planes around the world up to heights of 25,000 feet and finally, flying large jet airliners worldwide up to altitudes of 42,000 feet, I saw nothing that I could identify as a UFO (Unidentified Flying Object). However, I did see many things that at first glance were inexplicable, until closer inspection turned them into shadows of clouds or other meteorological illusions. Nevertheless, bizarre stuff finally happened to me in the last half of 1987, when I saw and heard weird things while climbing in the Northwest Cascade Mountains. Strange events that I still can't explain.

The first incident occurred during a routine climb of Mount Hood in northern Oregon. The start point for the south-face route is Timberline Lodge at an elevation of 6,000 feet, then follows an almost straight line on a north magnetic heading to the summit at 11,200 feet. I had passed through a height of 9,000 feet in the early morning hours when I caught the flash of an extremely bright light to the west of my position. I estimated the source to be one mile away and a thousand feet below. The sun, positioned behind me, had come over the eastern horizon one hour before, so I first assumed the bright light was a reflection off a mirror-like surface. The object was making slow direction changes above a broken layer of cloud, obviously airborne, but neither a light airplane nor helicopter. There was no noise, and my best guess because of the slow birdlike maneuvers, that it was indeed a large bird with a reflecting object attached to its body, which seemed illogical. After five minutes of watching, the light blinked off, and no object, bird or plane, was discernable! What it was, I still have no idea.

The second and third events occurred on a climb of Mount Jefferson, also located in Oregon. The south-face route on this volcano is best approached from a trail through old-growth Douglas Fir conifers that lead to Pamelia Lake, a body of water enclosed on three sides by steep forest-covered shorelines. Shortly after first light, I arrived at the perfectly calm lake on the early morning in question, shrouded by a solid cloud layer that obscured the surrounding ridgelines. A short time after reaching the lake, I heard the sound of something airborne above the lake, hidden by cloud; no engine noise, just rapidly increasing airstream almost to the point of an approaching sonic boom! I'd heard stories of wild geese and other large birds flying into clouds, becoming disorientated and plunging out of control into the ground. So that was my best guess, and I expected a large bird to come plummeting from the cloud and crash into the lake at high speed. The noise built up to a crescendo, then suddenly stopped—and nothing appeared below the cloud! To this day, I don't believe it was a bird; was it something else?

After leaving the lake, ascending a section of the Pacific Crest Trail (PCT) that provides access to the south-face route to the Jefferson summit, I continued to ponder what the heck I'd heard over the lake. I thought it possible that some military air operation was taking place on the mountain's slopes and forests, but there was nothing to see. I spent the rest of what was ultimately a long day into night, climbing to within a few hundred feet of the summit before descending and returning to my rental car at the Pamelia trailhead. The final three hours were in forest darkness, on a trail crowded on both sides by thick rhododendron bushes and dogwood trees, my progress illuminated by a weak, dying headlamp. Exhausted, hungry, and thirsty, I began to believe something was pacing me in the bushes on a parallel path. When moving, I imagined I could hear whatever it was, pushing its way through the undergrowth, until I stopped—and then it stopped too! Was there a bear stalking me, perhaps a cougar, or the mythical Bigfoot?

Since that long hike in the deep dark forest, spooked and close to panic mode, I've done many mountain walkouts at night, in places far away, like Nepal, Australia, New Zealand, as well as Alaska, New Hampshire, and Tennessee. I began to carry a powerful, fully-charged headlamp and accept that there are illusions during night hiking. The headlamp's side illumination gives the appearance that you're moving quicker than reality, making it seem like you'll never reach your destination and get out to safety, where forest monsters can't hide in the undergrowth. Tom Gummer, a pilot friend at UPS, who had grown up in Montana where he'd been an experienced hunter, told the story of being stealthily followed by a cougar. The big cat had paralleled him through heavy undergrowth, stopping when he stopped, then finally making a fast move to get in front and intercept him on the trail. Fortunately, it was daytime, and Tom was carrying his trusty 44-Magnum revolver, a handgun capable of stopping a Grizzly. From recollection, the cougar took off, and Tom lived to hunt another day.

Ten years after my scary night on Mount Jefferson, Stephen King wrote a book called *The Girl Who Loved Tom Gordon*, the fictional story of a 9-year-old girl who gets lost in the wilderness of southern Maine. In the dense dark woods, she's stalked by a massive creature that parallels her progress, leaving a trail of slaughtered animals and mangled trees. Reading the story brought back all the terrifying memories from Mount Jefferson and other dark green forests that cover the Cascade Mountains of the Northwest USA.

On the subject of Stephen King's books, I must tell the story of why I began bidding for flights to Portland in Oregon. The attraction had nothing to do with the city of Portland, but everything to do with Mount Hood, the 11,200-foot volcanic peak a one-hour drive east of the city. How did I know about Mount Hood? Thanks to Stanley Kubrick and his 1980 horror movie, *The Shining*, adapted from the book of the same name by Stephen King. Five years before I immigrated to the USA, in 1985, I saw the movie in San Antonio during a layover, waiting to fly a new Swearingen Metroliner to Singapore. In various parts of the movie are images of a snow-covered peak and the exterior of a large hotel on the mountain's slopes, supposedly situated in Colorado's Rocky Mountains. As a wannabe climber, I was fascinated by the actual location, which I later learned from the credits. It was Mount Hood, Oregon, a thousand miles west of Colorado, and the hotel was called Timberline Lodge.

Back in Singapore, and later, relocating to Queensland in Australia, I kept notes about the mystical and mysterious Mount Hood, eventually purchasing a VHS tape of the movie *The Shining*, to be scared again and again. In late 1983, I decided to become more than just an armchair alpine climber, vicariously inhabiting mountaineering ventures in books from Ed Hillary, Heinrich Harrer, Maurice Herzog, Eric Shipton, and Chris Bonnington. My transition from dreamtime climber to the real thing began with walking the Annapurna Circuit in Nepal, a 24-day 250-mile hike, including climbing and crossing Thorong La, a 17,700-foot mountain pass, near the Tibetan border.

One year later, I was motivated to acquire professional skills in alpine mountaineering, and the best place to do that was back on my pre-Antarctic turf, the Mount Cook National Park in New Zealand. Our instructors were from Alpine Guides based at the Mount Cook Village. Three Kiwis—Don, Kevin, Paul, and one German—Erwin. These four were top-class, hard-arse alpine climbers. For this two-week extreme course, tortured by these instructors, I showed up full of confidence, despite being in my mid-40s and 20 years older than the other six clients on the course. I don't recall being concerned about the high level of risk involved in the training or opting out of any potentially hazardous exercises ... and there were plenty of those. A sad note about our instructors: Irwin drowned, trapped under a glacier, two weeks after my training finished. Paul was killed in an avalanche on Mount Tasman in 2003.

Upon completing this comprehensive alpine mountaineering training, I came away knowing I was now prepared to attempt serious climbing on high snow and ice-covered mountains. The course had introduced the latest techniques and equipment, a quantum leap from my knowledge and usage in 1959 during my Air Force survival training for airplane operations in Antarctica. I returned home to Queensland with all the tools and skills needed for a planned adventure to climb a 20,000-foot, or higher, peak in Nepal during 1985. What I planned did not happen until 1992. In the meantime, the first big alpine mountain I was destined to climb was none other than Mount Hood, Oregon in 1987. How did I choose a relatively insignificant mountain on the international landscape that was in a remote corner of a country I had never planned to live in? As loopy as it sounds, I believe Mount Hood chose me.

In 1980, when I first viewed the movie, *The Shining*, I was intrigued by the various locations that Kubrick had used, in particular the Timberline Lodge. At that time, any plans to be a serious-minded mountaineer were at a nascent stage, if not totally vague. After all, I was living in Singapore, continuing to enjoy Southeast Asia's tropical pleasures after nine years in the location. So, the idea of visiting Timberline Lodge and climbing Mount Hood was never on my dance card. Nor was the city of Portland in Oregon. Since 1978 I had frequently visited the United States, traveling on a New Zealand passport with a multiple entry Business Visa. My visits were to take delivery of small US manufactured airplanes, then flying them to New Zealand, Australia, or Southeast Asia. I always enjoyed being in the United States, spending time in San Antonio, with layover stops in San Francisco, Hawaii, Indianapolis, Buffalo, Long Island, and Bangor, but I had neither the inclination nor desire to live in the USA—until the destinies forced my hand in early 1985.

Happy as a clam living in Queensland Australia, employed by a large copper mining company, flying their corporate jet-plane between Queensland and Bougainville Island in Papua New Guinea, I was planning to remain in place until retirement 15 years later. Then, with the worldwide price of copper falling in early 1985, I was laid off from my dream piloting job, at a time when both airline and general aviation pilots were in oversupply in Australia and New Zealand. After two months of seeking similar employment in Australia, no good offerings came my way, despite me being an overqualified (hotshot?) pilot, so, with great reluctance, I accepted a tentative offer from a corporate jet operation in Delaware, USA.

With the fates moving in serendipitous ways, after interviewing with the good folks in Delaware I encountered aviation people (or they encountered me?) who placed me into the emerging overnight air-freight business. Based in Louisville, Kentucky, I was soon flying to cities across the lower 48 states, with extended weekend layovers, including at Portland, Oregon. To quote John Muir: *The mountains are calling, and I must go.* In my case, it was Mount Hood. This semi-mystical journey was completed in the spring of 1987 when I first summited the mountain. Yet Hood's ascent was not an ending, but a new beginning beyond my wildest imagination, a world of adventure that has lasted 35 years and counting!

What was it like to be on this mountain made infamous by Stanley Kubrick? Although just a movie, the scenes filmed outside Timberline Lodge were of unforgettable terror. And so it was for me in the early morning of my first climb of Hood. A Portland climbing group's recommendation was to leave the Timberline trailhead no later than 4 a.m. to begin the one-day climb and descent. The primary reason to be off the summit no later than midday is to avoid rockfall from stones loosened in melting ice. Also, descending the lower ski field is hampered with softening snow by early afternoon. So on the day of that first ascent, after cautiously negotiating the winding snow-covered road leading to the Lodge, I arrived in the dark at 3 a.m. I spent 30 minutes completing the self-permit requirements in the Climbing Register, available in a corner alcove of the ski rentals building, situated below the actual Lodge.

In the early morning light, hiking through a dense fog, rounding the western end of the Lodge, I was unnerved to see an identical screenshot from *The Shining*. It was the final scene where mother and son are sliding down the steep snowbank that extended up to the highest windows ... escaping crazy Jack. The snowbank was precisely in place, the illumination and fog both identical, only the actors were missing. I captured the scene with a photo that still gives me the creeps. Being there that morning, so spooked, I was ready to turn back and run to the car, but instead, I reluctantly pushed on above the Lodge to a hedge of small Whitebark Pines, half-buried in snow. In Kubrick's movie, the trees and bushes near the Lodge don't move, but in King's novel and a later movie version, the trees display menacing motion and whisper dark warnings. I imagined it was happening that morning, though common sense suggested an illusion from the wind effect on the trees. Whatever was happening near the Lodge, I was relieved to be climbing fast, and well beyond, into the rising sun just appearing over the horizon.

After all the imagined drama, the 5,000-foot ascent to Hood's summit was pleasantly straightforward, some hard physical effort required, but not technically difficult for someone with a background of alpine training and experience. The south face climb from the Lodge was considered 'the dog route' (easiest route on the mountain), and yet, Mount Hood has been the site of dozens of climbing accidents and fatalities, including on the dog route. In May 1986, the year before my first climb, nine people in one group died on this route: seven high school students and two adults. They were ill-equipped, with no previous alpine experience, guided by incompetent leaders, then lost in the clouds when turning back for the descent to Timberline Lodge. Most followed the 'Fall-Line' (the direction downhill that a ball, rock, or body will fall) instead of using the recommended compass heading of magnetic south, ending up dying of hypothermia in gullies and ravines far from Timberline Lodge.

For the next 15 years, continuing to climb Mount Hood, I witnessed the constant presence of novice climbers and hikers with limited experience, inadequately prepared, and poorly equipped. But bizarrely, the most dangerous climbers, to themselves and others, who would show up on Hood were overly equipped—using ropes without understanding the essential techniques.

On the morning of May 30, 2002, I was relaxing at our residence in Vancouver, Washington, watching local TV news reports showing dramatic images from below the summit of a mountain I knew well, Mount Hood. The images were a live-feed from a news helicopter, with the airborne reporter explaining how a major climbing accident had occurred 200 feet below the final approach to the summit. Most of the victims had slid into the only crevasse on the slope, a feature commonly called a bergschrund. A gathering of climbers and search and rescue personnel were working along the lower lip of the crevasse, apparently awaiting the arrival of a Blackhawk helicopter from the Oregon National Guard.

Early information from unhurt climbers who had witnessed the accident indicated that a group of four climbers, roped together, had fallen from above the crevasse, and their rope stretched across the slope sweeping other climbers into the crevasse with them. For me, I was watching a déjà vu moment. I had climbed Mount Hood on the same route many times since 1987, mostly solo, sometimes with my wife or Australian climbing friends, always unroped! For experienced amateur climbers, which we were, boot crampons and ice axe were the only tools needed. Over the years climbing Mount Hood, I became more concerned when seeing roped teams moving on a fall line above us, crossing the steep slope leading to the summit. Their obvious ignorance of the potential danger by all moving together, without the use of fixed or running belays, was astonishing. They could kill me, my friends, and themselves.

Headlines in The Oregonian, *Portland's daily newspaper, would scream that it was just a 'freak accident.' It was not. It's a very common one, repeated over and over on numerous mountains. The most experienced mountaineer on Hood put it this way: "A rope without fixed protection is a suicide pact."* Laurence Gonzales in his book *Deep Survival*

In May 1994, I had completed a successful solo climb to the summit, and rhetorically asked myself, *Why do some climbers on this route persist in moving roped on steep sections? It would be less dangerous climbing solo. Is it because of the rockfall hazard or a lack of understanding of the techniques of roped travel?* This question came to mind when I was descending, passing four climbers from Chicago, all roped and moving together below the steep section, but they were in the process of turning back, so I didn't stop to give them a lesson on safety. As it happened, this missed chance would have spared them much grief. On the local Portland news the following day: *Four climbers from Chicago take a serious fall on Mount Hood—all injured, three seriously.* Were they roped and moving together near the summit? From that event, I predicted that one day there would be deadly consequences of a similar fall, with a rope sweeping unroped climbers off the slopes below. Eventually it happened in 2002, with three dead and six seriously injured.

One year after the accident I read an article in *The Oregonian* newspaper about a book that had just been published called *Deep Survival: Who Lives, Who Dies, and Why*. The author was Laurence Gonzales. In his book were two chapters devoted to the May 30, 2002 Mount Hood accident. Intrigued, I purchased a copy, read the two Hood chapters, and realized that this book spoke to me in many ways. It provided me with some answers as to why I was still alive at age 64, after taking so many risks in airplanes and on high mountains. It's not about lists of equipment you should take into the wilderness to survive, or the techniques of how to fly an airplane safely, instead, it contains advice like:

It's easy to demonstrate that many people (estimates run as high as 90 percent), when put under stress, are unable to think clearly or solve simple problems. They get rattled. They panic. They freeze. Muddled thinking is common in outdoor recreation when people get lost or injured or are otherwise threatened with harm. Laurence Gonzales, *Deep Survival*

2002: The House at the End of the World

Thoughts from Goode Beach, West Australia.
November 25, 2002

I WAS DREAMING at the end of the world. What had brought me to this place, this last foothold on the edge of the vast Southern Ocean? I was following the voyages of Captain Vancouver of the Royal Navy to the far reaches of his Pacific domain. Mostly, I had been living in the Pacific Northwest of North America's Washington State, in the old timber town of Vancouver, across the Columbia River from the city of Portland in Oregon. Down there, in the southwest corner of Australia, I was residing on Vancouver Point, above the beach where the well-traveled captain put in for water in 1791. During his short stay on this beach, he referred to the local flora as *deadly green herbage, interspersed with a few groveling shrubs or dwarf trees scattered at a great distance from each other.* It was obvious to my rainforest eyes that nothing had changed in two centuries. What the Captain had failed to record in the ship's log was the presence of prolific poisonous snakes lurking and slithering among the green herbage and groveling shrubs.

Awaiting the closing of a house purchase I had made at Goode Beach, I rented accommodation in a battered RV at the Frenchman's Bay Caravan Park. The family that owned and operated the park and general store appeared to be typical for this remote location in Australia. They were a middle-aged couple and a younger man I initially assumed was their son, a strange and somewhat scary individual. I silently began referring to the park as the *Bates Motel*, and imagined a Stephen King story that could be written about the place.

One evening strolling along the beach near the centuries old remains of the Norwegian whaling station adjacent to the Caravan Park, I saw what looked like two human heads on sticks in the sand. I reluctantly came closer in the last light of evening, expecting to see blood-soaked sand beneath these grizzly relics, the eyes and tongues picked out by the circling grey gulls. It was easy to imagine that some ancient Transylvanian ceremony had been enacted by the Park family with their thick, often unintelligible Slavic accents, incanting spells at the removal of these heads from two luckless travelers; their rental Britz Campervan now at the bottom of Salmon Pools, their mutilated bodies, sans heads, providing food for the prowling Great Whites.

I suppose I can blame my visual confusion that evening on too many glasses of excellent West Australian Shiraz; nonetheless, I never felt entirely safe visiting the general store until it was closed down and the Bates family moved away from the beach. I read somewhere that the captain of the Russian submarine K19, *The Widowmaker*, ordered his crew to drink plentiful quantities of red wine to reduce the effects of radiation sickness coming from their leaking nuclear reactor. If this remedy is true, then, when the big one comes, winos like me and the cockroaches will be all that survive. That's the perfect justification for guzzling down the Australian red wines until the Apocalypse or the Walking Dead stumble into town.

To purchase a house at the end of the world, ten miles south of the city of Albany, with Antarctica next stop south, and Africa, six thousand miles west, was a crazy idea, but I did it because I could. At the time, it seemed like an eccentric decision, but I had been making wacky choices for many years, and still kept coming up smelling of roses. Though, I must say, this action gave me a few sleepless nights, not that I doubted the financial returns from the purchase, or the great property and its location. Rather, it was the question of how the heck we were going to use the place in the years to come. Subsequently, we decided to take up summer residence there, returning to the USA for the northern summers. I alerted Australian and New Zealand friends and family that visits to our Albany residence would be mandatory. Surfing with the Great Whites would be optional; hiking the coastal headlands with the summer swarms of Dugite and Tiger snakes would also be optional, but attending daily tours of the nearby excellent vineyards would be compulsory.

Since 1995, Lucy and I had lived happily in a humble three-bedroom apartment, with little desire for anything more pretentious. My interest in the mountains had kept me content throughout the northern summers and limited the effects of cabin fever during the miserable winters by a combination of international trips to Australia, New Zealand, and Nepal. Also, I made regular visits to friends in southern California, and learned computer graphics as an enhancement to my summer mountain photography. Lucy was still occupied and happy at her local job with the occasional sortie with me into the mountains. We often looked for retirement properties in locations that offered an escape from the northern winter, and more specifically, with a spectacular seascape.

As a legal resident of the USA since 1985, my desired

location had been to live on the Californian coast somewhere between Santa Barbara and the Monterey Peninsula, but we didn't have US five million dollars to spend on the kind of place that would meet our requirements. US $500,000, which we did have, would have purchased a two-bedroom trailer home two miles inland, so that was not a choice. Neither was Hawaii: easy to get to, had a great winter climate and they all speak Yank, but where our limited funds would not buy a dog-box close to the water. So, the decision was narrowed to Australia. First choice, Queensland, where I'd lived and enjoyed from 1982 to 1985. Second choice was Perth where my second son, Christopher, had lived with his family for 20 years.

The problem was I considered the majority of Australia too hot during the southern summer, the time of year we expected to be there. I had always liked hanging out on surf beaches, but not all day, every day. I needed a location that offered a more temperate summer climate in a region that provided long distance hiking trails, a rugged wild coastline and some hills. Albany met all those requirements and I found the perfect coastal property that was adjacent to a national park and was the most southern house in Western Australia. Notably, it was very affordable, because in early 2003, the exchange rate between the United States and the Australian dollar allowed us to purchase the $820,000 property at Goode Beach for US $500,000. What could possible go wrong with this deal?

The city of Albany was an excellent small community: 250 miles south of Perth, surrounded by rich farmland that including great vineyards, more rainfall than most parts of Australia, and a rather well-mannered population of Aussies. Although not the only factor in choosing Albany, the presence in Perth of my son and his family was a definite plus. They say that in retirement you shouldn't follow your children, but my son Christopher and his three adult daughters were not planning to leave Perth anytime soon. It seemed that West Australians never want to be anywhere else and I was beginning to have the same desire. Another plus was that Chris and his family would be very happy looking after the property during the times we returned to the USA.

Lucy had a good job in Portland, Oregon, just across the Columbia River from Vancouver, so I returned alone to Albany in early 2003 to take possession of our new beachfront property at Goode Beach. It was an exciting period, living in the large white mansion on a cliff edge, overlooking Whalers Beach and Frenchman Bay, with great views of Flinders Peninsula and the islands of Michaelmas and Breaksea. Within a week of settling in to our new home I was invited to a small gathering of local Goode Beach residents, fine wine cocktail hour drinkers, curious about their new neighbor who had made the most expensive residential property purchase in Albany's history ... or so they said. With barely my first sip of wine swallowed, I was besieged by inquisitors, accusing me as a Yank of using my American dollars to inflate the local real estate values. In part, I responded that I was not a Yank, but a Kiwi, which really got them mad, commenting that was even worse, a Kiwi with American dollars! Belatedly, I pointed out that if they owned properties at Goode Beach, their property values had just been raised, which then had them whining about property tax increases.

Ironically, there seemed to be few original Australians living at Goode Beach. There were British, South Africans, Southern Rhodesians, Germans, Dutch, Canadians, and of course ... one Kiwi (me) and one Yank (Lucy). In all, an eclectic collection of international misfits amongst whom we felt quite comfortable. How did Lucy deal with them as a real Yank? As it happened, she adapted very well to the denizens of Goode Beach, in part because of their cosmopolitan makeup, but much to do with her recognition of their level of sophistication and they being just basically good people. Within a year she was elected the secretary of the Frenchman Bay Association, an active member of a choral/music group in Albany, and organizer of a very successful modern dance group.

My longtime climbing buddy, Mal Hill, flew over from Queensland to help me settle in, and Chris drove down from Perth, both helping with my transition from American retiree to Australian beachcomber. Without any furnishings in the house, no car in the garage, no kitchen or laundry appliances and no TV, phones, or computer, we had a busy time hunting down all this stuff in Perth and Albany. Fortunately, the large purchase costs were negated by the advantageous exchange rate, using US dollar funds from America. Mal, Chris, and I left final decisions on bedroom furnishings for when Lucy would show up later in the year. Color matching of sheets, duvets, and towels was not our forte.

When Chris returned to Perth, Mal and I did some necessary yard work on the steep sandy bank below the house, a bank that was slipping away toward the beach. That finished, we decided to do some local day hikes on Flinders Peninsula, then climb Bluff Knoll, the highest point (3,500 feet) in West Australia. Finally, before winter arrived, we backpacked a long coastal section of the Bibbulmun Track from William Bay, eastbound to the town of Albany. The necessary car ride to William Bay from Goode Beach was provided by Mike and Allison Mettum, close neighbors of mine. I had first met Mike when passing by his home at Goode Beach in 2002. Although our initial encounter was brief, I had quickly determined I was in the company of a most likable wag. My first question to Mike concerned his military background. Because he was wearing a red beret, jungle-green fatigue trousers, and walked with a pronounced limp, I had him figured as a retired SAS or Parachute Regiment soldier. Perhaps at the very least, a white-mercenary wounded in some obscure African country.

As I was to learn in 2003, Mike was not an ex-military man, but rather a fancier of unusual hats; the red beret was a particular favorite of his. It was true, however, that he had spent time in Africa, a naive Aussie country boy in the land of the lions and other big critters that scratch and bite. He told us the story of how, as an easy target working at the mines in Southern Rhodesia, he'd been scared by his local workmates telling horror stories of leopard attacks on the open plains.

Never stop your car and never, never get out of the car if you do stop!

So it happened that Mike borrowed a beat-up old car to go visit his lady friend, Allison, a nurse who worked in the big city. On the way back to the mine in the late afternoon, rattling along a rutted dirt road with almost non-existent brakes, he temporarily lost control of the vehicle down a rather steep section—and at speed hit a nasty bump that had the effect of separating the muffler and exhaust pipe from beneath. He slew to a stop, but not before one rear wheel slid slowly down into a roadside ditch. As he waited for the red dust to settle, the images of pouncing leopards flickered through his mind: he was on the open plains, alone, with enough leopard-hiding trees in the vicinity to be surrounded by a herd, a murder or whatever, of the beasts.

The engine stalled shortly before the car came to a stop. Mike's first rational action was to get the hell out of there. He turned the ignition; the engine started with a god-awful roar without the muffler, surely attracting every hungry predator for miles around. It was a pointless exercise: when he tried to drive forward, the rear wheel slid further into the ditch. It slowly dawned on him that he had no choice but to leave the relative safety of the car and somehow lift it from the ditch and quickly. It was almost dusk—time for leopards to feed!

Mike leaped from the car, ran around to the rear to see what he could do with the wheel in the ditch, all the while searching the immediate vicinity for leopards. He noticed the muffler and exhaust pipe lying back up the road, reluctantly comprehending that he'd need to retrieve them because the car was not his. He decided that the ditch problem could wait, and racing up the slope, grabbed the dismembered parts, turned, and sprinted back to the car. Halfway there the excruciating pain in his hands alerted him to the fact that he was holding a very hot muffler, recently separated from a running engine ... but the leopards were out there so he was not going to drop it even though the skin was peeling from his palms!

He reached the car, pulled open a rear door, heaved the offending parts onto the back seat, shedding burnt flesh in the process. Then it was back into the driver's seat, slamming the door and sitting shaking with fear and the shock of badly injured hands, he took deep breaths trying to fight back the panic so he'd be able to exit the vehicle one last time to solve the ditch problem and get the car moving while there was still some daylight. So he was out of the car again, moving fast, powered by terror and its adrenaline rush to lift the car in one superhuman move from the ditch and back onto the road. The rest is history:

Mike was not eaten by leopards, which really never existed in the area, but a story fabricated by his mates at the mine. He did, however, suffer with polio shortly after and thought there was some correlation between that and the Incredible Hulk performance he had staged in ghost-leopard country. He did eventually marry Allison and live happily ever after, but never could understand how he'd found the physical strength to lift a car that day on a lonely dusty road in Rhodesia.

Mike, Allison, their children and grandchildren, became lasting friends during our annual southern summer months in Australia.

By the beginning of 2005, Lucy and I were fixtures at Goode Beach, swimming each morning along the length of the dazzling white strand below our house, hiking the trails close to our property, and enjoying social gatherings with our neighbors. Unfortunately, I had been diagnosed with prostate cancer toward the close of 2004, and had a tough few months trying to make the best decision about treatment options. Both in Australia and the USA, there was a plethora of information about the best treatments, where to have it done, and by whom. In Australia I lacked the medical insurance coverage and was not impressed with their listed statistics of success and failure. Returning prematurely to the USA was not exactly what I wanted, but I did have excellent medical insurance there and my surgeon would be the doctor who had done the biopsy. He advised me that he had a record of three hundred successful radial prostatectomy surgeries. So that was my final choice, and one that was a total success. Nerve bundle retained, no urinary incontinence, and supposedly no cancer left, although years later I'm still in remission thanks to the war in South Vietnam and Agent Orange.

Within a few months after the operation I was able to return to Goode Beach, back to daily swimming, surfing, and sea kayaking in Frenchman Bay and extended backpacking hikes along the coastal sections of the Bibbulmun Track with Lucy. On our return to Vancouver in the USA, we hiked the 215-mile John Muir Trail in late summer, in what was becoming an annual pilgrimage. In 2007, Lucy finally backed out of this extreme activity, which she had named *Going to the Fat Farm.* I continued the yearly adventure through to 2016, despite total knee replacements in 2012 and 2013.

Our annual six months visits to Australia and Good Beach continued until early 2008 after we made the tough decision to sell the property and return permanently to the United States. Much of our justification to sell had to do with immigration problems we had with the Australian government, and we had recently lost visits from Chris and Tanja, who had moved permanently to Christmas Island. This also meant that we lost their friends and my granddaughters making regular appearances at the house. So this new situation had a lot to do with changing my perception of seeing Goode Beach and Australia as a permanent home. The nature of our magnificent house and its wonderful location needed the regular presence of family and friends to enliven and justify its uniqueness. Without them, the expensive four walls of a two million dollar property became nothing more than a mausoleum for two isolated, self-centered individuals.

Thanks to the input from Kevin Bovill, an Australian ex-Vietnam veteran, we were close to solving our impasse with the Australian Immigration Services, but fates decreed that would not happen with the surprise election of Kevin Rudd and his left-wing administration. With that game over, we decided to take the money and run. Our only loss was of the friendships we had made at Goode Beach. They were the best of people and the best of times.

2010: Matterhorn Peak Climb

The first indication of my failing knees

MATTERHORN PEAK is situated on the northern boundary of
Yosemite National Park, not far from the Californian town
off Bridgeport, and celebrated by Jack Kerouac in his book,
Dharma Bums. This particular adventure had been on my
books since June 2008 when I'd hiked north from Tuolumne
Meadows and up Spiller Canyon to Horse Creek Pass.
There, I'd camped below the southeast face of Matterhorn
Peak (12,300'), but didn't attempt a summit climb, despite
the route looking very straightforward. This time, I planned
to hike the extra distance, using the PCT to Matterhorn
Canyon and then up the side trail to Burro Pass
(unfortunately 22 miles each way), to climb the Class 2 route
on the southwest face of Matterhorn Peak. I discarded the
option of returning to Horse Creek Pass via Spiller Canyon:
lesser distance, but all off-trail hiking from the PCT crossing
at Spiller Creek, with hazardous and challenging route
finding ... and into a very isolated location for a solo
climbing guy like me.

Setting off from Virginia Lakes Resort with five days of
food, I planned on two days hiking to the base of
Matterhorn's southwest slope, one day on the mountain,
and then returning to Virginia Lakes in two more days. My

first camp was near the PCT crossing of Return Creek, the fast-running creek that flows down the length of Virginia Canyon. I discovered an excellent site on the creek's western side that didn't require the difficult crossing to the established campsites on the other side.

Being quite sure I had the location to myself, I took advantage of the warm water and calm sunny environment to strip off and wash in the creek, using a small amount of biodegradable liquid soap. One hour later, after eating dinner and then going to the stream to brush my teeth, the most bizarre event occurred. Looking down the creek, I saw many people perched on large boulders, perfectly still, like stone gargoyles attached to the granite. On closer inspection, they all appeared to be young women, staring at me, either appraising or condemning me for washing in the stream … or some other breach of hiking ethics? I must admit I was shocked by their sudden appearance, their complete silence, and in particular, their strange positioning on creek boulders, like birds on a perch … or worse, a surreal tableau of demons waiting for me. This was an image that returned a few days later after descending from Matterhorn Peak.

The closest gargoyle was squatting on a boulder in the middle of the creek … with dry feet! How did she get there? On a broom, maybe. I walked down the creek bank to where it was possible to converse with her over the sound of the rushing water. I opened the conversation by asking where they were camping because I was surprised to find them so far up from the established campsites on the eastern side of Return Creek. She explained that she was leading a group of 14 young women on a hiking/backpacking trip from Tuolumne Meadows to Twin Lakes, and because of the group size, had found it necessary to spread out some distance along the creek bank. My guess was their visit up near my 'isolated' camp was for ablutionary purposes …

and that my presence had interfered with that. Although not mentioned by the head gargoyle, I suspected at least one of them had seen me bathing in the creek, and my crime was not immodesty, but instead, using soap in the water! How I hate meeting these trail Nazis ... an excellent reason to practice stealth camping (which I thought I was doing at this place!) like an experienced PCT thru-hiker.

The next morning I packed up early and hit the trail by 7:30, hoping to get well ahead of the women's group that would also be heading north on the PCT. Ten minutes after leaving camp, I passed the crossing and saw the group over the creek, messing around, trying to get organized to get moving. I'd figured that such a large group of newbies would take forever to pack up in the mornings and not move fast along the trails. The day began with a gentle ascent to the Spiller Creek crossing, and then a tough climb to Miller Lake, followed by a long steep descent into Matterhorn Canyon, turning right onto the Burro Pass Trail.

For some reason, I made hard work of this trail to Burro Pass. It was difficult in places, all uphill, with numerous creek crossings, and from its midpoint to the Pass, good campsites were few. Through this area, both sides of the canyon fall steeply down to Matterhorn Creek, with sloping wet grassy areas close to the creek's edge. The few flat dry regions had been deliberately covered with tree dead-fall, presumably by park rangers, because of overuse. About half a mile below the Pass, I gave up the struggle that had been so tough and set up camp on dry ground between two granite slabs. Even here, on a rough rocky surface, I had to clear tree branches that had been dumped on the area. But it was flat, close to a small creek, and sheltered from the wind.

Unfortunately, I had a minor accident with my Thermarest sleeping mat, managing to pierce the fabric in two locations

382

on sharp rocks. To find the leaks, it was necessary to dunk the inflated pad in the creek … late in the day, with the sun behind the mountains and no quick way to dry the fabric for either the repair or for placing my non-waterproof sleeping bag on. Not precisely a desperate situation, but after an exhausting day, the last thing I needed was to rest directly on the hard rocky surface for the night. I finally stopped the leaks with duct tape patches and wrapped the mat with my waterproof jacket, pack cover, and pack liner … then lay down to sleep in grateful comfort.

R.J. Secor's *The High Sierra* describes the southwest side climb of Matterhorn Peak as Class 2, with the route guide: "Ascend the broad scree gully in the center of the southwest slope. This side of the peak is easily reached from Burro Pass." That's it! My plan for the climbing day was to leave the camp in place, ascend the trail to Burro Pass, and climb the southwest slope. Big mistake! On arriving at the Pass, I was greeted by six climbers who'd come up from the northern side, having backpacked in from Twin Lakes and spent the night camped by Piute Creek. Like me, they'd come to the Pass to climb Matterhorn Peak from the southwest slope, but were equally confused as to where the route began, despite one of them having done this many years before. After some discussion, we figured out that the route started from 600 feet below the south side of the Pass … where I'd just climbed from! If I hadn't been following Secor's instructions to the letter, the direct route would've been self-explanatory; the ascent actually began at the level base of the apparent cirque at the head of Matterhorn Canyon. Therefore hiking in from the south, as I had, there's no need to climb the 600 feet to Burro Pass … bummer!

The six male climbers, much younger than me, set off on a level traverse from the Pass toward the southwest slope gully. The terrain they were traversing was steep with rock outcrops and nasty little ravines, so I elected to go back down the trail for about 200 feet before setting out in a parallel traverse below them, on more comfortable ground. By the time I reached the climbing route, the six were already some distance above me on a steep grassy slope that leads to a well-watered ravine between large granite slabs. Above this ravine, the gully opened up again, eventually onto a rocky scree-covered slope. Above was the choice of two steep gorges composed of vertical rock buttresses, with loosely secured boulders on scree between … not the safest place to be with climbers ahead. I noted that they'd climbed the left gully, and as I got closer to making a choice between left or right, it became evident that left was the way to go because of a climbers use-trail marking the way.

With about 300 feet to reach the summit, I met the six on their way back down the slippery slope. They'd got to a small saddle about 100 feet below the summit … then run out of ideas and bravado. One had found his way up onto the summit rocks but said the experience had really spooked him. I didn't find this revelation very encouraging for my own endeavor and just hoped that he'd missed the correct route. I reached the saddle, which is relatively flat, with vertical rock on the summit side, but drops away to the east on a long scree slope down to Horse Creek Pass. This side of the mountain I was familiar with from my hike up Spiller Canyon back in 2008. It was apparent that the route from Horse Creek Pass would've been much more straightforward and safer than what I'd just experienced … and had to go back down in one piece! I believed that the route to the summit proper could be found on an eastern traverse below the vertical rock to the point that had a prominent staircase formation. But I decided not to find out; my knees were already sore, and the difficulty of the descent was uppermost on my mind ... get down from here safely, and as soon as possible.

It was not easy, and in places, downright dangerous with the pain and loss of flexibility in my knees. So I took my time, and twice had close calls; one with an extended slide on wet granite and the other after dislodging two large boulders ... one of which I'd been using for a handhold to swing my legs across a deep crack through a slab. When they came loose, I let go of the lower boulder and moved my leg back from the fall line; both boulders barely missed hitting my right knee and foot. This could have been a nasty accident, high on the peak, without any immediate help (the group of six had a long time gone from the mountain). As it turned out, the 14 gargoyles (or should I say gargirls!) had probably been watching my progress from afar; my yellow shirt would have been clearly visible from the trail up to Burro Pass. Thankfully, when I did reach the level area at the base of the climb, I spotted the party traversing up the path, 500 feet above me. Fortunately, I'd told their leader that I planned to climb Matterhorn Peak, and it became evident they'd been following my progress during the tortuous descent down the slope. From high above, the team whooped and yelled as I strolled safely across the level ground.

Before I dropped off the level area down to my tent on the Burro Pass Trail, I noted several perfect campsites on flat dry granite sand surrounded with boulders and slabs. This is where I should have struggled up to yesterday, and the knowledge went into my hiking memory-bank for future use. Settled safely back at my campsite, I had reason to pass on this knowledge to a group of 14 (Boy Scout Leader Course?) young men hauling hefty packs. They asked me where they could find good campsites, so I told them they'd just passed the best location, 500 yards back up the trail. I further explained that in the direction they were traveling, it would be at least one mile down the canyon before they found an area that was dry and reasonably flat. Their leader (of the day?) quickly dismissed my advice, and the group moved off, then unbelievably, not far below me, stopped to camp on sloping grassy wetlands near the creek bank; they could not have picked a worse spot to spend the night. Too stupid to survive!

I packed up early the next morning for my 22-mile return hike to Virginia Lakes Resort. As I set off down Matterhorn Canyon, I passed the sorry-looking group trying to dry their tents and equipment after what no doubt had been an unpleasant night. The scene reminded me of how much I enjoy traveling with PCT/JMT thru-hikers who know what they're doing in the wilderness. Not only do they pick good campsites, but carry half the load these poor saps were lugging. To my surprise, I passed another four hikers packing up in similar conditions. For some reason, they'd chosen to camp on the wet, sloping ground close to the creek, when there were dry alternatives on the other side of the trail. These guys were not talkative, and although they looked like military personal with buzz haircuts, muscular builds, and fitness, they weren't young and presented a somewhat thuggish aura. Possibly they were members of a military contractor from Iraq or Afghanistan. Whatever, I was pleased to be on my way and going in the opposite direction to these characters.

The rest of my trip out was uneventful. I felt much fitter, particularly on the first day from below Burro Pass to Return Creek, possibly because the only serious climb was out of Matterhorn Canyon up to Miller Lake. The remainder was all downhill, and thanks to Advil, I had my knee pain under control. I camped at the same location by Return Creek, this time without gargoyles or other campers nearby.

On the final day, hiking up Virginia Canyon to Summit Lake, I did have a 'Doctor Livingston, I presume' moment. As I struggled up from the canyon to Summit Lake on a nasty steep trail section with no switchbacks, I was passed by a day-hiker dressed in tennis whites, black socks, brogues, and a pith helmet. Was he British, I don't know, because he didn't respond to my quip re Doctor Livingston. Some people in the mountains just don't have a sense of humor!

This trip was the first time in many years that I'd gone into the Sierras solo to climb a peak for that specific purpose. It would have been much quicker and more comfortable with a strong partner. We'd have taken the cross-country route from Twin Lakes up the Horse Creek Trail to Horse Creek Pass, camped there at the head of Spiller Canyon, and climbed Matterhorn Peak on the short southeast slope. A maximum of 15 miles round trip. Being solo, I wasn't prepared to handle the steep talus below Horse Creek Pass with my wobbly knees, but in retrospect, it wouldn't have been any worse than what I experienced going up the southwest slope, and with 22 miles backpacking each way. Another choice would have been to approach the southwest slope from Twin Lakes, which is what the six climbers I met on Burro Pass had done. That route is 15 miles each way and could be done, including the climb, in three days. I can't remember my reasoning for not making this choice, but perhaps it had to do with my familiarity with Virginia Canyon and the PCT in the area. Nonetheless, it was a good shakedown and fitness training for my annual JMT hike, due to begin nine days later.

2017: Dying in the Forever Rain

Will I die this time, in this uninviting wilderness I once called
home or is this another Faustian delay.
Aren't my dues paid many times over?

SO GO THE REVERIES of an aging Immortal Man. I've often
said that in New Zealand, it's either raining, or it's about to
rain. As a mountain man from that country, it is senseless to
believe otherwise. Death stalks the mountain forests and
raging river flats of New Zealand in many unexpected
ways: rock and snow avalanches, river crossing drownings,
and in particular, hypothermia! The combination of continuous
rain with temperatures between freezing and 50 degrees
creates a deadly environment for the unprepared without
shelter.

Nevertheless, seduced by the presence of numerous
huts along the South Island tracks, I elected to leave my tent
behind to hike the St. James Walkway, thus off-loading two
insignificant pounds from my pack. On the fourth day while
hiking from Anne Hut to Boyle Flat Hut, a distance of 11
miles, light warm rain fell, leaving my core temperature
static and comfortable for the first seven miles. Shortly into
the eighth mile, a subtle temperature drop and strong wind
rapidly brought on the early signs of hypothermia. Alone,
after other hikers had moved ahead, I believed the game

was up. I would not survive hiking the additional miles to Boyle Flat Hut. No panic, no delusion, just resigned to dying in the country in which I'd been born. I wasn't physically struggling to survive. I did not, and possibly could not, run or walk faster to reach my intended destination, but just kept pushing ahead into the wind and continuous heavy rain. I hadn't yet reached the confusion and memory loss stage of advanced hypothermia, but I was shivering violently, and my breathing grew noticeably slower and shallower. I was sure that time was running out unless the rain stopped or I found shelter.

My only chance of survival would involve changing into the dry clothing buried at the bottom in my pack. But opening it risked getting everything wet, including my sleeping bag. With most hope gone, a grass-covered sign became visible in the distance, indicating a hut to my left. Staggering in that direction, a minimal structure appeared through the rain and mist … an old hunter's shed. With remarkable good fortune, I was able to save my own stupid hide, having learned a powerful wilderness lesson: Never leave home without a tent!

I was finally out of the rain that continued unabated for the next 12 hours. Inside the hut was cramped even for one person: three primitive stretcher bunks, a narrow bench for cooking, and most importantly—a fireplace, in which I was able to light a small fire with wet wood, using my propane stove burner for ignition. Within one hour I was restored to life; wet clothes drying by the fire, two hot drinks from my stove, and dressed in dry clothes from my backpack.

I was 77-years-old and back in the country of my birth, full of confidence to head into the Nelson and West Coast mountains of the South Island, not as a doofus wannabe 'Adventure Tourist,' but as a hotshot old-fart hiker who knows what he is doing. And it was true, I'm almost famous—but only in Reno: "That old guy, expat Kiwi, with titanium knees, the Tinman, who has hiked the John Muir Trail for the last 14 years, scrambled solo up difficult peaks and slew a few dragons in his lunchbreaks."

On Kiwi ground again, my overall impression was that the mountain huts were more than adequate, the river and creek crossings ... most with swing-bridges marginally safe, but the tramping tracks were atrocious. Hard to follow, poorly maintained, unformed in many sections and potentially hazardous without taking extreme care.

My survival in the forever rain along the Saint James Walkway track was much more good luck than proper planning. If I'd been carrying a tent, survival would have been assured well before allowing the rain, wind and temperature events to bring on a life-threatening hypothermic condition. My knowledge of the hut (Rokeby) that I literally stumbled upon had not featured in my self-briefing for the Walk. Finding it at such a critical moment was indeed a serendipitous discovery. Years later, I still wonder if I returned to that miserable valley whether I would actually find the hut again ... was it really there?

~

The desperate moments I've outlined above are a reminder of how seconds can make the difference between disaster and survival. In my 60 years of extreme adventure, mostly planned, but often accidental, the events I've described are small tips of an iceberg.

2021: It's Not Dark Yet, But it's Getting There

Thanks for the reminder, Bob Dylan

TWENTY-TWO YEARS ON, at age 82, I look back throughout my retirement as the very best years of my life. I'm still physically able to spend weeks backpacking in the high mountains of California, including climbing off trail over 12,000 feet cross-country routes. I've survived cancer, which has been in remission for 16 years, had two hernia operations, both knees replaced, and renewed eyesight from cataract surgery. For the past 12 years, Lucy and I have lived in what could be called a top-of-the-line captain's house, situated at an elevation of 6,000 feet on the mountains between Reno and Lake Tahoe, Nevada. The house stands on two acres of sloping ground surrounded by Ponderosa pine forest.

Overall, did I make the right decision of early retirement at age 60? Of course. I instinctively knew what the benefits would be for my long-term physical and mental health. However, I did possess a unique advantage, leaving employment with a well-established passion and experience to climb tall mountains and be permanently free to wander the great outdoors. And it came to be—bringing me all the way to my early eighties, not as fast on the hills as I used to be, but still out there on multiple day backpacking trips, as motivated and adventurous as always.

It is fair to say I have been taking risks in the mountains of America and elsewhere for 35 years, but now, as an octogenarian, shouldn't I be less reckless? Not so. If I had a death wish, I would be passed out on my basement couch, the TV recycling Netflix reruns, inebriated, waiting for the bliss of Joe's dementia. It has been suggested by close friends that I am essentially narcissistic, and in my estimation, a unique adventurer. As an example of my vanity, they often quote the description from my primary website: *The incredible mountain adventures of the High Sierra Kiwi, one of New Zealand's most unique mountaineers and pilots, yet unsung and ignored in his country of birth.*

Setting aside the braggadocio, it's getting closer to recognizing that my mountain dreams are slowly fading. That aside, I retain enough self-confidence to believe I can still survive in the mountains, but sometimes feel the physical limitations closing in. The training remains, and years of experience return to save my aging butt when the going gets tough, or worse, treacherous. Friends and family often remind me that I should not continue doing extreme physical activity in the outdoors as an octogenarian. Instead, I should realize I'm an 'elderly person.'

Of more concern to them, I often go out alone, and that's considered irresponsible since I'm in the zone for sudden heart attacks, strokes, and severe falling accidents. My crime is putting rescuers at risk searching for me or my mortal remains. Not a problem: they will find me, dead or alive, because I carry a Garmin Inreach SOS device that tracks my every move in the wilderness. Also, I've been told that I show no fear in the backwoods, climbing potentially dangerous routes, but they're wrong, because fear is one factor that has kept me very much alive.

As could be expected, I'm often asked by passing hikers, particularly those in their 60s, how I keep going at my advanced age, and the answer is in the question. Some will query my survival lifestyle choices: What's your diet? I eat everything put in front of me. What supplements do you take? None. Do you smoke? Yes, for 25 years until stopping at age 40. Do you drink (alcohol)? Yes, regularly, but not in the wilderness; too heavy to carry. I have to admit it's a lot of fun being an octogenarian and still hiking the mountain trails. May it continue into my 90s, although recently, I've been dreaming of my final resting place in the mountains I call home.

For many years I've experienced vivid dreams from my two passions: flying and mountaineering. More often now, the dreams include visits to my chosen location for the spread of my ashes in the High Sierra. Alive, I've been there many times. The outlook is breathtaking, surrounded by two peaks over 14,000 feet and many others over 13,000 feet. This view for eternity sits beneath a 3,000-year-old relic of a Foxtail Pine, with two crossed trunks, set in a series of granite ledges looking over a shimmering pond encircled with springtime grass and wildflowers.

© Peter William Tremayne, December 2021

.

Where in the World is Peter William Tremayne?

For more stories, adventures, and photos,
please visit Peter's websites:
highsierrakiwi.com
flyingkiwiusa.com

and his Vimeo channel: Peter W Tremayne

To contact Peter directly, please email him at:
harvardflyer@charter.net

Made in the USA
Columbia, SC
17 July 2022

63246679R00215